TEACHER DEVELOPMENT SERIES
Series Editor: Andy Hargreaves

CRITICAL DISCOURSES ON TEACHER DEVELOPMENT

CRITICAL DISCOURSES ON TEACHER DEVELOPMENT

edited by
John Smyth

CASSELL

Cassell
Wellington House
125 Strand
London WC2R 0BB

215 Park Avenue South
New York
NY 10003

1971145X

First published 1995

British Library Cataloguing-in-Publication Data
A catalogue record for this book is available from the British Library.

ISBN   0–304–33401–4 (hardback)
          0–304–33402–2 (paperback)

Typeset by York House Typographic Ltd.
Printed and bound in Great Britain by Redwood Books, Trowbridge, Wiltshire

Acknowledgements

Publication of this book was made possible, in part, through research funding from the Australian Research Council and the Board of Research of Flinders University of South Australia.

Contents

Notes on Contributors

Barbara Albrecht is an administrator at the Adams-Friendship School District in Wisconsin.

Nell Anderson is a co-ordinator of teaching English as a second language at the Wausau School District in Wisconsin.

Wilfred Carr is Professor of Education, University of Sheffield.

Marilyn Cochran-Smith is Assistant Professor and Director of Elementary Education, Graduate School of Education, University of Pennsylvania.

Noreen B. Garman is Professor in the Department of Administrative and Policy Studies, University of Pittsburgh.

Jesse Goodman is Associate Professor, School of Education, Indiana University.

Ivor Goodson is Professor in the Faculty of Education, The University of Western Ontario.

Jennifer M. Gore is Senior Lecturer in the Faculty of Education, University of Newcastle, Australia.

Peter P. Grimmett is Associate Professor, Faculty of Education, Simon Fraser University.

Andy Hargreaves is Professor in the Department of Education Administration, The Ontario Institute for Studies in Education.

Anthony Hartnett is Senior Lecturer, Department of Education, University of Liverpool.

David Hursh is Assistant Professor, School of Education, University of Rochester.

Connie Milz is a teacher of physical education at the Marshfield School District in Wisconsin.

Michael Naish is Senior Lecturer, Department of Education, University of Liverpool.

Jon Nixon is Professor of Education, Canterbury Christ Church College, Kent.

Cynthia L. Paris teaches in the School of Education and Human Services, Rider University, New Jersey.

John Smyth is Professor of Teacher Education and Director, Flinders Institute for the Study of Teaching, Flinders University of South Australia.

Henry St Maurice is Associate Professor and Director of Field Experience, Professional Studies, University of Wisconsin, Stevens Point.

Ronald Sultana is a Senior Lecturer in the Department of Educational Studies, University of Malta.

Kenneth M. Zeichner is Professor, Department of Curriculum and Instruction, University of Wisconsin, Madison.

Series Editor's Introduction

In Britain and Australia, they call it teaching. In the United States and Canada, they call it instruction. Whatever terms we use, we have come to realize in recent years that the teacher is the ultimate key to educational change and school improvement. The restructuring of schools, the composition of national and provincial curricula, the development of bench-mark assessments – all these things are of little value if they do not take the teacher into account. Teachers don't merely deliver the curriculum. They develop it, define it and reinterpret it too. It is what teachers think, what teachers believe and what teachers do at the level of the classroom that ultimately shapes the kind of learning that young people get. Growing appreciation of this fact is placing working with teachers and understanding teaching at the top of our research and improvement agendas.

For some reformers, improving teaching is mainly a matter of developing better teaching methods, of improving instruction. Training teachers in new classroom management skills, in active learning, co-operative learning, one-to-one counselling and the like is the main priority. These things are important, but we are also increasingly coming to understand that developing teachers and improving their teaching involves more than giving them new tricks. We are beginning to recognize that, for teachers, what goes on inside the classroom is closely related to what goes on outside it. The quality, range and flexibility of teachers' classroom work are closely tied up with their professional growth – with the way that they develop as people and as professionals.

Teachers teach in the way they do not just because of the skills they have or have not learned. The ways they teach are also grounded in their backgrounds, their biographies, in the kinds of teachers they have become. Their careers – their hopes and dreams, their opportunities and aspirations, or the frustration of these things – are also important for teachers' commitment, enthusiasm and morale. So too are relationships with their colleagues – either as supportive communities who work together in pursuit of common goals and continuous improvement, or as individuals working in isolation, with the insecurities that sometimes brings.

As we are coming to understand these wider aspects of teaching and teacher development, we are also beginning to recognize that much more than pedagogy, instruction or teaching method is at stake. Teacher development, teachers' careers, teachers' relations with their colleagues, the conditions of status, reward and leadership under which they work – all these affect the quality of what they do in the classroom.

This international series, Teacher Development, brings together some of the very best current research and writing on these aspects of teachers' lives and work. The books in the series seek to understand the wider dimensions of teachers' work, the depth of teachers' knowledge and the resources of biography and experience on which it draws, the ways that teachers' work roles and responsibilities are changing as we restructure our schools, and so forth. In this sense, the books in the series are written for those who are involved in research on teaching, those who work in initial and in-service teacher education, those who lead and administer teachers, those who work with teachers and, not least, teachers themselves.

This collection of papers, *Critical Discourses on Teacher Development*, examines some of the more disturbing and perplexing trends in teacher development at a time of rapid retrenchment in education and of fundamental shifts in the demands being placed upon teachers. In a world where teaching is often being delimited and deskilled by overly-stringent impositions of standardized testing and accountability procedures, and by reductions in the tasks of teaching in many places to instilling basic competencies in young people, the papers in this book try to rescue and reinvent a vision of teaching and of teacher development that is more moral, aesthetic, educational and political in nature.

These papers from some of the foremost critical scholars on teaching and teacher development around the world seek to strengthen the voices of teachers, to celebrate difference and diversity (not standardization and sameness) in teaching, to promote and support more critical reflection in teaching, and to acknowledge the processes of power and struggle that do and should suffuse the work of all teachers, of all those who help create the generations of the future.

The research and analysis of this book explores some of the least understood aspects of how teachers really do develop (or can be blocked in their development). It shows how teachers' work is intimately bound up with their lives. It shows how teacher collaboration can be an exciting opportunity but also a seductive trap. It demonstrates how politics is everywhere in teaching; how care is a ubiquitous (but much overlooked) feature of it; how reflection and research need to become more part of teachers' work and not just something other people do when they study teaching. This book is a fine compendium of critical and cutting-edge thought on teacher development. It does not offer instant models or other simple solutions. But it does provide deep reflection and true grit for understanding and acting on the course of teacher development in the rapidly changing workplaces and wider societies where the work of teaching must be done.

Andy Hargreaves
Ontario Institute for Studies in Education, Toronto
October 1994

Introduction

John Smyth

HOW TEACHING IS PERCEIVED

As we enter the closing part of this century there are real questions remaining unanswered as to what progress has been made in understanding teaching and the nature of teachers' work – and, by implication, how teachers grow and develop as individuals and as a professional group. What is becoming increasingly apparent is that there are a number of trends (not all of them novel) emerging worldwide that tell us much about how teaching is regarded – tendencies that include:

- intensifying the testing and the measurement of educational 'outcomes' through national and statewide testing;
- focusing on demonstrable, observable and performance aspects of teachers' work;
- requiring teachers to be increasingly explicit about what it is they do;
- defining competence in teaching according to static invariant standards derived largely from business and industry;
- requiring that teaching be reduced to some magical 'bottom line';
- rewarding teaching on the basis of 'merit pay' and 'payment by results', according to the extent to which teachers are able to demonstrate achievement-oriented learning gains in students;
- demanding, under the guise of accountability, that teachers show that what they do enhances the skills of students and, in turn, ratchets up the level of international economic competitiveness;
- ranking, rating and appraising teachers and placing schools in 'league tables' that compare one against the other;
- marginalizing teachers because they are regarded as self-interested 'producers', and, instead, favouring 'consumers', vaguely defined as parents and employers;

- treating teachers implicitly as if they cannot be trusted and are in need of surveillance through the use of 'performance indicators'.

While some of these may have been inevitable, and even carry with them a degree of superficial appeal because they require teachers to be demonstrably more accountable, efficient and effective in producing quality learning, they are also trends that are extremely worrying because of what they have to say about the perceived nature of the work of teaching.

Much of the implicit argument behind these approaches is that if standards of teaching can be determined and set (usually arbitrarily by people at a distance from schools), then surveillance and quality control procedures can be put in place to ensure adherence to what are claimed to be community expectations. The unfounded and unproven claim is that the current batch of economic problems can be blamed on teachers who have been less than diligent in the discharge of their duties, who act in self-interested ways and are incapable of pursuing the wider national agenda, and who are therefore in need of careful control, auditing and monitoring to ensure the production of acceptable educational outcomes. This is fanciful thinking, unsubstantiated by research, but it nevertheless has a good deal of currency in the wider community, especially in times when alienated youth finds it increasingly difficult to obtain non-existent jobs. While teachers may have become convenient whipping boys, the greater tragedy is that this kind of thinking is educationally regressive because the ideas informing it come from a view of a misty-eyed golden era of high standards that never really existed. Schools and teaching increasingly become treated as 'black boxes' in contexts in which the paramount considerations are inputs (to be severely circumscribed) and outputs or outcomes (that must increasingly be shown to be meeting national economic priorities).

In a particularly well argued paper, Maharey argues that what is occurring is part of 'a wider crisis of purpose in public education' which is emerging, he says, because 'the people who are driving education policy have little sympathy with our tradition of public education. They prefer a system based on choice and competition; the consumer and the market'.[1] The problem stems from a fundamental shift in the way we regard ourselves – from being citizens (having access to defined goods and services as members of society) to being consumers (purchasing goods and services, provided that we have the money). Being a consumer and having purchasing power is fundamentally and qualitatively different from being a citizen and having rights by virtue of a social contract with the state. The battle being waged is over what constitutes education and how the work of teaching and learning are to be advanced. It is a struggle over whose view of reality is to prevail, and it amounts to a battle over 'the intellectual and moral ideas that will guide the education system'.[2] All of this is not, as Maharey argues, about 'defending what we already have . . . . Education must change to meet new demands. The question we face, then, is not who will defend the past but who will define the future'.[3]

TEACHER DEVELOPMENT IN CONTEXT

Teacher development against this kind of backdrop, far from being a process of enlivening teachers and turning schools into critical and inquiring communities, becomes a process of ensuring cost cutting and of putting in place procedures to ensure compliance, docility and the creation of schools as institutions whose main concern is meeting the requirements of centrally devised diktats.

This displacement of purpose becomes glaringly apparent, according to Maharey, as the patently obvious is repeatedly reinforced and used as the sole basis for policy:

> Of course, during times when money is so short no one can complain about efforts to make efficient use of resources. The problem . . . is that cost cutting has now become the basis of policy where it impacts on the public sector and the education system in particular.
>
> No one actually says that education policy is driven by cost cutting. No one actually says that the state is seeking to reduce its responsibility. What they do say is that the deficit must be reduced; that schools should act like businesses; that capital works should be paid for by business sponsorship; that teachers should be paid less; that schools should be charged rent to introduce a little bit of market discipline . . . ; that it might be better if schools were privatised; that students should not look to the state to subsidise their education – but no one actually says all of this must be done in the name of cost cutting and rolling back the state.[4]

These are disturbing trends, made even worse by worldwide moves to centralize control over education, while shifting responsibility for the achievement of objectives onto teachers, in contexts of shrinking resources. We are hearing a lot, for example, about teachers 'delivering on performance-guaranteed outcomes'.[5] Let me see if I can be more explicit about the nature of some of these tendencies.

Recent, but as yet unproven, thrusts for competency-based approaches to teaching have their wider genesis in attempts by governments to use schooling as a tool of micro-economic reform, through a re-skilling of the workforce. We can find the evidence for this in:

UK	the establishment of the National Council for Vocational Qualifications (NCVQ);
Australia	the establishment of the National Office for Overseas Skills Recognition (NOOSR), the National Advisory

Committee on Skills Recognition (NACSR), the Vocational Education, Employment and Training Advisory Committee (VEETAC), the National Training Board (NTB) and, specifically in teaching, the National Project on the Quality of Teaching and Learning (NPQTL);

USA   the Commission on Skills in the American Workforce.

The competency-based approach to teaching and teacher development is a particularly good illustration of what is occurring. It has a number of defining and distinguishing characteristics:

- it is based on lists of benchmark criteria derived without consultation with the teachers to whom it is to apply;
- it works on the presumption that there are deficiencies in teaching, and that these can be 'fixed' by requiring that individual teachers adhere to a particularly narrow view of what comprises teaching, which is extremely problematic;
- it is compiled by outsiders at some distance from classrooms, and what are included as criteria of competence may bear little relationship to the way teachers in classrooms define what is skilled or competent practice;
- it starts from the presumption that non-teachers know best how teaching should occur, which is arrogant and likely to be very damaging to the image of teachers as an occupational group;
- it leads to teachers being excluded from decisions about what is important in their work, and when this happens, questions about the valued social and educational ends of teaching become subservient to aspects that are observable, technical and easily controllable. Such perspectives largely deny the profoundly moral, political, social and ethical nature of teaching as a relational activity;
- its undisclosed agenda is to silence teachers' professional judgement, and to impose in its place a preferred view of teaching that is allegedly value neutral but which, in reality, is constrained, contrived, easily quantified and compliant.

All of the creations of the state alluded to above derive from the same conservative educational think tanks. The unanimity of approach in countries as different and as widely dispersed as the USA, UK, Australia and New Zealand is so uncanny as to raise questions about whether in both diagnosis and pre-scription there has been some 'invisible hand'[6,7] at work crafting and replicating. The answer, I suspect, is that this is partly the case, but it is also true that all western economies encountered crises that required massive restructurings, as a result of the 1970s' oil shock and the uncontrollable inflation that followed, at much the same time. International agencies like the IMF, the World Bank and the OECD have certainly been important mediators as economies have sought both explanations and ways of extricating themselves from the bog. Muscular measures aimed at teachers and schools have been an extremely convenient rallying point for besieged governments at a loss to explain what is happening or what needs to be done. We can see this clearly in the way notions like 'quality', 'excellence' and 'skills formation', and their derivatives like 'competency' and 'performance' approaches to teaching, have been ideologically warehoused in organizations like the OECD. The nature of the 'policy borrowing' is also well documented by Finegold, McFarland and Richardson and their colleagues in their two-part 'Something borrowed, something blue?', an account that traces the international trends in educational restructuring from the 1970s through to the 1990s.[8]

The process of responding to global economic restructuring, and using schools as the wedge with which to do that, is an approach that has a good deal of appeal to it, and also one that is so naturalistic and commonsensical that it has become almost unassailable. As I have put it on another occasion, such technical/rational instrumental ways of thinking have become extremely persuasive, and it is not hard to see why:

> Because of the way in which capitalist systems in general have been able to ascribe the causes of our economic ills to the personal inadequacies of individuals (illiteracy, lack of incentive, and poor work habits among students), it has not been difficult to link this with the supposed systematic failure of schools to meet the needs of industry. The argument is such a compellingly simplistic one that it is proving almost impossible to dislodge – get students in schools to conform through more compliant forms of education, and all our economic woes will disappear.[9]

When teachers are treated in the demeaning and implicitly distrustful and unprofessional ways that occur through the processes alluded to above, moral questions arise about what messages this sends to students. The constructing of hierarchies of the kind that occur when teachers are treated as having limited professionalism inevitably conveys the message to students that it is acceptable to use increasingly muscular and distant ways of resolving complex problems. They learn that instead of understanding and appreciating diversity, idiosyncrasy and contextual nuances close up, it is more acceptable to deal with them by bureaucracy or administrative fiat. The nub of the matter is that students are given a lesson that institutional authority has more currency than the moral authority and credibility that attach to peer and collegial professional judgement on what is important about teaching.

'TEACHERS RECLAIMING TEACHING'

What is wrong, you may well ask, with this approach? While some change to education is inevitable as a consequence of broader economic restructuring, the overall direction ought to be the source of some worry. In response to an attempt to analyse what was happening to teachers' work, the Third International Teacher Development Conference at Flinders University of South Australia in 1993, on the theme 'Teachers Reclaiming Teaching', generated some valuable insights and suggestions from teachers. Among them were comments like the following from a primary teacher:

> The supposed failure of the education system to produce workers
> with adequate technical, cognitive and attitudinal skills has been
> blamed on teachers and provided the justification for massive
> changes. The new directions are characterised by a greater
> emphasis on vocationalism and technical education; moves
> towards privatisation of education and more direct influence of
> private companies on the curriculum; the introduction of
> performance 'tests' of both students and teachers for accountability
> purposes and greater competitive ethos, particularly between
> schools.[10]

But, as Sultana argued at the same conference, this new pragmatic regime has produced a circumstance in which 'moral, aesthetic, educational and political issues are reduced to technical problems, and value-based questions of "why" and "what" are reduced to technical questions referring to the "how"'.[11] The consequence is that the work of teaching is increasingly construed as a technical activity, where a competent teacher is one who is able to implement the policies of the government of the day effectively.

When given an opportunity, as the conference revealed, teachers expressed a set of views quite different from those of competency-based approaches. For example, they were concerned to work in ways that would try to contain burgeoning community expectations, by reintroducing clarity into what are considered to be the rightful responsibilities of teachers. White, a high-school teacher who attended the conference, put it that before teachers participate in furthering their own discomfort and overload they should ask questions like:

> Is this appropriate to achieve improved learning for me and my
> students?
>
> How can I gain control over the management of my own time?[12]

White claims that teachers need to be more forceful at resisting incursions into their time by politely acknowledging the importance of what is being asked for but firmly indicating that for the time being they are busy completing something else which is fundamental to enhancing the learning of students. He argues that polite deferral of additional duties by teachers ought to be on grounds that validate and authenticate the educational reasons for not participating because of prior existing commitments to improved student learning. In other words, he suggests that the case be presented on educational grounds that enable the practitioner to determine what is realistic and appropriate, based on the relevance of overall teaching plans. White also argues that teachers have a professional responsibility to quarantine time for themselves to remain in touch with educational change. As a practical example, he says:

> Come up with a priority list of problems/issues/ideas. Select one or two and use some non-contact time to answer the question: 'What must I do to clarify my understanding and use of —?' e.g. perhaps talk to —, read about —, visit —, and remember to reject involvement in other programs for the time being.[13]

Dummett and Wells, teachers who also attended the Teacher Development Conference, go further by suggesting positive actions in the form of questions by teachers, and of commitments of the following kind:

- we can think critically;
- we can learn to say no;
- we can reject jargon;
- we can resist corporate and military language;
- we can take control of our professional development;
- we can keep a log;
- we can start a register of tasks;
- we can celebrate and share successes;
- we can support each other.[14]

As a way of drawing this together, it can be argued that recent approaches to teaching and teacher development that celebrate and trumpet 'competency' and 'standards' approaches are very damaging for the following reasons:

1. They deny the richly nuanced nature of teaching and the fact that the way in which it is enacted is a consequence of working through complex personal, historical and contextual factors.
2. They silence the multiple voices and understandings of participants in classrooms, favouring instead the perspectives of people who sit at a distance from the realities of contemporary classroom life.
3. They rend teaching apart by the way in which they separate it from its present, its past and its future.
4. They fail to acknowledge the politics of inclusion and exclusion with regard to what is deemed to be important in measuring, observing and calibrating teaching.

5. They elevate particular viewpoints in the quest to designate what is important about teaching, without disclosing or acknowledging this.

6. They eschew the interconnectedness of theory, method and practice in teaching and the way in which each of these informs the other.

7. They leave unexplored the assumptions, theories and practices of teaching held by teachers, and how these have evolved.

8. They fail to celebrate difference and diversity, and instead seek to suppress them by promoting sameness, rationality, control and efficiency as virtues.

9. They colonize, appropriate and institutionalize teaching in the interests of dominant groups in society, particularly business and industry.

10. They fail to acknowledge classrooms as sites of struggle and contestation, not only over whose views of reality prevail but also over what versions of knowledge are important, and how these should be conveyed.

11. They make teaching appear as if it is a complete, coherent and unified process, when in reality it is characterized by uncertainty, rupture, dissonance, tentativeness, provisionality and self-disclosure.

These are issues that are picked up in various ways by the contributors to this volume as they argue over and present evidence of quite different discourses and practices upon which Teacher Development might proceed. For the very survival of teaching as we know it, we need to listen carefully to these other voices.

INTRODUCTION TO CONTRIBUTIONS

In Chapter 1, Noreen Garman makes the argument that discourse in teacher development, as in any other social practice, is crucial, and that the language within which the practices of teaching are conceptualized exercises a profound influence on shaping what occurs. In teaching it is demonstrably the case that language *is* power! Garman draws on recent US experience to show how the 1980s produced a cacophony of discourses on teacher development – one that was enslaving, followed by one that was allegedly empowering for teachers. The early part of the 1980s was (and to some extent still is) driven by a pervading rhetoric of economic/educational decline, where the 'bottom line' (sic) is teacher development for accountability. Garman describes how teacher development amounted to a form of exhortation in which the principal was deemed the instructional leader in the school, and ought, therefore, to be leading, managing and supervising programmes epitomized in the view 'we brought teachers up to snuff and so can you'. This was a process that was about teacher performance standards and model lessons for teachers to follow. Garman points out that in the latter 1980s educational reform was followed by educational restructuring (a kind of equivalent to perestroika) in which the rhetoric was that of teacher empowerment, with a more muted approach to principal leadership in which administrator-directed forms of teacher improvement were replaced with more seductive forms of teacher development that on the surface, at least, seemed to emphasize participation as an imperative. But even here all was not as it seemed, for, as Garman shows, the language of teacher empowerment of the late 1980s was qualitatively different from the 1960s' civil rights version of what the term 'empowerment' meant. Empowerment by 'authorization' (working within the limited confines of a given framework) was markedly different from empowerment by 'enablement' (the power created or realized by those who have previously been denied control over their lives). Garman illustrates how the perspectives of critical theorists, with their views of how teachers transform themselves intellectually, overcoming technical rationality and engaging in self-confrontation and collective social transformation, have considerable potential as a path to follow.

From the other side of the Atlantic, Anthony Hartnett, Wilf Carr and Michael Naish, in Chapter 2, carry forward the argument for reclaiming the language and the practices of teacher development. They outline what a framework of a theory of teacher development might look like in a modern democracy. They explain how the middle ground, construed as natural and commonsense, has been captured by the New Right, which has been able to construct the fiction of a need to return to a golden age of education where children knew their tables, their grammar and their manners; and they point out how alternatives can and should be shrouded in a 'discourse of derision' – incompetent teachers, falling standards and morality, and declining economic performance. The answer, it was argued, was to abolish teacher autonomy by telling teachers what to teach, how to teach and how to assess that teaching. Part of this has been buttressed by a practice-based view of teacher education currently in vogue.

Hartnett, Carr and Naish argue that if we are to take teacher development seriously, there is some major reclamation work to be done to provide quite a different context and set of circumstances in which the debate can move beyond the technicalities of teaching to focus on the historical, intellectual and moral issues of the role of teachers in the wider social arena – but in ways that take a 'principled view of democracy' and relate this to curricula, pedagogy and assessment. They see three key elements: (i) connecting teachers with social and political theory; (ii) locating them within a historical tradition; and (iii) re-establishing a democratic educational agenda.

Notions of democracy are themselves contested, and depending upon which view we opt for, an educative one (in which citizens participate through education in shaping their own future), or a representative one (in which there is political education for the ruling élite, and utilitarian education for the masses), quite a different set of implications comes into play for teacher development. A democratic approach would hold that teachers need to engage with other teachers in reflecting upon the nature of society, and the complex moral and political issues stemming from that. But this needs to occur, the authors would argue, in a historical situation that understands the role and function enacted by teachers – which in the UK has revolved around teachers for the élite, and teachers who were ideologically reliable and able to deliver guaranteed forms of social control over the masses. This has a contemporary counterpart in the prevailing need for teachers to establish and maintain control and classroom discipline. Teacher development of a democratic kind must, therefore, realistically grapple with the three elements of teachers as citizens, teachers as workers and teachers as persons.

Ivor Goodson, in Chapter 3, argues that to articulate an alternative discourse of teacher development we need to move beyond a narrow focus on 'teacher practice' and focus instead more broadly on 'teachers' lives and work'. This is important, he says, because with what is occurring in classrooms increasingly coming to be shaped by government guidelines and initiatives, there is a constant need to weigh how teachers negotiate the effects of these intrusions against the ways in which *they* interpret their work. Furthermore, to focus only on the practices of teaching is, in Goodson's view, to play into the hands of those outside schools who would gleefully set the agenda and define teachers as little more than mindless technicians. Producing a counter-discourse, and resisting this tendency to 'return teachers to the shadows', is dependent upon sponsoring teachers' voices (in a non-patronizing way) by giving them an opportunity to speak. Goodson sees this as working against the 'curriculum-as-prescription' notion that governments, bureaucracies and universities know best. He sees the processes of silencing and complicity operating in current official trends in education as being sustained, maintained and buttressed by a belief in managerialism as a way of keeping teachers at arm's length. While producing a counter-discourse might occur through approaches that seek to uncover the way we all *as students* came to internalize the norms of teaching, and thus to engage in different forms of socialization into teaching that were much more cognizant of our own unpenetrated histories, it might equally well happen through trying to move the private and oral histories of teachers' lives, which are largely trapped (not unusual for minority views), into more publicly accessible forms. Studying teachers' lives so as to produce teacher-centred forms of professional knowledge is one way to do this.

The 'trading point', according to Goodson, for teachers as researchers (insiders) and external researchers (outsiders) hinges on the different ways the two parties see the world and how this is negotiable and mutually informing. Within this ethical minefield Goodson sees considerable spaces for collaboration between 'story giver' and 'research taker' as each party exercises clear rights of veto in challenging the 'hierarchy of credibility' (the believability of the man at the top) which has been such a devastating put-down of teachers. Mapping who owns the data and who controls the accounts and reports becomes crucial in countering the tendency of officials to 'lie'. What is required are not only 'narratives of action' but also 'genealogies of context' that show the embeddedness of practices in history. Stories, Goodson says, do not exist apart from and outside the communities from which people derive their identities. We need better ways of enabling teachers to theorize about their worlds so as to minimize manipulation by outsiders.

Jesse Goodman's chapter (Chapter 4) recounts with insight the moral, political and epistemological issues that emerge when a group of university researchers engage with a school in working through a process of 'bottom-up teacher development'. While there is much exhortation on the desirability of such approaches, there is scant evidence of the complexity of what this means for schools as well as for outsiders. Goodman unfolds the manifold weaknesses of the 'purchase model' of school staff development (determining teachers' needs, then buying in an expert programme), and the 'medical model' (buying in consultants who are 'doctors of teaching' to study the symptoms, diagnose the condition and then recommend a 'treatment'). Goodman presents an alternative that is grounded in a collaborative/critical approach, that acknowledges its own ideological agenda, and that prominently pursues questions of its own power, expertise and commitment. In this model there is joint examination by the school (principals, teachers, students and parents) and outsiders; the problems are not pre-formulated; the process is one of engaging school people with their values, ideals, aspirations, dreams and visions, and seeing how these relate to the wider society; and the school identifies its own strengths and weaknesses.

Goodman describes how he and his colleagues worked in Harmony School in an up-front way, presenting themselves as having an agenda without any pretension of being detached, neutral or value-free. He says this produced tensions as the researchers tried to remain true to their espoused democratic convictions while trying to foster 'bottom-up' transformation in which school people are the agents of change. They sought to handle this by presenting ideas as being tentative and evolving, and therefore debatable and contestable. Trying not to be treated as 'experts' was difficult, and no matter what they did there was still a certain amount of deference. Questions about whether they were liberating or disenfranchising teachers in another way were never far from their consciousness. No matter what they said or did, they still had power in this setting. Similarly, they had to tangle with the question of whether it was possible for schools and outsiders genuinely to share an educational vision, and what constituted the nature of the common ground. Goodman and his associates struggled too with the question of 'what was to be gained by not working with them?', especially in schools antagonistic to their agenda. The dialogic model of teacher and school development which they presented, while not resolving all of the issues, at least enabled the issues to be put on the table.

Henry St. Maurice, Barbara Albrecht, Nell Anderson and Connie Milz argue in Chapter 5 that research *on* teaching (sic) is moving away from the notion of a Grand Theory (fostered largely by an outmoded process–product approach) at precisely the same time that governments are enacting policies and reforms that progressively silence teachers. It is very much a case, they say, of external changes that are more powerful than anything being developed by the teaching profession itself being imposed upon teaching. This is coming about in part because teachers are increasingly becoming enmeshed in a constructed illusion about 'professionalism' and in increasingly centralist policies designed to meet 'national educational goals'. This is not a uniquely American phenomenon, and it does raise pressing questions about how teachers might best respond to research, policy and practice being crafted by others. St. Maurice and his co-authors present a series of case studies that show how individual teachers struggled with the micro-politics of interpreting, contesting and re-defining what the prevailing discourses of teacher development meant for them. Starting from the everyday discourses of teachers they showed that truth for teachers was something that was continually bound by cultural and political considerations, and that what occurred in teacher development programmes was framed by ideology, interests and power. The three cases they examine show how teachers struggled to make sense, using journals, action research and clinical supervision with competing and conflicting versions of truth, as they encountered what it meant to work with colleagues in ways that were 'prudent' and 'sincere'. These cases are a poignant reminder that professional development is a problematic construct, that it can be used to trivialize teaching, but that it is also not reducible to a simple set of procedures and rules. Encountering the personal difficulties of confronting a valued colleague whose teaching is inappropriate, working in contexts where mutual trust are absent, and promoting conditions in which teachers are pre-pared to fight to overcome isolation do not provide answers, but they do provide a basis upon which to frame better pedagogical questions about what counts as meaningful professional development for teachers.

David Hursh, in Chapter 6, claims that developing as a teacher can be interpreted as a process of finessing style, adding to one's personal repertoire, and matching what one does with the perceived learning needs of students. This is often informed by the most altruistic of beliefs about teaching as a caring profession. This is one way of looking at it, but it is a limited view. Another way is to see teaching as not simply a process but an enterprise that has to be argued for, justified, and defended beyond mere individual preferences for style. According to Hursh, this alternative would involve teachers moving beyond seeing teaching as a matter of individual choice and situating it instead 'within the larger context of discourse and institutional structures . . . [to] explicitly connect their nascent critical and ethical interests to larger ethical and political questions'. Hursh portrays educational discourse as deriving its instrumental approach to indi-vidual and institutional choice from the discourse of philosophical liberalism. We are witnessing this dramatically at the moment, around the world, in a wave of discourse about autonomous, competitive, free-market choices with regard to schooling. What this conceals, Hursh argues, are questions about how a fair and just society and the common good outweigh individual good. This is expressed, for example, in the view that what is most important about teaching is 'what works'. Such views mask the fact that practices are not natural or given but are the outcomes of contested struggles between competing interest groups. The liberal view portrays these merely as differences in style rather than differences embedded in ethical, critical and political positions. Some of these discourses are dominant and accepted and, therefore, limiting – but they ought not be regarded as 'determining', Hursh says.

Teaching practices like 'tracking' were originally a response to the increasing diversity of students, but when they are accompanied by standarized testing, Hursh argues that they produce demonstrable and diminished life chances for students in the lower tracks. There are, he argues, other less competitive, more co-operative approaches to teaching and learning, but they require a reconceptualization of practices and structures, as well as of educational goals at various levels. Within an 'ethic of caring for students' it is possible to develop a discourse that questions the dominant one – one that is more just! What Hursh provides in this chapter is both a rationale and examples of how this might occur, through the ethnography he conducted of eight pre-service teachers in their final year of training. The teachers he worked with tended to justify their teaching on the ground of 'personal beliefs', rather than on the 'ethical or political requirement that schools promote justice or economic fairness'. These teachers, and they are probably not particularly unusual, tend not to see their practices as the 'outcomes of struggle'. This, Hursh says, probably stems in large measure from teaching having been historically regarded as women's work, and therefore more about means than ends – a rational rather than an ethical or political activity. But Hursh's case studies show how, from within the contradictions of liberal discourse itself, alternatives can emerge as teachers are provided with assistance and support in questioning 'what is taught, to whom, how, and for what purpose'.

Peter Grimmett, in Chapter 7, takes a particular instance of educational and curricular reform in British Columbia and discusses the implications this might hold for teachers to engage in classroom-based research as they explore the possibilities of a 'learner-focused curriculum'. Grimmett discusses both the principles behind this policy initiative and the manner in which government has sought to support teachers prepared to work as 'teacher research groups'. What is interesting about Grimmett's analysis is the manner in which, at least on the surface, it seems possible to integrate both systems objectives and the aspirations of teachers to pursue activities that give them the opportunity to create spaces and obtain genuine equity in their work; Grimmett describes this as a process of teachers 'finding their voices'. The themes that emerged from these teacher research groups (there were 11 of them) included: the emergence of a new professional discourse among teachers; a learner-centred focus based on a community of learners; a connectedness to students' prior knowledge and real world experiences; student ownership of learning; and a concern with how best to portray these forms of learning (assessment and reporting) to parents. The policy implications emerging from these teacher research groups were threefold: (1)

teacher research enabled participants to bring the educative agenda to the fore; (2) it provided the necessary support, stability and challenge of a community of inquirers; (3) it demonstrated the important nuances of the difference between learner-focused and learner-directed teaching. Grimmett makes it clear that while definitive conclusions are not possible at this stage, teacher research groups appear to have provided the kind of cultural conditions in which individuals and groups can experiment with the goals and principles of proposed change.

Ronald Sultana provides an especially fascinating illustration, in Chapter 8, of the way in which an alternative discourse of teacher development that is embedded in critical social theory was taken up by a social movement in Malta incorporating student teachers, teachers, university faculty and the wider community. He raises the important, and often unasked, question as to whether 'schools are the best places to promote emancipatory rationality?'. Sultana's view is that teachers occupy a contradictory class location in which they carry out their work, and that they are culturally (if not ideologically) incorporated into the centralized, exam-orientated bureaucratic school system (and Malta is no different from many other parts of the world in this respect).

Sultana describes how he uses case study materials and a version of the catechism method (organized around issues like 'preparation', 'relationships', 'pedagogy', 'control' and 'assessment') as a way of introducing normative dimensions into teaching, alongside the prevailing pragmatic view of 'what works'. All of this is part of a wider process of reconstructing education as a moral and transformative enterprise, and of seeing 'given' structural and cultural factors within which teachers work (routines, rituals, class size, timetables, hidden pedagogy and the like) as technocratic forms of life that ought to be reflected upon. The difficulty, Sultana says, is that teachers are deeply influenced by classical liberal traditions that perpetuate a culture of individualism and make it difficult to link the personal with the political. Some of the responses, like action research and the 'teacher as reflective practitioner' movement, actually exacerbate this. Micro-strategies that focus only on local circumstances fail to make use of the wider political spaces. Sultana's way of handling this in Malta has been through the engagement of student teachers in forms of 'responsible critique' during their five-week practical experience, as they form critical nuclei as part of a wider Moviment Edukazzjoni Umana (MEU) now numbering over two hundred. Activities of the MEU include meetings that make resolutions and form action groups – the formation of a parent pressure group to ensure better resourcing for village schools is one illustration of the latter; another is an action group to shift the discourse of vocational schooling away from an exclusively technicist orientation. A third developed its skills in media communications and developed its own newspaper, and an alternative theatre group acted out social relationships in schools, resulting in the production of a student charter of rights. All of this, Sultana argues, amounts to teacher education moving beyond mere spectatorship to a situation that Alain Touraine calls 'sociological intervention', in which a language for critique is created and pressure can be exerted for structural change.[15]

Andy Hargreaves, in Chapter 9, provides an analysis of how wider social changes are producing a set of imperatives for quite different forms of teacher development, despite the continuing prevalence of models that are clearly outmoded. He looks in depth at collaboration, not as an abstract construct but in its context of use – particularly the emerging conditions of unpredictability and rapid change known as 'post-modernity'. Hargreaves leads us through the features of collaboration that are seen as the solution to the problems of contemporary organizations, but he also warns us that collaboration is no sure-fire cure because of the sometimes unproblematic interpretations and realizations attaching to it: its confinement to the non-controversial; its promotion of conformity and 'groupthink'; its use, sometimes, as an administrative contrivance to secure teacher compliance. There are, Hargreaves says, promises inherent within collaborative approaches, but there are also challenges that teacher development has to grapple with. The way to do this, he says, is to have a clearer sense of the bigger post-modern picture, and the context within which collaboration is being proffered. He draws on Toffler's analogy of 'the moving mosaic' as a way of portraying the changing patterns of production, consumption and economic life, and the way in which flexibility, adaptability, creativity, opportunism, collaboration and continuous improvement are profoundly shaping us educationally and in other facets of life. This impact (manipulative in some senses) is being given its strongest expression in forms like school-based financing, school-based staff development, and the self-managing school, and all of the dangers relate to the way in which this new flexibility is determined and defined.

Hargreaves argues that the other aspect which has to be worked through is the micro-political and moral frameworks that inform these changes. He says that unless we are careful we can end up engaging in 'safe simulations' in which the presentation of image covers up moral, political and ethical emptiness. The way in which co-operative learning is used is a case in point. Hargreaves sees benefits and drawbacks in collaboration, but he also draws our attention to the way we can move beyond it by attending to the moral principles and the political and ethical discourses that inform and guide current conceptualizations of collaboration.

Marilyn Cochran-Smith and Cynthia Paris, in Chapter 10, take a particular form of collaboration, 'mentoring', and argue that this holds the greatest potential for reforming teacher development (and teacher education), provided that: it is based on teachers' ways of knowing, rather than on knowledge of effective teaching or hierarchical management bodies' knowledge about 'what is best practice'; it involves collaborator-to-collaborator, rather than expert-to-novice, relationships; school and social agenda, rather than narrow functional occupational socialization are the object of focus. The problem with the prevailing view of mentoring (especially in the USA) they argue, is that it is based on notions of 'coaching', 'research on teaching', 'best practice' and 'training' – all of which are outsiders' knowledge and language that deny (except rhetorically) insiders' knowledge of classrooms, students and teaching. Conceived in this way, mentoring becomes a way of reproducing current school practices, rather than critically examining teaching and the wider contexts within which it occurs.

Cochran-Smith and Paris offer an alternative vision of mentoring where teachers' ways of knowing are central and where teaching is regarded as fluid and socially constructed by communities of learners, including the way in which teachers treat the data of school life as diverse texts to be connected and interpreted and how they jointly construct and understand meanings about joint products based on closely observed children. The approach Cochran-Smith and Paris offer is not founded in technical-rational epistemology, hierarchical relationships, paternalistic relationships, or helping roles on the part of senior teachers – they see it as being far more complex than that. What they have in mind acknowledges power differentials and asymmetry, and sees instead relationships that are constructed around collaboratively understanding the work of teaching through openly acknowledging the analytical abilities of each of the parties. This view is also antagonistic to the notion that mentoring is fundamentally about the smooth induction of teachers into the prevailing system – rather, it is about challenging standard practices and policies, interrogating assumptions, questioning educational ends and goals, and producing (as distinct from reproducing) knowledge. In the authors' terms, mentoring is fundamentally about 'teaching against the grain' and regarding the prevailing structures of society as being far from inevitable or natural.

Jennifer Gore and Kenneth Zeichner, in Chapter 11, reinforce many of the shortfalls of teacher development alluded to in the previous chapter. For them, all of the exhortation about teacher empowerment and teachers as reflective practitioners amounts to very little, for three reasons: (1) teachers are still urged to replicate the practices of university-sponsored research, while neglecting theories and expertise in their own lived experiences; (2) an overwhelming and prevailing tendency towards means-end forms of thinking predisposes teachers to focus on technical questions of teaching technique while neglecting questions of curriculum and educational purpose; and (3) there is a focus on helping teachers to reflect individually. All of these, Gore and Zeichner say, give the illusion of teacher development, and even when they go beyond the charade they often still fail to address adequately questions of equity, social justice and to what ends (or purposes) teaching is a valued intentional social activity.

Gore and Zeichner examine the claims of emancipatory action research as an antidote to the closure of the technical-rational view of teacher development, and the possibility that this too may have 'become reinscribed in the very politics of truth it opposes' and be implicated in forms of domination of which it is not even aware. In essence, their argument is that even when the practices of action research are situated in discourses of enlightenment like critical social science, this is no guarantee that action research will (or can) deliver on its emancipatory promises. The argument is that, in fields like education, there is so much complexity, diversity and local identification of relevant issues and inequities that it is hard to see how individualized discourses like that of critical social science can produce social transformation. Drawing upon Michel Foucault,[16] Gore and Zeichner claim that the very manner in which action research intervenes (particularly the tendency to direct student research topics in pre-service teacher education programmes, individualizing approaches, and assessing the outcomes of student work) serves to produce forms of self-regulation and self-surveillance that amount to practitioner forms of the confessional and are expressions of the way that modern society operates so that individuals police themselves. Similarly, there are increasing entanglements of emancipatory action research with notions like teacher professionalism as action research is used by those (particularly in pre-service teacher education) who want to appear to be 'more scientific'. The claim being made is that the specific *practices* of action research themselves produce regulative and sorting effects as the *products* of action research become further trapped within limited educational circles. While not using this critique as a basis for suggesting that we abandon attempts at emancipatory action research, Gore and Zeichner claim that we need ways in which it might become more reflective of its own agenda, and they offer suggestions as to how this might occur.

Jon Nixon, in the concluding chapter, in a very fitting fashion demands that we revisit many of the issues raised in the previous chapters of the book. His claim that we live in the midst of an 'economic, technological and sociological earthquake' is a poignant reminder of the enormous complexities facing schools and of the heavy burden that teachers (and their professional development) carry in the process of trying to alter the trajectories and life chances of all of our children. He paints a bleak picture of the UK, but one that is little different from anywhere else in the Western world as schools are pushed in the direction of competition, market forces, and the management of image and impression, rather than being concerned with self-determination and agency, collaboration and mutual support – all in the face of a burgeoning underclass incapable even of 'getting their feet on the first rung of the ladder'. The challenge, for Nixon as for all of the contributors to the book, is how to create a cadre of teachers committed to creating a vision of professionalism that involves revisiting the core values of what teaching is supposed to be all about. 'What might teacher professionalism mean after the earthquake?' is indeed a relevant question.

Assailed from all sides, teachers are finding it increasingly difficult to develop a coherent response. Three possible responses are: 'We are doing a grand job – just leave us to get on with it'; 'We are changing – it's just that it takes time for these changes to have an impact on classroom practice'; and 'We are thinking about what we are doing and about the changes happening around us – our professionalism is dependent on our capacity to do just that'. Each of these responses has implicit within it a quite different view of teacher professionalism. Ultimately, however, Nixon claims that it will be teachers articulating core values that will give them the ability to move beyond merely proclaiming their autonomy – values like the centrality of learning to the educational enterprise; student self-determination; supportive relationships and breadth of achievement. Each of these themes needs to be open too to the possibility of different starting points that acknowledge student disaffection, and are able to explore its genesis; place a premium on students feeling they belong to a learning community; regard learning as a continuum, with multiple entry points; highlight individual progression, based on student opportunity to talk and write about their own learning; and establish partnerships with parents based on respect for the child. Endorsing these values means schools viewing themselves as having to move on several fronts simultaneously, in contexts where there is a strong element of reciprocity, and in climates that are decidedly hostile and oppositional. All of this, Nixon claims, amounts to a politics of refusal – a refusal to allow teaching to be atomized and separated in to a series of meaningless technical operations.

Herein lies the challenge; herein lies the possibility of creating a more educative and socially just world!

NOTES AND REFERENCES

1. Maharey, S., 'The crisis of purpose in public education'. *Delta*, **47**, pp. 11–18 (p. 11), 1993.

2. Ibid., p. 11.

3. Ibid.

4. Ibid., p. 12.

5. Smyth, J., 'A study of participation, consultation and collective bargaining in the teaching profession in Australia'. Paper commissioned by the International Labour Organization, Geneva, December 1993.

6. Jonathan R., 'State education service or prisoners' dilemma: the "hidden hand" as source of education policy'. *British Journal of Educational Studies*, **38** (2), pp. 116–32, 1990.

7. Soucek, V., 'Post-fordism: an economic rationalist attempt at making or unmaking capitalism'. Unpublished manuscript. Perth, Western Australia, 1992.

8. Finegold, D., McFarland, L. and Richardson, W. (eds.), 'Something borrowed, something blue? A study of the Thatcher government's appropriation of American education and training policy'. Parts 1 & 2. *Oxford Studies in Comparative Education*, **2** (2), 1992, and **3** (1), 1993.

9. Smyth, J., 'A critical pedagogy of classroom practice'. Paper presented to the ninth 'Curriculum Theorizing and Classroom Practices' conference, Bergamo Conference Centre, Dayton, OH, USA, p. 36, 1987.

10. Matheson, L., 'Teachers reclaiming teaching'. *South Australian Institute of Teachers Journal*, **26** (7), pp. 10–11 (p. 10), 1994.

11. Sultana, R., 'Conceptualizing teachers' work in a uniting Europe'. Paper presented to the Third International Teacher Development Conference 'Teachers Reclaiming Teaching', Adelaide, p. 18, December 1993.

12. White, G., 'Teachers Reclaiming Teaching'. *South Australian Institute of Teachers Journal*, **26** (7), pp. 10–11 (p. 10), 1994.

13. Ibid., p. 11.

14. Dummett, K. and Wells, D., 'Teachers Reclaiming Teaching'. *South Australian Institute of Teachers Journal*, **26** (7), pp. 10–11, 1994.

15. Touraine, A., *Solidarity: Poland 1980–81*. Cambridge: Cambridge University Press, 1982.

16. Foucault, M., *Michel Foucault: Power/Knowledge. Selected Interviews and Other Writings*. C. Gordon (ed.). New York: Pantheon, 1980.

Chapter 1

The Schizophrenic Rhetoric of School Reform and the Effects on Teacher Development

Noreen B. Garman

DISCOURSES IN EDUCATION

During a supervision training session entitled 'Principals as Instructional Leaders' the discussion turned to the topic of the supervisor's personal style. One principal asked the trainer, 'No matter what I say about her teaching, Norma gets defensive. What can I say that will change that?' The trainer answered, 'It's not what you say, it's how you say it that really matters.'

The trainer, of course, missed the point. Educational practice, as well as public policy, is made of language. Whether as text or talk, discourse is central to the processes of education. It really is *what* you say that matters. Practitioners would do well to understand the way their rhetoric shapes their practice as well as how policies provide the linguistic manoeuvring embedded in their work. Rhetoric focuses on the use of language, and, in the classic sense, looks at how language might influence the thought and conduct of an audience. In recent times, however, there has been a renewed emphasis on language and power as two different aspects of the same phenomenon, recognizing that language is not simply an instrument for describing events, but is itself a part of events, shaping their meaning.

There is also a recognition that the language of education is a political language. (Some would argue that all language is political if we take a broad definition of 'political' to mean the use of strategies of power and control to deal with people in social situations.) In any case, practitioners are often accused of being politically naïve. In a recent conversation with a group of teachers the issue of education as a political enterprise came up. The group as a whole found the idea distasteful, and one teacher suggested that politics referred to dealing with people in opportunistic, manipulative or devious ways. As we talked about his notion of 'political', however, the teachers began to agree that even the distasteful meaning had direct relevance to educational policy and classroom practice. They all came to the conclusion that teachers, perhaps by choice, tend to be politically naïve.

There exists a substantial amount of scholarly literature in which it is maintained that political language can and does significantly influence the thinking of the politically naïve.[1] Edelman has argued that political language can shape political beliefs, and that these beliefs can in turn be evoked in self-serving ways by political leaders.[2] Educational leaders are political leaders, and it is important for us to develop an ear for their rhetoric since it represents their linguistic manoeuvring through the discourse of educational communities.

Cherryholmes describes educational discourse as that which ranges from 'what is said in elementary classrooms, teacher education classes, and research findings reported at conferences and conventions, to what is written in high school textbooks, assessment exams, and research articles in professional journals'.[3] In other words, remnants of discourse can be found in the various artefacts of educational activities such as administrator workshops as well as policy documents. As Foucault has shown, disciplined discourse does not represent 'great continuities of thought, beneath the solid, homogeneous manifestation of a single mind or of a collective mentality' but rather 'discontinuity and rupture'.[4] It is difficult, then, to grasp the various linguistic manoeuvrings in educational discourse, yet our professional lives depend on understanding how the production of discourse is at once controlled, selected, organized and redistributed by what Foucault calls 'the societies of discourse', a group of individuals held together by structured knowledge in their field.[5] In education there are many such 'societies of discourse'. We are not held together by common understandings of our language and, for this reason, the attention to educational rhetoric is crucial.

During the decade of the 1980s the discourses in education became charged with the rhetoric of school reform. Educational issues began to hit the front pages of local newspapers as government political figures discovered their value. The intention of this chapter is to examine the discourses of various groups during this period, especially as they centre on two major concepts central to teacher development: instructional leadership and teacher empowerment. I will argue, through an explication of the rhetoric associated with these concepts, that educational policy and practice had undergone a dramatic shift in position in a short period of time. Prescriptive forms of teacher development were being questioned even as state departments of education were investing heavily in instructional leadership programmes for administrators, ostensibly to upgrade teacher quality. The discourse began to give way to the more seductive rhetoric of teacher empowerment, and the cumulative effects of the two movements had particular consequences for teacher development.

SCHOOL REFORM RHETORIC IN THE 1980S

One thing we can say about the decade of the 1980s: it brought a great deal of public attention to education in general and to teacher development in particular. Almost every social advocacy group in the USA had shown some proclivity for shaking up the educational establishment about a particular vested interest. As a part of the flurry, state legislators introduced an unsurpassed number of education-related bills, increased state aid, examined the findings of hundreds of state-level task forces and commissions, and generally sent a barrage of signals to educators and school districts about school reform.[6] Many of these state efforts predated the infamous *A Nation At Risk* report[7] which gave national prominence to educational reform by suggesting that primary and secondary school education in the USA was a national disgrace, and 'if an unfriendly foreign power had attempted to impose on America the mediocre educational performance that exists today, we might well have viewed it as an act of war'.[8] Most significantly the opening lines of the report sounded what was to become a dominant theme: 'Our Nation is at risk. Our once unchallenged preeminence in commerce, industry, science, and technological innovation is being overtaken by competitors throughout the world'.[9] Its provocative language infused it with a sense of urgency, and the rhetoric of economic/educational decline was the clear message. By the middle of the decade national policy reports continued to link the need for school reforms to industry's concerns for international competitiveness.

A major policy report was launched by the Carnegie Forum on Education and the Economy in May 1986. *A Nation Prepared: Teachers for the 21st Century*[10] was put together by the Task Force on Teaching as a Profession, an influential group of high-profile industrialists, government officials and famous educators. It provided a highly visible policy link between national economic concerns and teacher quality. Once again a report's opening line announced: 'America's ability to compete in world markets is eroding', and continued by saying 'There is a new consensus on the urgency of making our schools once again the engines of progress, productivity and prosperity.' In this new pursuit, one of the remedies for 'the key to success lies in creating a profession equal to the task – a profession of well educated teachers'.[11] Thus the concern for teacher development found its way into government policy rhetoric (if not into funding sources).

Similarly, other documents making statements to influence national policy were issued about the same time. *Investing in our Children: Business and the Public Schools* was prepared by the Committee for Economic Development and focused on two issues, employability of students and teacher quality.[12] *Technical Excellence in America: Incentives for Investment in Human Capital*, issued by The Center for Strategic and International Studies, recommended that heavy investment be made in science and maths teachers.[13] *Creating Responsible and Responsive Accountability Systems*, a report by the US Department of Education, called for more accountability instruments as 'fair and reliable measures of performance'.[14] It recommended that data on accountability 'must be tailored to what individual teachers actually do (for example, how they teach), which usually requires a variety of different kinds of information, including classroom observation'.[15] Implicit in the report is the notion that teacher development is clearly tied to systems of accountability.

The above mentioned documents are a few examples of the massive number of reports issued in the 1980s. By the middle of the decade it seemed as if we were awash in education commission reports. In less than a year following the publication of *A Nation at Risk* more than 260 'blue ribbon commissions' had been created across the nation, established supposedly to attack the problem of poor and mediocre educational institutions.[16]

Ironically, there is little evidence that these commissions made plans for communicating directly to educators. Those involved with *A Nation at Risk* and *A Nation Prepared*, for instance, relied on strategies of power politics outside the education community. As Hlebowitsh points out, the sources used to influence public policy as well as public opinion included access to bases of prestige, competence, money, legal authority and mass communication.[17] Both reports were successful in achieving a mandate for change because they had a number of political sources at their disposal. They were buoyed by a media blitz that caused many (particularly state department officials, superintendents, principals and local school board members) to re-evaluate their school programmes in light of their recommendations.[18] Teachers became the reluctant recipients (some say, victims) of the rhetoric since one of the strongest signals throughout the reports was the call to upgrade teacher quality.

Instructional Leadership vs. Teacher Empowerment: The Schizophrenic Rhetoric of the 1980s

Pennsylvania, like most other states, responded to these political initiatives by focusing on teacher evaluation and, specifically, on the training of administrators to do a better job of evaluating teachers. In other words, teacher evaluation became synonymous with teacher development. In 1983 the governor issued a white paper that included a charge to the state department of education to 'train administrators to supervise teachers effectively and evaluate them fairly'. Under the guise of *instructional leadership*, supervision/evaluation became the primary vehicle for teacher development and school reform in Pennsylvania. The state Department of Education developed a model two-day workshop for its Executive Academy so that regional intermediate units throughout the Commonwealth could conduct training for administrators. The model workshop was called 'Fair and Effective Supervision and Evaluation Practices', and it featured Madeline Hunter's teaching/supervision model, which linked a prescribed version of teaching to in-class supervision. This became the prototype for activities in most school districts. Often referred to as a type of school-based accountability programme, it was the centrepiece for the instructional leadership movement.

More than 1,700 principals, supervisors and other central office administrators, representing 78% of Pennsylvania school districts, attended these workshops. They then returned to their districts to train selected 'enlightened' teachers in the teaching portion of the model. (Teachers were sold the portion as 'Hunter's teaching model' and rarely realized that it was really a supervision model.) Administrators and teachers often went to the intermediate units for more extensive training. In many Pennsylvania schools the teaching portion was put into the district's teacher evaluation system. Thus Pennsylvania became another 'Hunterized' state.[19] The significant point here is that during this time a great deal of effort and resources were given over to acclimatizing the principals and teachers to the instructional leadership role that principals were being asked to assume.

By the mid-1980s another strong message was beginning to get front-page attention, in some cases to counter the heavy-handed side-effects of the instructional leadership movement. *Teacher empowerment* began to be the new challenge. *A Nation Prepared: Teachers for the 21st Century* was issued in 1986 and was interpreted by many as the national call for teacher empowerment because it recommended that there be 'a profession of well-educated teachers prepared to assume new powers and responsibilities to redesign schools for the future'. Now policy-makers were echoing the words of Associate Justice William O. Douglas who lamented that 'those in power want only to perpetuate it'. We were being told that giving teachers greater power was the way to improve education. But the real difficulty was to persuade those in power – in particular, principals, – to share their power. Now, I find this a genuine schizophrenic irony. *We spent the first half of the decade training principals to assume more power over the teachers' domain, and during the second half of the decade we ask 'Why can't principals empower teachers?'.*

MESSAGES IN THE INSTRUCTIONAL LEADERSHIP LITERATURE

In addition to the state-sponsored training programmes for administrators, the literature of instructional leadership during the early 1980s gave clear messages about the meaning of the concept. Made legitimate through the 'effective schools' research and programmatic efforts,[20] instructional leadership became the central concept of the school improvement initiatives. As Greenfield suggests, 'More and better "instructional leadership" is invariably the exhortation one hears in calls for reform and in attendant prescriptions for school improvement.'[21] Although there were earlier references in literature which touted the importance of the principal's role in the school, in *Instructional Leadership* Mackenzie and Corey noted that it is the principal who is viewed as the 'instructional leader of his school'.[22] Thus a cherished assumption is established in the educational literature: the school principal is a critical actor on the school scene, and the effectiveness of instruction and achievement of children can be tied directly to efforts by a strong school principal to lead, manage and supervise teachers and school programmes. The exhortation linking the role of the principal to instructional leadership and school improvement has a long history in education and is as robust today as in the 1920s.[23]

In 1988 ERIC issued one of its composite documents identified as ERIC/CEM *Value Search on Instructional Leadership* which contained 160 articles assembled by the staff as 'relevant to the concept of instructional supervision'.[24] (Composite works were assumed to be important to practitioners and appeared in journals and resource indexes between January 1982 and May 1987.) A content analysis of the major themes and messages in each article revealed the explicit and implicit meanings and assumptions regarding the concept of instructional leadership.[25] The primary theme which dominated the ERIC articles was that instructional leadership meant improving teachers through more in-class supervision and teacher evaluation. Articles such as 'Bringing together teacher evaluation, observation, and improvement of instruction',[26] or 'Courageous teacher evaluation proves principal's prowess',[27] advised principals to back up their impressions of teachers' performances by using documentation and offered suggestions for developing evaluation schemes that supported the improvement of instruction. The article 'We brought teachers up to snuff and so can you'[28] described a plan for instructional improvement that required principals to take part in several workshops and activities to learn how to analyse what goes on in the classroom. Principals then directed teacher in-service training by conducting staff meetings, small seminars and classroom observation, followed by teacher conferences. The plan described here is a common procedure, mentioned earlier, which uses the Hunter teaching/supervision model. Similarly, 'Moving toward excellence: the principal'[29] described opportunities for teacher improvement and development by 'setting teacher performance standards and instilling a "lesson model" for teachers to follow'.

The message is clear. It is the principal who is responsible for improving instruction and developing teachers' practice. It is the principal who must be trained to recognize good teaching, often by learning a prescribed five-step model of teaching. It is the principal who will teach the teachers about teaching practice. Instructional leadership will be accomplished through evaluation of teachers by principals using a standardized version of teaching.

There are, of course, other themes related to instructional leadership in the ERIC compilation. Principals are advised to consider curriculum development, monitoring student progress, aligning student achievement with curriculum and instruction, and encouraging collaboration and collegiality of teachers as part of the role. *The subliminal message in the literature and in the training programmes, however, is that principals should exercise strong authority and control to make their schools effective.* In his chapter 'Administrative control and instructional leadership', Peterson discusses the importance of understanding control mechanisms for effective leadership.[30] He cites six major control mechanisms that 'direct, restrict, or form behaviors, goals and motivational states of principals'. 'Supervision', he says, 'is predominantly a directive control, used to prescribe behavior and communicate expectations.'[31] Thus, within the lore of educational administration the meaning of instructional leadership is identified with the image of a strong principal with firm control who spends a good deal of energy in classrooms helping teachers to improve their work.

By the turn of the decade, however, educational writers were attempting to reconceptualize the meaning of leadership and supervision. Leithwood insisted that ' "Instructional leadership" no longer appears to capture the heart of what school administration will have to become'.[32] Sergiovanni argued that we should seek substitutes for leadership and warned that 'the more professionalism is emphasized, the less leadership is needed. The more leadership is emphasized, the less likely it is that professionalism will develop.'[33] Gordon's notion of a paradigm shift is embedded in a concept of 'new supervision',[34] while Starratt,[35,36] intending to start a discussion among the education community, called for abolishing supervision as we know it and concentrating on teacher development 'after supervision'.[37]

THE CALL FOR TEACHER EMPOWERMENT

'Teacher empowerment' became a rallying concept for the education community as well as policy makers in the latter 1980s. In a rhetorical switch, school reform began to be referred to as school restructuring. A headline in the *Providence Sunday Journal* on 18 February 1990 signalled 'Exit School Reform, Enter Restructuring of US Education'. In the article Frank Newman, president of the Education Commission of the States, said, 'To improve our schools we need a total redesign of our educational system.'[38] Marc Tucker (who was responsible for the Carnegie Report *A Nation Prepared*) called it a 'cultural transformation'. He described the difficulties of radically changing people's roles and likened it to the then Soviet Union. 'Gorbachev is trying to mobilize masses of people who have never had much control of their lives and aren't sure how to handle it when given the opportunity. The same thing has to occur in our schools. They call it perestroika. We call it restructuring.'[39] Initiatives were now under way as teacher participation schemes, such as site-based management, teacher decision-making, and lead teachers, appeared in the name of teacher empowerment.

In Pennsylvania two initiatives were begun by Governor Robert Casey: passing of a law which mandated procedures for ongoing professional development programmes at the district level[40] and the establishment of a state Lead Teacher Program in which the governor proclaimed his support for empowerment.[41] Act 178 was heavily supported by both state teacher unions, especially after it was reported that the state legislature was considering legislation which would mandate a master's degree for permanent certification. Act 178 provided for certification to be obtained through local control of professional development programmes with a high level of involvement by local teachers on the professional development committees responsible for content. The Lead Teacher Program had less enthusiastic support from the Pennsylvania State Education Association (PSEA), which is the major teacher union in the state. It described its position as one of 'cautious interest'.[42]

Thus, in a short span of three years, the Pennsylvania State Department of Education put into place two competing initiatives. Spawned by two opposing rhetorical movements, instructional leadership versus teacher empowerment, the administrator-directed forms of teacher improvement began to give way to more seductive forms of teacher development, with teacher participation as an imperative. However, the opposing rhetoric at the national level often resulted in heated statements of position by those engaged in the discourse. When he was Secretary of Education, William Bennett announced his view of teacher empowerment as a union power play. He called the advocates 'peddlers of the union-hijack reform philosophy'.[43] Gene Geisert, a former school superintendent and now a professor and an author, also stated that he opposed 'the drive toward teacher empowerment as a union juggernaut intended to put unions in the driver's seat and take away the principal's authority'.[44]

The term 'empowerment' was used in the 1960s as a mustering call for the liberals in the civil rights movement. 'Taking control of your own life – refusing to let external authority tell you how to be' was a rallying cry for blacks and feminists during the consciousness-raising phase of their movements. Ironically, in the 1990s empowerment was co-opted by the conservative Bush administration, most notably by Jack Kemp, the Housing Secretary, who pushed Bush to become the 'empowerment president'.[45] Kemp advocated at the US Conference of Mayors that they should 'empower poor people' to have more control over their own lives, adding that 'welfare programs had become a trap, not a springboard'.[46] Many political analysts read this empowerment message as a justification by the federal administration to cut the budget on welfare programmes.

Two Etymologies for Empowerment

As far as we know, the term 'empowerment' originated in written form in 1645. This earliest citation in the *Oxford English Dictionary* reports that 'empower' meant to authorize or to license. In 1681 another use of the term emerged: to enable or permit. According to the first definition, some person or formal body with power approves or sanctions the transmission of power to another person or formal body. In the second definition a person or authorizing body provides an opportunity for another to develop power. The emphasis on the idea of direct transmission is lessened, and the implication is that responsibility for empowerment is shared by both parties.

The difference in these two etymological definitions appears to be subtle, yet the distinguishing features are significant for discourse in education. In the first meaning, someone 'empowers' someone else, generally by imparting specific knowledge and skills that allow the other to work within the existing social system. Sears and Marshall call this *empowerment-by-authorization*.[47] People are empowered to work within the limited framework provided by those who do the empowering. In the second definition, *empowerment-by-enablement*, educators become empowered or enabled in different ways. Their power is created or realized by them – not received from or bestowed by others. In this conception, according to Sears and Marshall, 'empowerment is a deeply personal process of meaning-making within particular historical, cultural, and economic contexts'.[48] When one talks about empowering people, the intent is to enable them to recognize, create and channel their own power. The intent is not merely to share limited institutional power. Scholars such as Nyberg provide elaborate considerations for the understanding of power and authority within the discourse of empowerment.[49] Still, there are those who would argue that no matter how one speaks of empowering another person, it assumes a hierarchy of power and control that one holds over another.

Critical Theorists Contribute to the Discourse

One significant body of discourse is carried on in the educational community by scholars known as critical theorists. Within this discourse they argue that teachers can transform themselves intellectually, overcome technical rationality, grow in awareness of both the overt and the hidden curriculum and encourage reflective practice, self-efficacy and self-confirmation through collective action and social transformation. This discourse reflects a political vision toward teacher emancipation and is viewed as a means toward an end, a 'project of possibility'.[50] Common among these scholars is the belief that teachers must acquire the knowledge, skills and power to transform the existing social order both individually and collectively. Critical theories are grounded in such works as Friere's notion of emancipation,[51] Fay's theory of social change and educative process,[52] and Gramsci's notion of hegemony,[53] to mention only a few.

Situated within the discourse are implicit and explicit examples of the meanings and practices of teacher empowerment. In general, scholars suggest that empowered teachers should be concerned with a variety of issues, such as the ways in which local, state and national policies impact upon them, and how these policies promote particular practices that favour some forms of knowledge over others; how dominant modes of discourse in educational practices are constructed, maintained and circulated within and beyond the school; how the conditions under which teachers work and the political importance of these conditions either limit or allow what they can do; and how they give meaning to their lives through historical, cultural and political forms.

As empowered individuals, teachers are expected to aspire to an emancipatory praxis[54-56] and to the creation of schools as democratic spheres.[57] They are told that they must learn the language of critique and possibility;[58] uncover the dominant political interest in curriculum planning, school texts and school policy;[59,60] explore the relationships of schooling and the production of meaning;[61] scrutinize the hidden curriculum within their own teaching and the school in general, and form collaborative alliances with progressive movements outside the school.[62] Furthermore, teachers are advised to work toward establishing a structure in which they have adequate time to work creatively and collectively toward elimination of the rules and regulations that disempower them.[63-65]

Another part of this critical discourse emanates from feminist scholars who consider issues of gender, particularly the historical and social implications of teaching as 'women's work'. Martin argues that considerations of gender are central to the reconstruction of educational theory and practice necessary for emancipation for all women, not just for a few.[66] She criticizes the mainstream dynamics of educational policy which typically have been male dominated. Lather asserts: 'If we want to understand and change the work lives of teachers, issues of gender are central.'[67] Critical of theorists and scholars who have 'marginalized' issues of gender in their studies of teachers, Lather writes: 'To disallow gender in our analysis of teacher work is to not tap into the potential feminism offers for bringing about change in our schools.' If this 'absent presence', the invisibility of gender, is maintained, there will be little hope for restructuring the public schools, which have 'grown up around women's subordination'.[68]

Melenyzer, however, points out that 'teachers, those who are practicing [sic], living, and seeing teacher empowerment and disempowerment, have remained silent'.[69] Certainly within the discourses mentioned above, there are no classroom teacher voices represented in the call for teacher empowerment. The term seems to be central to the rhetoric of those who supervise teachers, write policies to upgrade teaching quality or study teachers' work. Ironically, teachers are the recipients rather than the initiators in this teacher empowerment reform. Teachers are truly the 'silenced practitioners'.[70] It might be said that teachers are disempowered when it comes to the discourse of empowerment.

Effects on Teacher Development: The Come-and-Go Syndrome

Reformers, as well as critics of current reforms, have continually reminded us that innovative programmes of teacher development have been part of the educational scene for the past century. As I have argued, the reforms of the 1980s have been particularly chaotic. In a short period of time the rhetoric which drives policy and practice about the improvement of instruction switched from direct administrative control to indirect teacher participation. In three short years the initiatives in Pennsylvania, as well as in other states, went from instructional leadership to teacher empowerment, with a flurry of energy and resources given over to both. Little attention has been given, however, to the cumulative effects on school personnel of their investment in these programmes, which they often see as come-and-go. We all know about the come-and-go syndrome in schools. We hear it in the teachers' lounge and during in-service programmes. Administrators despair over what one principal calls 'the bad attitude from the Snarks' (uncooperative teachers). It is clear that we hear the effects of the come-and-go syndrome on teacher attitudes, yet we know very little about the residual effect over time of these programmes, often seen by the teachers as administrative broken promises.[71] Teachers manifest feelings of anger and resistance and/or cynicism and hopelessness. One teacher spoke poignantly about her overriding sense of betrayal. She had participated in an innovative programme with enthusiasm and commitment, trusting that such involvement would result in increased professional autonomy. She, like others, invested much time and energy and hope in the programme, becoming an advocate even against many of her 'jaded' colleagues. As she said, 'I was zealously promoting it as an avenue for professional growth to the teachers.' Within the bureaucratic structure of the school, however, the stated intention of the programme became distorted as it was played out in the daily lives of the teachers. She felt she had been 'sold out', betrayed in the eyes of her older colleagues who could say 'I told you so'.[72] Each time this situation occurs, teachers become less willing to give their professional attention and loyalty in the name of teacher development. Moreover, those who design teacher development experiences never seem to take into account this disposition of come-and-go and, more important, the feelings of betrayal that have already settled over the educational community.

Teacher empowerment efforts are being created to address some of the relentless ills of the teaching profession: isolation from one's colleagues in teaching; lack of career advancement; the need to accommodate or resist bur-eaucratic controls; the feelings of betrayal when one's commitments are diminished. These are the everyday concerns that keep teachers disempowered. We must recognize the pitfalls of putting people into positions of responsibility with little sensitivity to prevailing conditions and little understanding of what it takes to create an authentic teacher development experience with genuine collegiality.

NOTES AND REFERENCES

1. Geis, M. L., *The Language of Politics*. New York: Springer-Verlag, 1987.

2. Edelman, M., *Political Language: Words that Succeed and Policies that Fail*. New York: Academic Press, 1977.

3. Cherryholmes, C., *Power and Criticism: Poststructural Investigations into Education*. New York: Teachers College Press, p. 3, 1988.

4. Foucault, M., *The Archaeology of Knowledge and the Discourse on Language*. New York: Pantheon Books, p. 4, 1972.

5. Ibid., p. 40.

6. Pipho, C., 'A decade of education reform'. *Phi Delta Kappan*, **74** (4), pp. 278–9, 1992.

7. *A Nation at Risk: The Imperative for Educational Reform*. National Commission on Excellence in Education Report. Washington, DC: US Government Printing Office, 1983.

8. Ibid., p. 5.

9. Ibid., p. 5.

10. *A Nation Prepared: Teachers for the 21st Century*. Carnegie Forum on Education and the Economy's Task Force on Teaching as a Profession Report. New York: Carnegie Corporation, 1986.

11. Ibid., p. 2.

12. *Investing in our Children: Business and the Public Schools*. A statement by the Research and Policy Committee of the Committee for Economic Development. New York: Committee on Economic Development, 1985.

13. *Technical Excellence in America: Incentives for Investment in Human Capital*. Washington, DC: Georgetown University Center for Strategic and International Studies, 1984.

14. *Creating Responsible and Responsive Accountability Systems*. Report of the OERI State Accountability Study Group. Washington DC: US Department of Education, 1988.

15. Ibid., p. 39.

16. Peterson, P. E., 'Did the education reports say anything?' *Brookings Review*, **2** (2), pp. 3–11, 1984.

17. Hlebowitsh, P., 'Playing power politics: how a nation at risk achieved its national stature'. *Journal of Research and Development in Education*, **23** (2), pp. 82–8, 1990.

18. Ibid.

19. Garman, N. and Hazi, H., 'Teachers ask: is there life after Madeline Hunter?' *Phi Delta Kappan*, **69** (9), pp. 669–72.

20. Achilles, C. M., 'A vision of better schools'. In Greenfield, W. (ed.), *Instructional Leadership: Concepts, Issues and Controversies*. Newton, MA: Allyn & Bacon, 1987.

21. Greenfield, W., 'Moral imagination and interpersonal competence: antecedents to instructional leadership'. In Greenfield, W. (ed.), *Instructional Leadership: Concepts, Issues and Controversies*. Newton MA: Allyn & Bacon, 1987.

22. Mackenzie, G. N., and Cory, S. M., *Instructional Leadership*. New York: Bureau of Publications, Teachers College, Columbia University, 1954.

23. Greenfield, op. cit., note 21, p. 57.

24. *Value Search on Instructional Leadership*. ERIC Clearinghouse on Educational Management. Eugene, OR: University of Oregon, 1987.

25. Garman, N., 'A rhetorical analysis of the concepts, instructional supervision and teacher empowerment representing conflicting practices for supervision'. Research report. University of Pittsburgh, 1990.

26. Reyes, D., 'Bringing together teacher evaluation, observation and improvement of instruction'. *Clearing House*, **59** (6), pp. 256–8, 1986.

27. Grier, T. B., 'Courageous teacher evaluation proves principal's prowess'. *Executive Educator*, **9** (2), pp. 17–19, 1987.

28. Jacobson, W. C., 'We brought teachers up to snuff and so can you'. *Executive Educator*, **6** (2), pp. 41–6, 1984.

29. Brown, E. D., 'Moving toward excellence: the principal'. Paper presented at the Annual Meeting of the National Association of Secondary School Principals, New Orleans, 25–29 January 1985. ERIC D. 254944.

30. Peterson, K. D., 'Administrative control and instructional leadership'. In Greenfield, W. (ed.), *Instructional Leadership: Concepts, Issues and Controversies*. Newton, MA: Allyn & Bacon, 1987.

31. Ibid., p. 144.

32. Leithwood, K., 'The move toward transformational leadership'. *Educational Leadership*, **49** (5), pp. 8–12, 1992, p. 8.

33. Sergiovanni, T., 'Why we should seek substitutes for leadership'. *Educational Leadership*, **49** (5), pp. 41–9, 1992, p. 42.

34. Gordon, S., 'Paradigms, transitions and the new supervision'. *Journal of Curriculum and Supervision*, **8** (1), pp. 62–76, 1992.

35. Starratt, R. J., 'A modest proposal: abolish supervision'. *Wingspan*, **8** (1), pp. 14–19, 1992.

36. Starratt, R. J., 'After supervision'. *Journal of Curriculum and Supervision*, **8** (1), pp. 77–86, 1992.

37. Ibid.

38. 'Exit school reform, enter restructuring of US education'. *Providence Sunday Journal*, RI, 18 February 1990.

39. Fiske, E., 'Finding a way to define the buzzword of American education: how about perestroika?' *New York Times*, 14 February 1990.

40. Act 178 went into effect on 15 December 1986 and represents a professional development law which governs teachers who have not attained their permanent certification. It mandates that schools must set up committees to scan personal needs of the professional staff systematically and develop programmes to meet individual and school-wide needs. Committees must be constituted to include a representative of the professional staff as well as community members. Although those with permanent certification are not mandated by law to be involved, it was assumed that they would be encouraged through the on-going activities to participate. In reality, school

administrators put heavy pressures on their staff to participate in total. These efforts are tied to the rhetoric of shared decision-making and site-based management.

41. The Lead Teacher Program was recommended by the Carnegie Report *A Nation Prepared*, op. cit., note 10. It called for schools to restructure their teaching force and create a new category of Lead Teacher with the proven ability 'to provide active leadership in the redesign of schools and in helping their colleagues to uphold the high standards of learning and teaching' (p.618). In February 1988 Governor Casey initiated the Pennsylvania Lead Teacher Program [sic], patterned after other state programmes. He charged the Secreary of Education with establishing a 46 member committee, and by November of that year the committee had issued a document, *The Profession of Teaching in Pennsylvania: A Report on Lead Teachers*, Harrisburg: Pennsylvania Department of Education, 1989, which described a lead teacher as 'one who works with other teachers in classrooms, where they observe, demonstrate, guide, suggest, critique and applaud'. It was emphasized that 'the approach of the Lead Teacher Programs in Pennsylvania has been to encourage collegiality . . . and to focus on the improvement of instruction' (p.8). The state provided for the funding of nine centres throughout the state serving 250 of the 501 school districts which have some form of Lead Teacher Program. The nine Lead Teacher Centers [sic] were established to provide teachers with leadership training which, in some cases, included a heavy dose of the state's earlier version of clinical supervision.

42. Cordell Affeldt, director of professional programs for PSEA, said in a personal interview: 'The reason we took that position is that the concept of Lead Teacher sounds intriguingly positive, but we are experienced enough in the affairs of public schools to know that good ideas can often be ruined on their way to implementation in the real world. And because we so frequently hear stories from teachers who have experienced the most negative interpretation or misapplication of an idea on a local level, it would be inappropriate for us at the outset to say this is wonderful because so many of our members would not experience it that way. And indeed, experience with this program has borne that out.'

43. Hechinger, F., 'More power for teachers: is it a "union juggernaut" or a path to better schools?'. *New York Times*, 8 November 1989.

44. Ibid.

45. DeParle, J., 'Bush blurred message on home front', *New York Times*, 3 February 1991.

46. *New York Times*, 24 January 1991.

47. Sears, J. and Marshall, D., 'An evolutionary and metaphorical journey into teaching and thinking about curriculum'. In Sears, J. and Marshall, D. (eds), *Teaching and Thinking about Curriculum*. New York: Teachers College Press, 1990.

48. Ibid., p. 17.

49. Nyberg, D. A., 'Power, empowerment and educational authority'. In Jacobson, S. L. and Conway, J. A. (eds), *Educational Leadership in an Age of Reform*. New York: Longman, 1990.

50. Simon, R., 'Empowerment as a pedagogy of possibility'. *Language Arts,* **64** (4), pp. 370–82, 1987.

51. Friere, P., *Pedagogy of the Oppressed.* New York: Seabury Press, 1970.

52. Fay, B., *Critical Social Science.* Ithaca, New York: Cornell University Press, 1987.

53. Gramsci, A., *Selections from the Prison Notebooks.* New York: International Publishers, 1971.

54. Giroux, H. A. and McLaren, P., *Critical Pedagogy, the State and Cultural Struggle.* Albany, NY: State University of New York Press, 1989.

55. Smyth, J., 'International perspectives on teacher collegiality: a labour process discussion based on the concept of teachers' work'. *British Journal of Sociology of Education,* **12** (3), pp. 323–46, 1991.

56. Smyth, J., 'Problematizing teaching through a "critical" approach to clinical supervision'. *Curriculum Inquiry,* **21** (3), pp. 321–52, 1991.

57. McLaren, P., 'Language, social structure and the production of subjectivity'. *Critical Pedagogy Networker,* **1** (2–3), pp. 1–10, 1988.

58. Simon, op. cit., note 50.

59. Apple, M. W., 'Is there a curriculum voice to reclaim?' *Phi Delta Kappan,* **71** (7), 526–30, 1990.

60. Giroux and McLaren, op. cit., note 54.

61. Aronowitz, S. and Giroux, H. A., *Education Under Siege: The Conservative, Liberal and Radical Debate over Schooling.* South Hadley, MA: Bergin & Garvey, 1985.

62. Apple, M. W., 'The deskilling of teaching'. In Bolin F. S. (ed.), *Teacher Renewal: Professional Issues, Personal Choices.* New York: Teachers College Press, 1987.

63. Giroux, H. A., *Ideology, Culture and the Process of Schooling.* Philadelphia: Temple University Press, 1981.

64. Giroux and McLaren, op. cit., note 54.

65. Smyth, op. cit., note 56.

66. Martin, J. R., *Reclaiming a Conversation: The Ideal of the Educated Woman.* New Haven: Yale University Press.

67. Lather, P., 'The absent presence: patriarchy, capitalism and the nature of teachers' work'. *Teacher Education Quarterly,* **14** (2), pp. 25–38, 1987.

68. Ibid., p. 30.

69. Melenyzer, B. 'Teacher empowerment: narratives of the silenced practitioners'. Unpublished dissertation. Indiana University of Pennsylvania (p. 158) 1991.

70. Ibid.

71. Ceroni, K., 'Promises made, promises broken: a literary criticism of the lead teacher experience in Pennsylvania'. Unpublished dissertation. University of Pittsburgh, 1995.

72. Ceroni, K. and Garman, N., 'The empowerment movement: genuine collegiality or yet another hierarchy?' In Grimmett, P. and Neufeld, J. (eds), *Teacher Development and the Struggle for Authenticity*. New York: Teachers College Press, pp. 141–61.

Chapter 2

Education, Teacher Development and the Struggle for Democracy

Anthony Hartnett and Wilfred Carr

'It is now sufficiently clear that the teacher to whom you give only a drudge's training, will only do a drudge's work, and will do it in a drudge's spirit.' (Matthew Arnold)[1]

INTRODUCTION

Teacher education, like education in general, is under serious attack. During the 1980s in the USA (under Reagan) and in the UK (under Thatcher) the right triumphed. In the UK, as always in the vanguard of progressive social and political change, the 'great moving right show'[2] continued with the election in 1992 of a Conservative government for a fourth consecutive term, but with a substantially reduced majority. In education the signs are that the move to the right is continuing with gathering momentum.

During the last decade education has moved up from low politics and low importance to high politics and the serious political league. The old arguments, vocabularies and academic specialisms are no longer adequate. This essay outlines what a theory of teacher development in a modern democratic society might look like. It concentrates on the situation in England, but it is hoped that the analysis it offers will have insights and implications for other societies.

Teacher development: the background

In England the status, development and public recognition of teachers have suffered particularly badly from the achievements of the Right. It sometimes seems as if the right has taken over all the best arguments and rhetorics and annexed all the 'best' words such as 'excellence', 'quality', 'standards', 'discipline', 'choice', 'freedom', 'parents', and 'autonomy'.[3] In addition, the right has constructed 'moral panics and folk devils'[4] around 'loony left councils', 'remote and ineffectual educational theorists', 'political extremists' and 'union militants'. It made effective and sustained use of highly selected accounts of *causes célèbres* such as Bennett's ineffable study of teaching styles,[5] and the William Tyndale, McGoldrick and Honeyford cases.[6] In its writings the right has constructed the fiction of a past 'golden age' in education, when everything, as in the Hovis advertisement, was bathed in sunlight and children always knew their tables, their grammar and their manners. The right also constructed a range of plausible characters and moral entrepreneurs able to take the messages to a wide audience: the down-to-earth experienced headmaster of northern origins (who had actually come to public notice in London) – Sir Rhodes Boyson; learned and cultivated professors – Scruton and O'Hear; and the sensitive liberals who had been damaged by the militant left – Baroness Cox and Ray Honeyford. With its other friends and collaborators it promoted a new cultural style of pamphlets and reports developed in what are incongruously called 'think-tanks'.

The result was that the right created a 'discourse of derision' and a 'mobilization of bias'[7] and established a view that state education was 'in crisis'. This was echoed, magnified and repeated in the press and on television. Teachers sustained the brunt of the attack. They were incompetent, responsible for the falling standards in education and in morality, and even for the decline in the UK's economic performance. Since the central educational problem was *teachers*, it had to be solved by dealing with their selection, training and performance. Above all it was teachers' autonomy that had to be abolished. Accordingly, they have now been told what to teach, how to teach it, and how to assess it to see if it has been taught successfully. They are managed by the senior management teams and controlled by the bureaucrats. They are to be appraised and, if they are found wanting, they are to be sacked. The entire process of teacher education and development has come in for a similar attack. Initial teacher training has been subjected to tight centralist and bureaucratic control.[8] It was proposed (in 1992) that schools should become the dominant partner in training.

What might be called 'the traditional establishment' of teacher education expressed, in private, grave doubts and serious *angst* about government policy. But in public, and during the early stages of the changes, its members co-operated with the government and its agencies and quangos. Some aspects of policy (such as the National Curriculum, and the privatization of HM Inspectorate) were seen by many managements as 'nice little earners' in financially hard times. But the real *trahison des clercs* had come a lot earlier in the work of the educational philosopher Professor Paul Hirst. From the safe haven of Cambridge University, he had put the theoretical case for a practice-focused view of teacher training.[9-13] This focus has been reinforced by his successor at Cambridge, Professor David Hargreaves.[14] Their work, combined with the effective attacks of the New Right, played a significant part in the failure of the *institutions* of teacher education to develop coherent intellectual and moral arguments for taking teacher development seriously in a modern democratic society. It also made an effective political defence of the area that much more difficult. When the government started to push, teacher education was ready to fall into the black hole.

PART ONE

AN EMERGING DISCOURSE ON TEACHER DEVELOPMENT

Teacher development: a perspective

This essay puts forward the outlines of a theory of teacher development for a society in which democracy is taken seriously. It sees teacher development to be concerned with the processes, insights, structures and ideas which enable teachers to reflect about, and improve, their practices throughout their careers. It places great significance on the context in which the initial education of teachers takes place, as well as on their development during their working lives. It attempts to shift the debate away from the often technical minutiae of local issues about teacher education, and back to the historical, intellectual and moral issues about the nature of the good society and of the good life, and to the role of teachers, schools and education in helping to imagine, construct and maintain them. It proposes that in a developed democratic society teachers should be a critically reflective group which is given difficult and complex tasks to do. Teachers' status, prestige, development and education has to reflect the complexity and social importance of these tasks.

In pursuing this argument the essay suggests that an adequate democratic theory of teacher development has to do three things: first, it must connect with more general social and political theories about such issues as democracy, social justice, equality and legitimacy. It has to demonstrate the implications of a principled view of democracy not just for educational systems but also for the way in which educational institutions should be run. It also has to relate these ideas to curricula, pedagogy and assessment.

Secondly, it must be located within a particular historical, political and educational tradition and context. Teachers do not work and reflect in a social vacuum. They act within institutions, structures and processes which have a past and a social momentum. Within the UK, for example, educational traditions in Scotland are quite different from those in England.[15, 16]

Thirdly, a theory of teacher education has to re-establish a democratic political agenda and to develop constituencies in the wider society for this work so as to bring about the changes which are required. In addition it must relate to the specific interests of teachers as citizens, workers and persons. We now examine each of these requirements in turn.

CONNECTING WITH SOCIAL AND POLITICAL THEORY

Education is irrevocably linked to politics and power (who gets what, when and how), and in modern industrial and post-industrial societies there are contested and different viewpoints about the nature of the good society and the good life. These differences may be both justifiable and enduring. Modern societies which claim to be democratic have to develop institutional and political processes which enable these conflicting viewpoints to co-exist. This contestable nature of society is especially important in education because schools play a central role in what Gutmann calls 'conscious social reproduction'.[17] This means that in a democratic society children need space and resources to make informed and rational choices about the kind of life that they want to lead, the sort of society that they want to live in, and the sort of people that they want to become.

Two views of democracy

The relationship between education and democracy is complicated by the fact that democracy, like education, is a contestable notion. For our purposes we can distinguish two broad approaches to the notion of democracy. First, there is the classical/moral tradition which dates back to the Greeks where democracy is seen as essentially educative: preparing individuals to participate in the political and cultural life of the society. Democracy here is a moral notion identifying a form of social and political life which speaks to fundamental human values. It requires a general education for all its citizens so that they have experience of both ruling and being ruled. All citizens participate in shaping their society by contributing to deliberations about the form and characteristics of the common good. Education, therefore, has to develop in citizens the kind of character and the kind of intellect that enables them to choose rationally between different ways of life. It follows from this that a central task for educational institutions, through curriculum, pedagogy and assessment, is to encourage in students a capacity to engage in a critical appraisal of dominant social norms and contemporary institutions.

Secondly, there is the contemporary or representative conception of democracy. This approach regards the classical ideas as impractical and unrealistic in modern industrial societies. All that democracy can offer is a system that allows the people a choice of rulers. Voters choose between rival policies offered by competing political entrepreneurs or élites. The political apathy and indifference of much of the electorate that such systems may engender are taken to be of positive value and to play an important part in the maintenance of a stable society. Under this model of democracy political education will be marginalized and policy will be formulated by leaders rather than through public deliberation and debate. Such a conception might even encourage a two-tier educational system: for the future élite an education appropriate to leaders, and for the mass of the people vocational and instrumental schooling to fit them for their future occupations.

These two approaches to democracy have quite different implications for teacher development. In this section we limit our discussion to examining the consequences of the classical view.

'Classical' democracy and teacher development

What Gutmann calls a principled theory of democratic education[18] has to deal with two central questions: who should have the authority to make decisions about education, and what should be the moral boundaries of that authority? There are at least three possible answers to the first of these questions, namely the state, parents, and individuals. Gutmann shows how there are justifiable limits to anyone having exclusive rights to authority in education and suggests that a democratic state is 'therefore committed to allocating educational author-ity in such a way as to provide its members with an education adequate to participate in democratic politics, to choosing among (a limited range of) good lives, and to sharing in the several sub-communities, such as families, that impart identity to the lives of its citizens'.[19] Gutmann goes on to argue that there should be a limit on state and parental authority in education because some authority has to be ceded to professional educators. She proposes two principles which determine this limit: non-repression and non-discrimination.

Under the principle of non-repression the state, and groups within it, are prevented 'from using education to restrict rational deliberation of competing conceptions of the good life and the good society'.[20] Conscious social reproduction, which is the primary ideal of democratic education, means that 'communities must be prevented from using education to stifle rational deliberation of compet-ing conceptions of the good life and the good society'.[21]

The principle of non-discrimination requires that 'all educable children must be educated'. This is essential to support conscious social reproduction. Discrimination often represses, at least temporarily, the capacity and even the desire of minority groups 'to participate in the processes that structure choice among good lives'. Thus the principle of non-discrimination precludes any group, and the state, from denying anyone education on irrelevant grounds.

Democratic citizens are persons partly constituted by sub-communities (fami-lies, religious groups etc.). Yet they are also free 'to choose a way of life compatible with their larger communal identity because no single sub-community demands absolute authority over their education, and because the larger community has equipped them for deliberating and thereby participating in the democratic processes by which choice among good lives and the chance to pursue them are politically structured'. The democratic state teaches the virtue of the 'ability to deliberate, and hence to participate in conscious social reproduction'.[22]

Teachers are, therefore, central to a principled democratic theory of educa-tion. Society is dependent upon the quality of their judgements, values, know-ledge and sensitivities, in particular in social contexts, to negotiate acceptable solutions to issues of authority in education; to sustain the development of democratic values in the wider society; and to creating a social environment in which children can deliberate about, and reflect critically upon, the nature of the good life and the good society. It is teachers who should be a centre of resistance to totalitarian, centralist and utopian thinking and control within society. They are a critical pivot between the state, parental power, institutional power and the development of democratic values and attitudes in each new generation.

Given these requirements teachers from their initial training have to grapple with complex moral and political issues. These include an examination of the assumptions and limitations of their own education and how this might inhibit access to education and to democratic values by other groups; insight into diverse cultural values and differences and how these differences are often translated into education failure; an understanding of schools as social institutions whose norms and practices might create obstacles to education and solidify the differences between cultures;[23] an understanding of how to connect with, and establish a rapport with, a wide range of cultural, class, ethnic and gender groups. As Gutmann puts it, teachers have to 'be sufficiently connected to their communities to understand the commitments that . . . students bring to school, and sufficiently detached to cultivate among their students the critical distance necessary to reconsider commitments in the face of conflicting ones'.[24]

Liston and Zeichner suggest that 'Teacher educators must enable prospective teachers not only to formulate good reasons for their educational plans but also to identify those social beliefs and conditions of schooling that are obstacles to a democratic education.'[25] Gutmann likewise puts forward reasons why 'democratic educators ought to be concerned about the conditions under which teachers work . . . . It is the teacher's job to ensure that restrictions are not placed on students' rational deliberation and that students are able to consider critically different ways of living.' Gutmann goes on to suggest that 'The structure of teachers' work contributes to . . . the ossification of office.' In other words, teachers have too little autonomy and as a result teaching in the state schools becomes rigid, settled, and fixed.[26] She further suggests that political action by teachers, in unions, might 'pressure democratic communities to create the conditions under which teachers can cultivate the capacity among students for critical reflection on democratic culture'.[27]

In a society which claims to take democracy seriously these issues have implications for all levels of teacher development and educational practice. They will influence the content, control and focus of the curriculum: what is taught, how it is taught, and the assessment of what has been taught. They also have consequences for how schools should be run. We explore some of these issues in the next section, and in greater detail in a forthcoming book by Carr and Hartnett.[28]

LOCATION WITHIN A HISTORICAL TRADITION

A democratic educational system, in the classical moral sense outlined in the previous section, both presupposes and requires a democratic society. Education necessarily plays a part in helping to bring about such a society, but it is not sufficient. A theory of teacher development needs, therefore, to be located within a particular historical tradition so that structural factors which that tradition embodies and which impede the development of democratic education can be made explicit. Among these are the characteristics of the educational system, especially those that relate to teacher development, and the specific political contexts in which teachers have to work. In this section we make some comments about these factors.

Background

Mass state education came to England late. As Green suggests, 'England was exceptionally slow to develop a national system of elementary schools.'[29] This system was started in the mid-nineteenth century when Liberalism was the key idea in the intellectual environment. There was a prejudice against state activity, and voluntary action was preferred. As the system developed, it had to fit into an existing class-based society and into a political system which was only slowly granting votes to adults. Through the monitorial system and the Revised Code of 1862 a sound and cheap system of schooling, which was supposed to teach the lower orders their social place, and also numbers, words and the bible, was put into place. The 1902 Act carefully distinguished secondary (i.e. grammar) school education from that provided by elementary schools. It also limited secondary education to a minority. This was 'exactly 100 years after Napoleon had created the *lycées* in France and almost as long since the USA and the German states created public secondary schools'.[30]

One way of characterizing educational change from the mid-nineteenth century to the second half of the twentieth century is to say that during the first part of the period, selection and differentiation were based explicitly on class lines. There were different schools for different classes. During the twentieth century selection gradually became individualized, so that 'bright' children could be selected for schools for 'bright' children, and membership of social categories became translated into individual failure and success. In the 1960s and 1970s comprehensive education brought some limited gains to democratic advance, but it moved selection and differentiation into schools and can be characterized as the period of 'the egalitarian dream'.[31]

A 'sponsored' system

From this quick sketch, it can be seen that, first, the system has developed in a fragmented, voluntaryist and uncoordinated manner. At no time have the questions 'what should be the main characteristics, structure and form of the entire educational system so as to meet the requirements of a developing, participatory democratic society?' and 'what kind of teacher education and development does this require?' been asked. Rather, the system is a 'sponsored' one[32] in which the main problem is the early identification of, and the distinctive education for, the intellectual élite. There have, of course, been political and social forces operating against this,[33] but generally the needs and requirements of the élite have had a disproportionate impact on the institutional structures, on curriculum, on pedagogy and on assessment. The continuous political concern has been how to protect the élite (via selective secondary schooling, special papers at GCSE, A level etc.) rather than with how to shape education in a way consonant with a fully democratic society. This has meant that each level of education has spent much of its time preparing a minority for the level above it rather than preparing everyone for life in a democratic society along the lines that our earlier discussion has suggested.

Secondly, as the system is a sponsored one, it is obsessed with grading, sorting, and selecting pupils, which is a characteristic of an élite system. This has continued in new forms in the twentieth century. From 1902 the question was one of selecting pupils for secondary schools; from 1944, with the introduction of the 11+ examination, it was one of selecting pupils for a secondary school 'relevant to their needs'; from the 1960s to the 1980s it was one of selecting pupils within comprehensive schools; from 1988, it was one of grading and sorting pupils (from the age of seven) by means of the byzantine and bureaucratic procedures of the 'National' Curriculum.[34]

Thirdly, élite schools are of key importance. Green calls the 'public schools' the 'most notorious of Britain's old institutional anachronisms and the most out of place in a modern, supposedly democratic society'.[35] They demonstrate how far England is from the classical model of democracy and are the educational equivalent of the largely vanished 'rotten boroughs'. Via these schools, privilege and status can be bought on the open market. Elite schools have also acted in collusion with the state system (much like private medicine) to actually subvert the state system. They have done this by being seen as the 'gold standard' by which the rest of the system is judged. Their criteria of success (high grades at GCSE and A level, and entry to ancient universities) became the criteria by which all schools are judged. Furthermore, the fact that such schools give low significance to teacher education is taken to provide grounds that formal teacher development can be regarded as a disposable luxury in the state system too.

Fourthly, Grace has shown that the relationship between teachers, teachers' unions and the mechanisms of the state is central to understanding how education has developed since the nineteenth century.[36] The 'state', and the control that it exercises, plays a crucial role in teacher development. The government and its agencies have significant power over criteria for selecting teachers; teacher training; the number of teachers; the pay, status and conditions of work of teachers; opportunities and resources for personal and professional development; the public regard in which education and teachers are held; and, lastly, the relationship of education and teachers to general social policy, and their role in bringing about what the government takes to be the good society and the good life.

Finally, under the English system, not only have the status, conditions and pay of and opportunities for teachers, especially those in state schools, been poor but also teacher education has always had low status and prestige. In the nineteenth century it was on the periphery of secondary education, and in the second half of the twentieth century it is in higher education but on its margins.[37]

A 'control' system

In addition, English traditions of teacher education have been infused with religion and focused on issues of control, order and management. From the beginnings of mass schooling, authority, power and control were of overriding importance. This placed the competence and quality of teachers, especially their ability to control children, at the centre of the agenda. In the nineteenth century there were worries about crime, pauperism and lack of religious practice, and the aim was to try to determine 'through the capture of educational means, the patterns of thought, sentiment and behaviour of the working class . . . . Supervised by its trusty teacher, surrounded by its playground wall, the school was to raise a new race of working people – respectful, cheerful, hard-working, loyal, pacific and religious.'[38] As Grace argues,[39] the notion of the 'trusty' teacher had two elements: ideological reliability and social control. 'Ideological reliability' was 'expressed initially in notions of religious and moral character of the teacher and in notions of his or her respectability'.[40] Goodness, as was to be expected, was preferred to mere cleverness. As Kay-Shuttleworth put it, the elementary teacher should be 'the gentle and pious guide of the children of the poor' and not 'a hireling into whose mind had sunk the doubts of the sceptic and in whose heart was the worm of social discontent'.[41]

Teachers also had to be competent and efficient in social control expressed in notions of management, discipline and good order. As the Newcastle Commission argued in 1861, the success of teachers required the maintenance 'of exact order and ready and active attention as the first necessity and after that as much kindness to the children as is compatible with a habit of entire obedience'. The existence of large groups of pupils and poor facilities ensured that teachers 'could not educate . . . only subjugate'. With 'large classes, cramped space and an arid curriculum, the strategy of a survivor–teacher had to involve dominance, hierarchy and respect'.[42]

Contemporary theories of teacher education

These historical concerns with ideological reliability and social control are reflected in the contemporary work of what might be called the semi-official theorists of teacher education, whose first item in a list of 'teaching competence' is the ability to 'establish and maintain discipline and classroom management'.[43] They are also echoed in the work of the New Right.

Both semi-official theorists and the New Right also draw support from two very disparate strands in the traditions of teacher education in England, one derived from the élite schools and the other from the 'teachers of the people'.[44] The former tradition is a subject based view of what it takes to make a person a competent teacher. It regards schooling as uncontested and a matter of transmitting well-established knowledge.

For teachers of the people, on the other hand, schooling is a highly contested area, with a good proportion of pupils not prepared to accept what is on offer without question. These teachers may have to rethink their ideas and re-educate themselves to cope with the gap between their own education and aspirations and the culture, values and attitudes of those whom they teach. For many of them, especially those in primary schools, subject knowledge is not merely (if at all) what they have learnt on a degree course.

The view (derived from the élite school tradition of teaching) that teacher education should be school and subject based; that discipline and order are central to the process; that schooling is uncontested; and that good teachers know their subjects and learn on the job, is seen in the publications of the New Right[45-47] and in the policies and practices of Conservative governments in the UK towards education. Through their policies on the curriculum, teachers' pay and conditions, teacher education, appraisal, and grant maintained status, and in many other ways, these governments have reduced the capacity of classroom teachers to play an active role in the creation of a more open system of schooling and of a properly democratic society, and moved them towards the role of operatives in a system which is managed centrally by politicians and their officials.

THE LONG REVOLUTION: RE-ESTABLISHING A DEMOCRATIC EDUCATION AGENDA

A theory of teacher development which speaks to classical democratic values has to make explicit what structural changes are required in particular educational systems and in the nature and direction of the wider society. It also has to suggest a political agenda and identify political processes and forces which are likely to give it support. This democratic agenda involves seeing teachers at three inter-related levels: as citizens, as workers and as persons.

Teachers as citizens

Teachers, like all citizens in a democratic society, have to reflect on, and decide about, the sort of society and the kind of life that they want. As Gutmann has shown, this will produce conflict, controversy and variety within the broad framework of democratic values. Political and social theory provide a rich source of perspectives, approaches and viewpoints here. If teacher development is disconnected from politics and from its historical and ideological roots, it, like schooling, will replace conscious social reproduction with unconscious social reproduction of the status quo.

Educational change therefore has to be part of wider political change. As such it has to link with other bodies, interest groups and political parties at international (for example, the European Union), national, regional and local levels. Failure to achieve this would make educational reform similar to whistling an attractive tune from the top of a mountain in a force ten gale: the tune may be nice, but its influence is nil.

As we suggest elsewhere[48] key questions in this area include how power is to be distributed; how educational institutions should be controlled and run; what form of teacher professionalism is appropriate; and what kinds of curriculum, pedagogy and assessment are consonant with a democratic society. One challenge, like that taken up in the past by Arnold, Tawney, Clarke, Williams and others[49] is to find those who can speak for education and whistle the tunes in such a way that people hear them and support them. It is not democratic for the Right to insist that theirs is the only tune, or that it should make the most noise.

Teachers as workers

The second level of analysis is that of the teacher as a worker with a career. Here a whole series of questions arise about what is an appropriate way for schools to be run in a democratic society. The contemporary growth within schools of managerialism and its concomitant bureaucracy is unlikely to create an institutional climate in which teachers can encourage conscious rational deliberation amongst their pupils and students about the good life and the good society, and all that is required by the democratic educational aims of 'conscious social reproduction'.[50,51]

To see classroom teachers as mere operatives – agents for others – that is, people who carry out an agenda set entirely elsewhere, is to subvert the development of democratic education. The tradition of the 'Great Head', and of authoritarian structures of control, likewise makes rational deliberation virtually impossible.[52] Under a developed democratic system, teacher development for classroom teachers would be a career process. It would require time for reflection on a day to day basis and it would need regular time away from classrooms.

Teachers as people

Finally, teachers are persons and have a right to have some say about the form and content of their private and professional lives. A bulwark against totalitarianism, authoritarianism and utopian centralist planning is to allow individuals space and resources to develop their own agendas and insights. The centre, as became clear in Eastern Europe, rarely knows best. In practice this means that all teachers should be able to choose, uncoerced and for themselves, what kind of teacher development they want. In hard political times, of course, if individual teachers and small groups of teachers wish to preserve the traditions of democratic education, they can only do this by subverting and changing the official agenda. In good times they can work with the political currents.[53]

CONCLUSION

A fully developed democratic theory of teacher development, therefore, needs to be connected to political theory and located in a historical tradition, and it has to re-establish a political agenda to gain support for itself. It has to see teachers as citizens, workers and persons. Where contemporary New Right thinking has tried to deintellectualize the issues, it has to reassert the need for serious intellectual work on educational issues; where education has been depoliticized, it has to show how politics and education are inextricably linked; and where the 'discourse of derision' has demoralized and demotivated teachers, it has to have the imagination and the style to recreate and redevelop the vision of democratic education for a properly democratic society. This task will not be easy, but, as Raymond Williams suggested, a long revolution is unlikely to happen quickly.[54] One thing is certain. As the commissars and apparatchiks of Eastern Europe found in agriculture, it is impossible to produce potatoes by ideology and rhetoric alone. You have to have the support and commitment of those who do the work: the peasants. In the same way, there can be no educational advance without classroom teachers. They do the work of education, and their knowledge, imagination, sensitivities, and skills are central to that advance. And that means that teacher development is, too.

NOTES AND REFERENCES

The issues dealt with in this essay are discussed more fully in a forthcoming book by Wilfred Carr and Anthony Hartnett.[28]

1. Wardle, D., *English Popular Education 1780–1915*. Cambridge: Cambridge University Press, 1976, p. 105.

2. Hall, S., *The Hard Road to Renewal*. London: Verso, 1988.

3. Knight, C., *The Making of Tory Education Policy in Post-War Britain 1950–1986*. London: Falmer, p. 91, 1990.

4. Cohen, S., *Folk Devils and Moral Panics*. Paladin, 1973.

5. Bennett, N., *Teaching Styles and Pupil Progress*. Open Books, 1976.

6. Jones, K., *Right Turn: the Conservative Revolution in Education*. Hutchinson Radius, 1989.

7. Ball, S. J., *Politics and Policy Making in Education*. London: Routledge, 1990.

8. Hartnett, A. and Naish, M., 'Teaching teacher trainers their place'. *Education*, **22**, p. 458, 1987.

9. Hirst, P. H., 'Educational studies and the PGCE course'. *British Journal of Educational Studies*, **23** (3), pp. 211–21, 1985.

10. Furlong, V J., Hirst, P. H., Pocklington, K. and Miles, S., *Initial Teacher Training and the Role of the School*. Milton Keynes: Open University Press, 1988.

11. Hartnett, A. and Naish, M., 'The PGCE as an educational priority area'. *Journal of Further and Higher Education*, **5** (3), pp. 88–102, 1981.

12. Hartnett, A. and Naish, M. (eds), *Education and Society Today*. London: Falmer, 1986.

13. Carr, W. (ed.), *Quality in Teaching: Arguments for a Reflective Profession*. London: Falmer, 1989.

14. Beardon, T., Booth, M., Hargreaves, D. and Reiss, M., *School-led Initial Teacher Training: The Way Forward*. Cambridge Education Papers, No. 2. Cambridge: Department of Education, University of Cambridge, 1992.

15. Davie, G. E., *The Democratic Intellect: Scotland and Her Universities in the Nineteenth Century*. Edinburgh: Edinburgh University Press, 1961.

16. McPherson, A. and Raab, C. D., *Governing Education: a Sociology of Policy since 1945*. Edinburgh: Edinburgh University Press, 1988.

17. Gutmann, A., *Democratic Education*. Princeton, NJ: Princeton University Press, 1987.

18. Ibid.

19. Ibid., p. 42.

20. Ibid., p. 44.

21. Ibid., p. 45.

22. Ibid., pp. 45–6.

23. Liston, D. P. and Zeichner, K. M., 'Teacher education and the social context of schooling: issues for curriculum development'. *American Educational Research Journal*, **27** (4), pp. 610–36, 1990.

24. Gutmann, op. cit., note 17, p. 77.

25. Liston and Zeichner, op. cit., note 23, p. 613.

26. Ibid., p. 615.

27. Gutmann, op. cit., note 17, p. 79.

28. Carr, W. and Hartnett, A. *Education and the Struggle for Democracy*. Cassell, forthcoming.

29. Green. A., 'The peculiarities of English education'. In Education Group II, *Education Limited*. Unwin Hyman, pp. 6– 30 (p. 7), 1991.

30. Ibid., p. 8.

31. Carr and Hartnett, op. cit., note 28.

32. Turner, R. H., 'Modes of social ascent through education: sponsored and contest mobility'. In Halsey, A. H., Floud, J. and Anderson, C. A. (eds.) *Education, Economy and Society*. Free Press of Glencoe, 1961.

33. Lawn, M., *Servants of the State: the Contested Control of Teaching 1900–1930*. London: Falmer, 1987.

34. Hartnett, A. and Naish, M., 'The sleep of reason breeds monsters: the birth of a statutory curriculum in England and Wales'. *Journal of Curriculum Studies*, **22** (1), pp. 1– 16, 1990.

35. Green, op. cit., note 29, p. 14.

36. Grace, G., 'Teachers and the state in Britain: a changing relation'. In Lawn, M. and Grace. G. (eds), *Teachers: the Culture and Politics of their Work*. London: Falmer, pp. 193–228, 1987.

37. Taylor, W., *Society and the Education of Teachers*. Faber & Faber, 1969.

38. Johnson, R., 'Educational policy and social control in early Victorian England'. *Past and Present*, **49**, pp. 96–119 (p. 119), 1970.

39. Grace, G., 'Judging teachers: the social and political contexts of teacher evaluation'. *British Journal of Sociology of Education*, **6** (1), pp. 3–16, 1985.

40. Ibid., p. 5.

41. Quoted by Grace, op. cit., p. 5.

42. Ibid., p. 6.

43. Beardon *et al.*, op. cit., note 14, p. 28.

44. Grace, op. cit., note 36, p. 197.

45. Hillgate Group, *Learning to Teach*. Claridge Press & Educational Research Centre, 1989.

46. Lawlor, S. *Teachers Mistaught: Training in Theories or Education in Subjects?* Centre for Policy Studies, 1990.

47. O'Hear, A., *Who Teaches the Teachers?* Social Affairs Unit, 1988.

48. Carr and Hartnett, op. cit., note 28.

49. Silver, H., *Education and the Social Condition*. Methuen, 1980.

50. Gutmann, op. cit., note 17, p. 15.

51. Inglis, F., *The Management of Ignorance: A Political Theory of the Curriculum*. Oxford: Basil Blackwell, 1985.

52. Carr and Hartnett, op. cit., note 28.

53. Lawn, op. cit., note 33.

54. Williams, R., *The Long Revolution*. Harmondsworth: Penguin, 1961.

Chapter 3

Studying the Teacher's Life and Work

Ivor Goodson

TEACHERS, RESEARCHERS AND PRACTICE

This chapter is primarily concerned with exploring the question of which strategic focus might be employed when teachers (as researchers) and externally located researchers (normally in faculties of education) collaborate. I take the view that a narrow focus on 'practice' and on practical stories in collaborating on research, a panacea that is politically and academically popular at the moment, will not take us too far. A much broader focus on the teacher's life and work is required, and this position is advanced in this chapter.

This is for two main reasons. First, practice is a good deal more than the technical things we do in classrooms – it relates to who we are, to our whole approach to life. Here I might quote C. Wright Mills; he is talking about scholars, but it is relevant to any member of the social scientific community. He said 'The most admirable thinkers within the scholarly community . . . do not split their work from their lives. They seem to take both too seriously to allow such disassociation, and they want to use each for the enrichment of others.'[1] So I would want a form of research which links the analysis of the teacher's life and work together. Secondly, the interactive practices of our classrooms are subject to constant change, often in the form of new government guidelines – initiatives like destreaming, as in Ontario at the moment. These initiatives outside the classroom – what I call preactive actions – set crucial parameters for interactive classroom practice. Preactive action affects interactive possibilities. In their collaborative research, teachers as researchers and external researchers need to focus on both the preactive and the interactive. What this means in short is that we need to look at the full context in which teachers' practice is negotiated, not just at interaction and implementation within the classroom. If we stay with the focus on practice then our collaborative research is inevitably largely going to involve the implementation of initiatives which are generated elsewhere. That in itself is a form of political quietism.

To avoid this fate, the preferred value position of this chapter comes close to that of the teacher as a researcher. But even the 'teacher as researcher' slogan, while it carries the essence of my value position, seems to me to bring a number of problems. First, in implying that the teacher becomes the researcher of her or his own practice, it frees the researchers in the academy from clear responsibility in this process. I, however, think that such people have a primary, and much neglected, responsibility for complementing and sustaining the teacher as researcher.

Associated with this, I am against the notion that the focus of the teacher as researcher should be mainly upon practical knowledge and practice-based stories: an assumption in a good deal of the literature in this area. I am opposed to this assumption because the parameters to practice, whether they be biographical or political, cover a very wide terrain. To narrow the focus to 'practice as defined' is to make the focus of research a victim of historical circumstances, particularly political tendencies. At the moment, the New Right is seeking to turn the teacher's practice into that of a technician: a routinized and trivialized deliverer of predesigned packages. To accept those definitions and to focus on 'practice' so defined is to play into their hands.

The teacher as researcher of practice will ideally seek to criticize and transcend such definitions of practice. But, and this is a crucial limitation, if we focus on practice in this way, the initiative for defining our starting point passes to politicians and bureaucrats. In short, they will retain the power of agenda setting. It would, I think, sponsor more autonomous and critical research if we adopted a wider lens of inquiry for studying the teacher's life and work.

TEACHERS' VOICES AND STORIES

The focus on practice, or practical knowledge, in teachers' voices and stories has coincided with a period of conservative restructuring of schooling. As long as this focus remains uncoupled from any analysis of this restructuring, the two initiatives make reasonable bedfellows. So on the one hand powerful interest groups restructure schooling and practice; on the other hand teachers are given a voice to comment on their practical knowledge. Practice is restructured at the point at which it is allowed a voice. A voice and a story which celebrate only practice create a valuable covering noise, an apparently quite emancipatory noise, while that very practice is narrowed and technicized.

So you may say: 'I am a teacher who tells stories that ignore social context.' So what! I can see that that is a theoretical problem for an educational scholar like you. Why should I worry – 'They're still good stories.' The reason why I should worry is that stories do social and political work as they are told. A story is never just a story – it is a statement of belief and of morality, it speaks about values. Stories carry loud messages in both what they say and what they do not say. They may accept political and social priorities without comment, or they may challenge those priorities.

Why would teachers' stories, particularly those directed to the personal and practical aspects of their work, be such a problem? Educational scholarship notwithstanding, why would such teachers' stories be a problem for teachers generally? How can giving someone a voice, especially one so long silenced, be anything but a good thing?

Let us briefly review some of the changes currently going on in teachers' lives and work. Then let us see how stories of the personal and practical knowledge of teachers respond to such change. How, in short, do personal and practical teachers' stories respond to the forces that construct their work?

Changes in teachers' life and work

Martin Lawn has written powerfully about teachers' biographies and of the way in which teachers' work has been rapidly restructured in England and Wales. The teacher, he argues, has moved from 'moral responsibility', particularly with regard to curricular matters, to a narrow technical competence. Teaching, in short, has had its area of moral and professional judgement severely reduced. He summarizes recent changes in this way:

> In the biographies of many teachers is an experience of, and an
> expectation of, curriculum responsibility not as part of a job
> description, a task, but as part of the moral craft of teaching, the
> real duty. The post-war tradition of gradual involvement in
> curriculum responsibility at primary and second level was the
> result of the wartime breakdown of education, the welfare aspects
> of schooling and the post-war reconstruction in which teachers
> played a pivotal, democratic role. The role of teaching expanded as
> the teachers expanded the role. In its ideological form within this
> period, professional autonomy was created as an idea. As the post-
> war consensus finally collapsed and corporatism was demolished
> by Thatcherism, teaching was again to be reduced, shorn of its
> involvement in policy and managed more tightly. Teaching is to be
> reduced to 'skills', attending planning meetings, supervising
> others, preparing courses and reviewing the curriculum. It is to be
> 'managed' to be more 'effective'. In effect the intention is to
> depoliticize teaching and to turn the teacher into an educational
> worker. Curriculum responsibility now means supervising
> competencies.[2]

Similarly, Susan Robertson has analysed teachers' work in the context of post-fordist economies. She too argues that teachers' professionalism has been drastic-ally reconstructed and replaced by a wholly 'new professionalism'.

> The new professionalism framework is one where the teacher as
> worker is integrated into a system where there is (i) no room to
> negotiate, (ii) reduced room for autonomy, and (iii) the commodity
> value of flexible specialism defines the very nature of the task. In
> essence, teachers have been severed from those processes which
> would involve them in deliberations about the future shape of

their work. And while many teachers are aware that change is taking place and talk of the 'good old days', few are aware of the potential profundity of that change even when it is happening in their midst. Clearly educators have been eclipsed by a core of interests from the corporate sector and selected interests co-opted in the corporate settlement.[3]

The response of teachers' stories

Teachers' personal and practical stories typically relate anecdotes about their work and practice. So stories in the new domain described by Lawn and Robertson will be primarily stories about work where moral and professional judgement plays less and less of a part. Given this starting point, such stories will speak about that which has been constructed. By focusing on the personal and practical, such teachers' stories forgo the chance of speaking of other ways, other people, other times, and other forms of being a teacher. The focus on the personal and practical in teachers' stories is, then, an abdication of the right to speak on matters of social and political construction. By speaking in this voice about personal and practical matters the teacher also loses a voice in the moment of speaking, for the voice that has been encouraged and granted, in the realm of personal and practical stories, is the voice of technical competency, the voice of the isolated classroom practitioner: the voice of 'ours not to reason why, ours but to do or die'.

COLLABORATIVE INSIGHTS INTO THE SOCIAL CONSTRUCTION OF TEACHING

In studying the teacher's life and work in a fuller social context the intention is collaboratively to develop insights into the social construction of teaching. In this way, as we noted earlier, teachers' stories of action can be reconnected with 'theories of context'. Hence teaching these stories, rather than passively celebrating the continual reconstruction of teaching, will move to develop understandings of social and political construction. It is the move from commentary on what is to cognition of what might be.

The crisis of reform

Studying the teacher's life and work as social construction provides a valuable lens for viewing the new moves to restructure and reform schooling. Butt *et al.* have talked about the 'crisis of reform' when so many of the restructuring and reformist initiatives depend on prescriptions imported into the classroom but developed as political imperatives elsewhere. These patterns of intervention develop from a particular view of the teacher, a view which teachers' stories often work to confirm.

All their lives teachers have to confront the negative stereotypes – 'teacher as robot, devil, angel, nervous Nellie' – foisted upon them by the American culture. Descriptions of teaching as a 'flat occupation with no career structure, low pay, salary increments unrelated to merit' have been paralleled with portrayals of teaching as 'one great plateau' where 'it appears that the annual cycle of the school year lulls teachers into a repetitious professional cycle of their own'.

Within the educational community, the image of teachers as semi-professionals who lack control and autonomy over their own work and as persons who do not contribute to the creation of knowledge has permeated and congealed the whole educational enterprise. Researchers have torn the teacher out of the context of classroom, plagued her with various insidious effects (Hawthorne, novelty, Rosenthal, halo), parcelled out into discrete skills the unity of intention and action present in teaching practices.[4]

In some ways the crisis of reform is a crisis of prescriptive optimism – a belief that what is politically pronounced and backed with armouries of accountability tests will actually happen. I have recently examined the importance and salience of the belief in curriculum as prescription (CAP):

CAP supports the mystique that expertise and control reside within central governments, educational bureaucracies or the university community. Providing nobody exposes this mystique, the two worlds of 'prescriptive rhetoric' and 'schooling as practise' [sic] can co-exist. Both sides benefit from such peaceful co-existence. The agencies of CAP are seen to be 'in control' and the schools are seen to be 'delivering' (and can carve out a good degree of autonomy if they accept the rules).[5]

However, there is a substantial 'downside' to this 'historic compromise':

There are costs of complicity in accepting the myth of prescription: above all these involve, in various ways, acceptance of established modes of power relations. Perhaps most importantly the people intimately connected with the day-to-day social construction of curriculum and schooling – teachers – are thereby effectively disenfranchised in the 'discourse of schooling'. To continue to exist, teachers' day-to-day power must remain unspoken and unrecorded. This is one price of complicity: day-to-day power and autonomy for schools and for teachers are dependent on continuing to accept the fundamental lie.[6]

In another context I also said: 'In addressing the crisis of prescription and reform, it becomes imperative that we find new ways to sponsor the teacher's voice.'[7]

Life histories

The challenging contextual insights which come from studying the teacher's life and work in a collaborative manner can be eloquently instanced in some of the work of Kathleen Casey. Take, for instance, her study of the reasons why progressive women activists leave teaching. She notes from the beginning that many of the more conventional studies work from a functionalist managerial perspective:

> A certain set of taken-for-granted assumptions control the way in which the problem of teachers' attrition has normally been defined, one which presumes managerial solutions. Inquiries have generally been oriented by administrative demands for a stable workforce.[8]

Casey decided to develop life history narratives of contemporary women teachers working for social change. She tape-recorded 33 such narratives in five American cities in 1984-5. In studying teacher attrition she notes the broad range of taken for granted assumption which go beyond the mere definition of the problem:

> A limited number of research strategies have been employed in investigating this topic. Former members of the teaching profession have often been traced statistically, rather than in person, and information has typically been collected from such sources as district files, state departments of public instruction, or through research-conceived survey.[9]

The subject, then, has been scrutinized either at a statistical distance or by employing data collected 'from above' and beyond the teachers themselves. In effect the teachers' voices have been silenced, and the research paradigms employed have confirmed and echoed that silence.

> The particular configuration of selectivities and omissions which has been built into this research frame slants the shape of its findings. By systematically failing to record the voices of ordinary teachers, the literature on educators' careers actually silences them. Methodologically, this means that even while investigating an issue where decision-making is paramount, researchers speculate on teachers' motivations, or at best, survey them with a set of forced-choice options. Theoretically, what emerges is an instrumental view of teachers, one in which they are reduced to objects which can be manipulated for particular ends. Politically, the results are educational policies constructed around institutionally convenient systems of rewards and punishments, rather than in congruence with teachers' desires to create significance in their lives.[10]

Teachers' attrition, when seen from the perspective of women teachers' life histories, comes to be seen as something growing from the life and work and social context of teaching:

> Teaching takes on a distinctive meaning in these narratives; it becomes much more than the paid employment for classroom work in a specific school. Many women define being a teacher as a fundamental existential identity. When she was unable to get a teaching job, one woman explains, 'I cried and cried because I was really upset. You know, I wanted some meaning to my life, and some meaning for having gotten that education.' Another woman mourns the loss of her profession in this way: 'I'm a teacher at heart. I will always be a teacher. And I miss teaching. I miss teaching.'[11]

Casey notes that the women in question celebrate an 'ethos of nurturance and growth' – 'a "tendency" which is discouraged by the management structure'. She also notes that a 'major explanation' for teachers' attrition is in fact the antagonism between teachers and administrators.

When seen through the perspective of women teachers' life histories, 'teachers' attrition' can be seen, conversely, as teachers' liberation from 'the conditions under which these women have laboured'. In this case they miss teaching and their work with children, but the social context of teaching and the politics of administrative hierarchy mean that many of them move gladly to the range of 'positive alternatives they have chosen'.[12]

Louis Smith and his colleagues chose to study educational innovation over the 15 years of Kensington School through the life history approach. Their justification turned on reintroducing 'the person', in this case 'the teachers', into the assessment and analysis of educational innovation:

> It seems self-evident that the 'person' is an important item in any description and analysis of educational innovation. Some analytic accounts have minimized this aspect of innovation. We believe the excerpts raise a major sub-issue in the nature of the conceptualization of the person in the study of innovation . . . . It has to do with the kind of personality theory to which students of innovation appeal. At times we feel we are beating the proverbial dead horse to note that the substance of the theory we have been developing is a far cry from the dominant behaviourist view in much of the innovation literature, in much of educational psychology, and in much of the educational research community. Behavioural objectives, time on tasks, mastery learning, school effectiveness, are sounds that emanate from drums and drummers distant from the language and perspectives of the innovators we

have studied and the language and theory in which we have chosen to couch our own interpretations and speculations.[13]

Once again, then, life history study helps to reformulate our understanding of innovations in education. Before these have been seen as primarily technical or political processes. Smith *et al.* show how 'there are personality processes at work as well'. Hence they argue:

> Now when we think of school improvement we have a conception which we can use to approach any proposal for change. That seems useful for consultants asked to help, for administrators who are pushing an agenda, and for teachers who may be less than willing actors if not pawns in the process of school improvement and educational change.[14]

Smith's work provides life history portrayals of teachers, worked into a broad contextual understanding of the school in what he calls, with admirable grandeur, a 'nested systems model'. We capture how teachers' life histories are lived out within, and constantly reformulate and reconstrue, the social contexts of schooling.

This capacity to reformulate and reinterpret the prescribed agendas of schooling is often captured in the detailed life history portrayal of teachers at work in their classroom contexts. An example is the study by Butt *et al.* of Glenda – at the time teaching English at the International School of Islamabad. In this life history portrayal we see how she grows confident enough to reach the stage were she can go beyond what is prescribed with confidence and competence, where her class discussions really take off and engage her children: 'The teacher's guide was closed and the students' workbooks were returned to the bookroom. The culture and knowledge within the classroom was infinitely more exciting.'[15]

Butt *et al.* cryptically note: 'In our future work with other biographies it will be interesting to investigate the role of curriculum guidelines in the worklife of teachers.'[16] By situating that inquiry within 'the worklife of teachers' we can see how life history work develops its own momentum in the search for theories of context in teachers' working lives.

CONCLUSION

If your worldview as expressed in stories is primarily personal and practical, then you are accepting a definition of yourself as you speak. The story that is told thereby acts as an agency which individualizes the teacher as cultural worker. We see then how the paradox of teachers' voices resolves itself.

Teachers' personal and practical stories and voices are being encouraged at a time when more and more teachers are being held accountable and having their work prescribed, interrogated and evaluated. At first sight this seems paradoxical – two movements running in a different direction. In fact this is not the case: both movements may play the same role of narrowing the teacher's area of professional competence and judgement, of social and political outreach.

This pendulum swing towards teachers' stories actually comes, in my view, at a somewhat unpropitious time. It sets up one of the paradoxes of postmodernism: that at precisely the time that teachers are being 'brought back in', their work is being vigorously restructed. Teachers' voices and stories are being pursued as bona fide reflective research data at a time of quite dramatic restructuring. In fact, at precisely the time that the teacher's voice is being pursued and promoted, the teacher's work is being technicized and narrowed. As the movement to celebrate teachers' practical knowledge grows, it is becoming less and less promising as a focus for research and reflection. As teachers' work intensifies, as more and more centralized edicts and demands impinge on the teacher's world, the space for reflection and research is progressively squeezed. It is a strange time to evacuate traditional theory and pursue personal and practical knowledge.

A promising movement might then 'throw the baby out with the bathwater'. At a time of rapid restructuring, the timing of these moves seems profoundly unfortunate. To promote stories and narratives, without any analysis of structures and systems, shows how the best of intentions can unwittingly complement the moves to uncouple the teacher from the wider picture. Stories and narratives can form an unintended coalition with those forces which would divorce the teacher from a knowledge of political and micropolitical perspectives from theory, from broader cognitive maps of influence and power. It would be an unfortunate fate for a movement that at times embraces the goal of emancipating the teacher to be implicated in the displacement of theoretical and critical analysis.

NOTES AND REFERENCES

1. Mills, C. W., *The Sociological Imagination*. London: Oxford University Press, pp. 195–6, 1959.

2. Lawn, M., 'From responsibility to competency: a new context for curriculum studies in England and Wales'. *Journal of Curriculum Studies*, **22** (4), p. 389, 1990.

3. Robertson, S. L., 'Teachers' labour and post-fordism: an exploratory analysis'. Edith Cowan University, Perth, WA. Mimeo, 1993.

4. Butt, R., Raymond, D., McCue, G. and Yamagishi, L. 'Collaborative autobiography and the teacher's voice'. In Goodson, I. F. (ed.), *Studying Teachers' Lives*. London: Routledge, pp. 51–98, 1992.

5. Goodson, I. F., 'Studying curriculum: towards a social constructionist perspective'. *Journal of Curriculum Studies*, **22** (4), pp. 229–312, 1990.

6. Ibid., p. 300.

7. Goodson, I. F., 'Studying teachers' lives: an emergent field of inquiry'. In Goodson, I. F. (ed.), *Studying Teachers' Lives*. London: Routledge, pp. 1–17, 1992.

8. Casey, K., 'Why do progressive women activists leave teaching? Theory, methodology and politics in life history research'. In Goodson, I. F. (ed.), *Studying Teachers' Lives*. London: Routledge, pp. 187–208 (p. 187), 1992.

9. Ibid., pp. 187–8.

10. Ibid., p. 188.

11. Ibid., p. 206.

12. Ibid., p. 207.

13. Smith, L. M., Kleine, P., Prunty, J. J. and Dwyer, D. C., 'School improvement and educator personality: stages, types, traits or processes?' In Goodson, I. F. (ed.), *Studying Teachers' Lives*. London: Routledge, 1992.

14. Ibid., p. 165.

15. Butt *et al.*, op. cit., note 4, p. 84.

16. Ibid., p. 89.

Chapter 4

Working with Teachers to Reform Schools: Issues of Power, Expertise and Commitment

Jesse Goodman

Although faculty development is often viewed merely as a means to 'improve' the instructional abilities of teachers, it is also a potential strategy for initiating substantive school reform. As I have discussed elsewhere,[1] since the direct ownership and involvement of teachers and principals is required in any significant school reform effort, faculty development often becomes the most important feature of such projects. As its title suggests, this chapter examines several issues that potentially can emerge when external reformers participate in faculty development/school reform ventures.

During the last two decades, efforts to reform education through faculty development in the United States have reflected a decisively 'top-down' style of in-service education. As Bullough and Gitlin state:

> Following a model common to many businesses and institutional
> bureaucracies, [recent] school reform efforts have been directed
> from the top down. That teachers need to be told what to do and
> how to do it has come almost to be taken for granted, a given of
> policymakers.[2]

In most industrial, western societies, teacher development programmes have been designed 'consciously or unconsciously in assumptions rooted in bureaucratic control', which has eroded teachers' autonomy and intellectual involvement in their work.[3] In contrast, Bullough and Gitlin[4] note that democratic thinking reformers view teacher development projects as an opportunity to create more egalitarian schools and societies and typically argue for the 'bottom-up' transformation of education. The hope is that, like workers who challenge the policies of corporate management, teachers will provide the impetus for democratic reforms in schools.[5]

Although the concept of 'bottom-up' teacher development is ideologically appealing, the question of how to carry out such a project is not so easily understood. How do democratic thinking reformers work with teachers in the establishment of 'bottom-up' school reform? What does it mean to participate in teacher development projects within an ethos of democracy? What issues confront external reformers who become involved in such efforts?

Based on a review of pertinent literature and on my colleagues' and my own experiences during the last three years spent working as external change agents with five elementary schools located in the mid-western part of the United States, this chapter explores a number of issues confronting democratic thinking reformers who participate directly in teacher development projects as a means to reform education substantively. After a brief statement about who 'we' are, the first section describes the guiding characteristics of our work with teachers. The next section discusses issues of power, expertise and commitment that have emerged from our involvement in teacher development projects. These sections begin to investigate the difficult questions of what assistance democratic thinking reformers can offer to (and hopefully influence what happens in) today's conservative schools.

HARMONY SCHOOL EDUCATION CENTER

From July 1987 to June 1988, I and two research assistants were involved in an interpretive study of Harmony School. The stated purpose of Harmony is to create an education that fosters the democratic empowerment of teachers and students. For a few years after completing the field work I was busy analysing data and writing various papers, articles and, eventually, a book based on my study of Harmony's elementary school.[6] I learned a great deal about education and society from this research project, and thought about how other schools might benefit from working with Harmony. Towards the end of 1990, I approached Harmony School with the proposal to create a 'centre' in their school, in conjunction with Indiana University, for the purposes of assisting other schools involved in reform efforts and promoting scholarly discourse on topics of democracy and education. After nearly eight months of conversations about the potential possibilities and costs of expanding Harmony's role, the Harmony School Education Center was established. At present this centre consists of a small number of professors and graduate students and of Harmony's teachers, administrators and students who have participated in outreach ventures with several public schools and/or a number of research projects. Although this paper discusses the collective work of these individuals, it is important to note that as I am the sole author of this paper, only one version of these events is being portrayed.

KEY CHARACTERISTICS IN FACULTY DEVELOPMENT PROJECTS

Since, from our perspective, working directly with teachers and principals is crucial to substantive school reform, much of our time during the last two years has been spent exploring questions of what it means to participate in what are often referred to as faculty development projects. As Bullough and Gitlin note,[7] working with teachers to reform schools substantively is a complex task. Unfortunately, few illustrations of democratic approaches to teacher development or in-service education currently exist.

The most prevalent approach to faculty development in the United States is the 'purchase' model. This approach usually involves central administration (in some school districts, a few representative teachers participate in this decision) determining that teachers need information about a particular topic and then hiring an 'expert' who provides the necessary content. Perhaps the most popular example of this 'purchase' approach during the last decade in the US has been Madeline Hunter's curriculum planning model.[8–11] In this situation, teachers are told that the way to improve the education in their schools is for them to follow the steps developed in Hunter's instructional model. Teachers then take a series of 'workshops', or in some cases even university classes, that 'teach' teachers the mechanics of Hunter's model. Once teachers learn what to do, they are expected to follow 'the programme'. There are literally hundreds of faculty development consultants who utilize the 'purchase model' in the US. They sell their 'reforms' for everything from disciplining students to curriculum planning, to teaching particular subjects (e.g. maths, spelling, science, sex, drugs), to co-operative learning, to test-taking.

Another common approach to faculty development might be referred to as the 'medical model'. The medical model is often seen as valuable in cases where central administration has identified a particular school in which the 'performance' of teachers and students has declined (often as measured on standardized tests' scores) and consultants have been brought into the school to determine what is 'wrong'. Departments of education associated with state governments will often utilize the medical model to evaluate a given school. In this case, consultants come into a school and 'examine' it much as a doctor examines a patient. The primary goal of the medical model consultant is to diagnose the school's 'illness' and then recommend the appropriate 'treatment'. For example, Kerr argues that schools hire a 'doctor of teaching' to help teachers become more competent.[12]

In spite of their popularity, there are several problematic aspects of these approaches to faculty development and school reform. First, they are based upon an assumption that the 'difficulties' of a given school can be accurately determined by a relatively small number of individuals, and that these 'problems' are usually isolated from other aspects of the school and society. As a result, the 'solution' is also fairly easily determined and implemented by having teachers and principals follow the directives of the designated 'expert'. In each case the educational reform is viewed as a process of fixing schools or teachers. There is little recognition given to the view that faculty development and educational reform can be based upon the visionary thinking or reflections of teachers and principals. What is most disturbing is that both of these approaches assume that teachers and principals should play a relatively passive role in determining the scope and substance of a given school's faculty development project.

Constructing an 'approach' to faculty development/school reform projects has been a complicated process. In our work we have drawn most heavily upon John Smyth's and Ann Lieberman's ideas related to collaborative and clinical teacher development and school reform.[13–18] In reflecting on our work with teachers and administrators, we find that two characteristics, the value of collaborative/critical inquiry and the need to be openly ideological, are particularly noteworthy.

Collaborative/Critical Inquiry

In contrast to the previously mentioned approaches to faculty development, our work in teacher development is based upon an initial *collaborative examination* into the school and social culture by ourselves and the teachers, the principal, and perhaps parents, students and others associated with a given school. The importance of this *joint* inquiry cannot be over-emphasized. Although many schools in the United States share common problems, each school has its own particular sets of traditions, structures, personalities, styles of inter-actions and faculty biographies.

Rather than coming to a school as experts with the 'problem' (e.g. teachers do not plan correctly) and the 'solution' (Hunter's model) already determined, we enter faculty development projects as participants in a series of shared investigations into the nature of a given school's situation and the context within which this school operates. Typically, these inquiries involve examinations into not only the daily problems and difficulties found in a given school but also the social and pedagogical values, assumptions and presuppositions of the teachers, the principal, the district administration and the local community, as well as our own views and values as external reformers. During these inquiries, special efforts are made to engage teachers in discussions about their ideals, values, dreams, and visions of education, and the relationship between these concepts and their images of the 'good' society.

It is vital that teachers and other school personnel learn how to investigate the strengths and weaknesses in their own schools, rather than relying on external diagnosticians. Even when we have recognized a problem and have ideas about how it could be solved soon after entering a given school, we avoid sharing our speculations prematurely. First, we have come to realize that we might be incorrect in our assessment, and in these cases we end up damaging our relationship with the teachers and/or the principal. Secondly, even if we are correct, a premature disclosing of our analysis might result in defensiveness or in an unnecessary dependency on us as the people with the 'answer'. It is the teachers, the principals and other interested parties who must recognize the problems of a given school and generate the resolutions to these problems. As external reformers, we typically draw attention to some practical or theoretical aspect of a particular situation or provide alternative solutions that may not have been considered, but the goal of our work during these joint investigations is to help teachers and other school personnel gain 'insight' into what is going on around them, within them, and between them and other people in their school and the society in which it exists.

Ideology

Another important characteristic of our work in faculty development projects is our commitment to be openly ideological. Conventional approaches to faculty development assume a 'value neutral' position. External consultants typically do not present themselves as individuals with an educational agenda of their own. These consultants position themselves as 'neutral' by indicating to schools that it is not their business to tell schools what their purposes, goals or actions should be.[19] Rather, most consultants articulate the ambiguous view that the purpose of their work is merely to help 'improve' teachers' performance. By assuming this 'value neutral' position, educational consultants passively accept the dominant values and goals of particular schools. If schools want to raise children's scores on standardized tests, or improve the scope and sequence of their curriculum, then it is the role of the faculty development programme to help schools reach this goal. If a school (or school district) wants help in determining what its goals are to be, external consultants will help it to articulate these goals (using various communication design processes), but they will not advocate any particular set of goals for this school to adopt. Many school consultants present themselves as individuals without educational or social visions of their own. However, at the same time, these consultants are often very sensitive to the prevailing views and values in the public discourse on school reform. This sensitivity is then used as a way to obtain clients. For example, during the 1970s many consultants offered workshops for teachers on 'student-centred' education. During the last decade there has been a plethora of faculty development/school reform programmes designed to help schools get ready for the new 'information technology age' coming to the United States.[20,21]

If particular ideas in these faculty development programmes are presented by consultants, there is an effort to site their suggestions within a value neutral, 'research says' context. The impression given is that a particular belief or practice is advocated as a result of certain research findings rather than as a reflection of ideology. However, anyone familiar with education research understands all too well that one can find 'research findings' to support any number of positions on a given educational topic or practice. In reality, consultants' values and beliefs are used consciously or unconsciously to screen the 'research' they bring to a situation. School reform consultants are no more protected from political and social influences than are other individuals. By draping their suggestions in claims of 'scientific neutrality', they amplify the importance of their views, placing teachers and principals in the position of 'passive knowledge consumers'. Using 'scientific findings' as part of a faculty development project is particularly insidious because the biases inherent in such comments are difficult to detect and are unlikely to be brought to light or challenged by others with different attitudes. Instead, these biases themselves become part of a stifling practice of 'scientific' school consultation. Although consultants armed with 'research' firmly believe that, as long as they are not conscious of any political or educational agenda, they are neutral and objective, in fact they are only unconscious.

In working with teachers, we have learned that it is important to be 'openly ideological', or what Pink and Hyde would refer to as 'proactive'.[22] At any given time, we have thoughtfully constructed views concerning, for example, the relationship between school and society; epistemology; curriculum development; power relationships in schools; learning processes; the nature of childhood; and the organizational structure of schools. Teacher development projects offer us an opportunity to engage in praxis, that is a process by which theoretical analysis of pedagogy and society is used to inform our practice as external reformers working with school faculties, and this work in schools is reflected upon in an effort to inform our on-going theorizing. In this fashion we are perpetually constructing a working analysis of schooling and social life as the foundation for our work with teachers and principals.

As previously mentioned, we share Dewey's view that education should help young people create a more democratic culture.[23–25] Democracy is seen not merely as a set of governmental structures and political rituals but as a way of community life.[26] As a way of life, democracy implies an appreciation for individual diversity and freedom balanced by values of social responsibility, compassion and the 'common good'. We view faculty development projects as an opportunity to explore with teachers and principals the creation of an education that will help empower themselves and their students to create a more democratic and caring society than at present exists in the United States.

In an effort to be forthright about our own pedagogical and social agenda, we articulate our values and visions in general terms during initial meetings with teachers and principals. We suggest to teachers and principals that one of the things we have to offer them is 'our perspective'. Practically speaking, we have found it useful to discuss these perspectives soon after initial contact has been made so that principals and teachers can make informed decisions about whether or not they wish to work with us. As a result, we are rarely in the position of spending a great amount of time in a given school only to discover later that the teachers and principal have an agenda significantly different from our own. As will be discussed in the following section of this paper, this openly ideological stance requires that special attention be paid to questions of power and commitment that arise between democratic thinking reformers and the teachers and principals seeking assistance.

Although it is useful to draw distinctions between various approaches to faculty development in an effort to 'map out' our understanding of this phenomenon, in actual situations these distinctions become blurred. For example, after several visits to one school in which we had become deeply involved, the teachers decided to 'create', rather than merely 'manage', the curriculum in their classrooms. However, they expressed reservations concerning their abilities to fulfil this responsibility. Responding to this concern required us to adopt a role similar to 'purchase' consultants. We conducted several 'workshop' sessions to inform these teachers about one way to design a classroom-based curriculum (from a critical perspective),[27] and we provided regular assistance and feedback as they developed and taught various units of study throughout the school year. Depending upon the specific needs of a school, we have assumed many roles in working with teachers and principals, including in-service educators (e.g. teaching specific strategies such as those related to 'whole language' instruction); librarians (i.e. finding and providing resources for specific instructional projects); sounding boards for new ideas; grant writers and editors; facilitators for individual and group brainstorming and problem-solving sessions; intermediaries to state officials; mediators of conflicts among teachers, principals, central administrators and/or parents; coordinators of school-to-school visitations and networking; public advocates for the schools with which we work; and liaison officers with other teachers and administrators involved in similar reform efforts (e.g. the Institute for Democracy and Education, Coalition for Essential Schools, Rethinking Schools Collective). When working with schools, we have discovered the importance of not letting one's 'approach' artificially limit the range of actions that may be needed to assist a given school.

QUESTIONS OF POWER, EXPERTISE AND COMMITMENT

Power and expertise

There is an intrinsic tension associated with our work in faculty development projects. The question before us is: how do we remain true to our convictions to reformulate education towards social and critical democracy[28] and at the same time foster the 'bottom-up' transformation of education in which teachers and principals assume the primary role as change agents? To insist that teachers and principals adopt an 'outsider's' ideology as a pre-condition to working together is something of a contradiction if one also advocates 'grass roots' school reform. Although we believe in our vision of schools and society, we want teachers and principals to create their own goals and visions on behalf of their students and community.

In working with schools, we have attempted to create relationships which allow us not only to facilitate teachers' and principals' ideas but also to share openly our own views and values related to any given topic. Several strategies are employed in order to establish this open dialogue without us, as external reformers, being viewed as the 'experts' with 'the answers'. In our initial contacts with a school, we consciously present our 'ideology' as broadly conceived, tentative and evolving, rather than as a 'grand theory' or 'the truth'. We communicate, verbally and through our actions, our belief that all ideas, values and visions, including our own, are inherently 'vulnerable'. In addition, we approach each school as a place where we can learn something about education as well as a potential site for the creation of democratic pedagogy. In discussing specific issues with teachers and principals, our contributions are presented as simply 'our ideas' that are not inherently better or worse than the ideas of the people with whom we are working. To guard further against the possibility of our 'suggestions' becoming 'directives', we encourage teachers and/or principals to make all final decisions in subsequent meetings without us. By emphasizing the power of teachers and principals to make final decisions, we are free to express our views with minimal risk of being coercive.

However, the dynamics of power found in faculty development and school reform situations are not so easily understood or resolved. As previously mentioned, once we are involved with a particular school, the distinctions between various approaches to faculty development consultation become obscured. As a result, the nature of power imbedded within these relationships can take unsuspecting turns. In some circumstances, we have found ourselves in what appears to be the role of 'experts' even though we ideologically reject this position and have practised the strategies previously mentioned. For example, in one school in which we spent considerable time involved in a major faculty development and school reform effort,[29] it was not uncommon for the teachers and the principal to present their ideas about particular matters (e.g. curriculum content, instructional activity, relationship with students or parents) for our feed-back. In these situations, we often found ourselves in the role of 'legitimizing' the teachers' and the principal's views. If we supported their ideas, then their confidence increased. When we offered them critical feedback, they often modified their thinking or actions in accordance with our analysis of the situation. By being placed in the position of 'experts', in most situations we were able to furnish these teachers with 'authoritative endorsement' for educational practices, curricular content and/or social visions which they intuitively believed were good but which had never been 'sanctioned' by anyone 'in power' (district supervisors or individuals with advanced university degrees) prior to our involvement. During the last two years, we have legitimized teachers' aspirations to design an original, school-based curriculum; to develop thematically integrated units of study; to teach multi-aged groupings of children; to establish instructional practices that cultivate children's 'multiple intelligences';[30,31] to create curricula that sensitize children to people in the world who have been historically marginalized and to humans' relationship with the world's eco-system; to broaden the school governance to include parents and students; and to develop approaches to 'discipline' that promote students' personal and social responsibility, respect for human diversity, and ethic of caring.[32] When inquiries are made about their programme, these teachers and principals often justify their actions, in part, by invoking my name and university affiliation.

From our perspective, being viewed as 'experts' facilitated the empowerment of these teachers and principals who, in turn, were able to utilize our involvement as 'experts' to gain additional school-level autonomy. However, these interactions from another perspective could be seen as teachers, once again, deferring to outside 'experts'. Instead of providing 'authoritative support' to ideas 'presented' to us, our interactions could potentially be viewed as teachers 'submitting' their ideas for our 'approval', thus reifying a 'service' role that keeps teachers largely powerless.[33] Our uneasiness with this latter perspective is exacerbated by the gender and racial composition of the participants. All of the teachers and the principal in this school were women and evenly divided across racial lines (50 per cent Afro-American and 50 per cent Euro-American), whereas, in almost every session, the consultants were white men. It would not be difficult to conclude that our relationship with this school implicitly bolstered the system of patriarchy which affirms men's control over women so prevalent in the United States.

What role have we played in this school? Did we help 'liberate' or 'oppress' these individuals? Does situating oneself as an 'expert' lead to the disenfranchisement of, or can it facilitate, in certain circumstances, the empowerment of, teachers? How do we come to understand the power relationships embedded in such situations? Did the fact that it was the teachers and principal who gave us the power to act as 'experts' (rather than our 'professional status' or supervisors in the district hierarchy) make our interactions empowering rather than disenfranchising for these individuals? Is it significant that our role of 'experts' only emerged after working together for an extended period of time and after a deep level of trust was established between us and the teachers and principal? Although these teachers and this principal have indicated to us that our interactions have left them feeling empowered, have they been victims of 'false consciousness' who cannot recognize their own oppression? There are many subtle dynamics at work in these situations, and the value of one's work with people is not easily evident.

Commitment

In addition to our concerns about power, we also have questions about commitment, especially as we assume the role of *public advocates* for the schools with which we work. Since many of our suggestions and ideas encourage teachers and principals to make substantive alterations in the education of their students and are thus viewed as potentially 'risky', when a school embraces our ideas in relation to a given situation, we communicate our willingness to assume equal responsibility and provide whatever support is possible to defend these views and practices if challenged. Schools such as the one previously discussed, that in general terms share our social and educational visions, clearly make for good partners in faculty development and school reform efforts in spite of the confusion that may arise from such relationships. However, as Finkelstein points out, these schools are difficult to locate during the present conservative times.

> For the first time in the history of school reform, a deeply materialist consciousness seems to be overwhelming all other concerns . . . . Contemporary reformers seem to be recalling public education from its traditional utopian mission – to nurture a critical and committed citizenry that would . . . extend the workings of political democracy . . . . Americans, for the first time in a one-hundred-and-fifty-year history, seem ready to do ideological surgery on their public schools – cutting them away from the fate of social justice and political democracy completely and grafting them instead onto élite corporate, industrial, military, and cultural interests.[34]

We have found few schools that initially share our visions of education and society. Most schools approach us because they express a desire to do something 'innovative' or 'different', but they have few ideas of what 'it is' they want to do.

In these situations, we actively search to find 'common ground' between the values and visions of the teachers and principal and our own. While many of the teachers and principals in these schools have, to some extent, 'bought into' the conservative agenda of the 1980s we, like others,[35–37] have found that most teachers have a deep sense of caring and public service. We have consistently been impressed with teachers' genuine desire to put the welfare of children before all other concerns. In our discussions with teachers and principals, most individuals do not find it difficult to agree that schools should be more interested in educating young people to help create a more compassionate and democratic society than in merely serving as vocational training sites for industry. We have found that many teachers seem willing to 'let go' of previously held values rooted in an industrial, technocratic ideology if given 'authoritative support' to do so. As Grumet implies,[38] teachers in these schools deeply resonate to values imbedded in a more feminized pedagogy. The values of caring and democracy have been useful to us in exploring with teachers ways to reform interpersonal power relationships (student/student, student/teacher, teacher/teacher, teacher/principal), the curriculum, and the types of educational experience found in particular schools.

There are, of course, schools that want to work with us that may agree with our social and educational values in broad terms, but wish to, or have little choice, due to local or state 'mandates' but to continue pedagogical practices such as punitive-based discipline, tracking, standardized testing, or textbook-based curriculum that to us contradict these values. What should our reaction be to this situation? Should we continue to work with these schools when our involvement may implicitly endorse practices that we believe do not serve the interests of or may even harm the students? If we decide not to work with these schools, what does this decision suggest about our commitment to public education?

In exploring this situation, we have borrowed from Glickman's reflections.[39] The most important question to ask is: what is gained by not working in these schools? Unless our departure will cause a major disruption (which it will not), the objectionable practice(s) will certainly continue. Although our 'reputation' may be protected because people will not be able to say that we support schools that condone such (an) abhorrent practice(s), there seems little to gain from leaving such a situation. Perhaps we will find ways of altering the conditions that keep the practice(s) entrenched. Our response is to be patient, raise questions, offer suggestions, articulate images of democratic pedagogy, try to understand others' perspectives, experience obstacles and look for opportunities.

Patience is also necessary because our assessment of a given situation may be wrong. For example, in the previously mentioned school the teachers and principal decided that all students and staff should wear 'uniforms' (white t-shirts with the school logo and navy blue pants, shorts or skirts). At first we viewed this decision as unwise, since it seemed to reflect an ethos of social conformism that would strip students of their individuality. However, as it was a 'magnet' school, students came to this building from all over a large metropolitan area. The student body included children from vastly different social, racial and economic backgrounds. The decision to have uniforms came from a sensitivity on the part of both teachers and parents to those students who lived in poverty and who would be spending hours each day next to children who lived in affluence. Uniforms in this situation were viewed as a way to help children go beyond the 'clothes that one wears' and discover other attributes upon which to establish friendships. In short, uniforms at this school promoted the development of authentic relationships among the students and a sense of community within the school. At the same time, teachers were sensitive to our concerns and were quick to affirm students' individuality as reflected in their work and personalities. As we look back on our initial assessment, we can see how easy it is to let one's ideology degenerate into dogma.

However, what if a school is 'doing harm' to students, and our work is to no avail? Do we call a press conference and denounce what is going on? Would anyone from the press even come? Although there are given situations in which public repudiation is warranted (such as Kozol's account of the racist brutality he witnessed in the Boston public schools),[40] in most cases this does not seem like a particularly useful response. If little headway is being made to reform a given school, then at some point it seems only natural to put our energies in other places. How do we know when this time comes?

As Glickman points out,[41] much depends upon our own sense of hope. It makes sense to leave when we have lost hope that the teachers and principal are still interested in asking questions, reflecting on experiences, or examining possibilities. Notice that our decision is not based upon our hope that the school will eventually do what we wish it would do. People who are moral, well informed

75

and thoughtful will often disagree with each other, and we view this disagreement as both useful and intelligent. Only when we lose hope in our abilities to generate an atmosphere in which we can learn from each other does it seem time to leave a particular school. Making a commitment to engage in faculty development projects suggests a moral obligation to 'hang in there'.

CONCLUSION

This chapter has explored several issues related to working in faculty development/school reform projects. As 'outsiders' to these schools, democratic thinking educators need to consider carefully what it means to 'assist' a faculty in its efforts to reform substantively the education that exists within its walls. Questions of power, expertise, and commitment are of special concern to individuals who may be called upon to act as consultants and who operate from an openly ideological position. While we have gained some insight into these issues, more of this self-reflective scholarship (what Krall refers to as 'autobiographical research'[42] is needed).

Although we have learned much in the previous two years, we have not yet initiated serious study into the dynamics of democratic forms of faculty development. Interpretive research that would illuminate the meaning that various participants (e.g. teachers, administrators, parents, students, outside consultants) give to a particular project would be especially helpful. As Schamroth and Blanchard state, 'Too often . . . it is administrators, researchers, or advisers (outsiders to the classroom) who give the public version account of teaching and curriculum development.'[43] Research that illuminates what Mikhail Bakhtin refers to as 'heteroglossia',[44] the interweaving of the many voices that exist in a given social phenomenon, would help us get beyond the surface layers of understanding and uncover the way in which different people may (and often do) create different meanings from the same experiences. The result would be a richer and more complex comprehension of faculty development.

NOTES AND REFERENCES

1. Goodman, J., 'Working in schools: emancipatory theorizing and educational reform'. Paper presented at the American Educational Research Association meeting, San Francisco, April 1992.

2. Bullough, R. and Gitlin, A., 'Schooling and change: a view from the lower rung'. *Teachers College Record*, **87** (2), pp. 219–37 (p. 219), 1985.

3. Sachs, J. and Logan, L., 'Control or development? A study of in-service education'. *Journal of Curriculum Studies*, **22** (5), pp. 473–81, 1990.

4. Bullough and Gitlin, op. cit., note 2.

5. Although students occupy the 'bottom' position in schools, they rarely have the maturity, knowledge, verbal skills, institutional longevity or power base needed to foster emancipatory reforms in schools.

6. Goodman, J., *Elementary schooling for critical democracy*. Albany, NY: State University of New York Press, 1992.

7. Bullough and Gitlin, op. cit., note 2.

8. Batesky, J., 'In-service education: increasing teacher effectiveness using the Hunter lesson design'. *Journal of Physical Education*, pp. 89–93, September 1987.

9. Hunter, M., 'Knowing, teaching and supervising'. In Hosford, P. (ed.), *Using what we know about teaching*. Alexandria, VA: Association for Supervision and Curriculum Development, pp. 169–203, 1984.

10. Hunter, M., 'What's wrong with Madeline Hunter?' *Educational Leadership*, **42** (5), pp. 57–60, 1985.

11. Hunter, M., 'Well acquainted is not enough: a response to Mandeville and Rivers'. *Educational Leadership*, **46** (4), pp. 67–8, 1989.

12. Kerr, D., 'Teaching competence and teacher education in the United States'. *Teachers College Record*, **84** (3), pp. 525–52 (p. 545), 1983.

13. Smyth, J., 'A teacher development approach to bridging the practice-research gap'. *Journal of Curriculum Studies*, **14** (4), pp. 331–42, 1982.

14. Smyth, J., 'A critical pedagogy of classroom practice'. *Journal of Curriculum Studies*, **21** (6), pp. 483–502, 1989.

15. Lieberman, A., 'Collaborative work'. *Educational Leadership*, **43** (5), pp. 4–8, 1986.

16. Lieberman, A., *Schools as Collaborative Cultures: Creating the Future Now*. Bristol, PA: Falmer Press, 1986.

17. Smyth, J. and Henry, C., 'A case study experience of a collaborative and responsive form of professional development for teachers'. Paper presented to the Australian Association for Research in Education conference, Canberra, Australia, November 1983.

18. Lieberman, A. and Miller, L., 'School improvement: themes and variations'. *Teachers College Record*, **86** (1), pp. 4–19, 1984.

19. Schein, E., *Process Consultation: Its Role in Organization Development*. Menlo Park, CA: Addison-Wesley Publishing, 1969.

20. Banathy, B., *Systems Design of Education: A Journey to Create the Future*. Englewood Cliffs, NJ: Educational Technology Publication, 1991.

21. Reigeluth, C., 'The search for meaningful re-form: a third-wave educational system'. *Journal of Instructional Development*, **10** (4), pp. 3–14, 1987.

22. Pink, W. and Hyde, A., *Effective Staff Development for School Change*. Norwood, NJ: Ablex Publishing, 1991.

23. Dewey, J., *Democracy and Education: An Introduction to the Philosophy of Education*. New York: The Free Press, 1966.

24. Goodman, J., 'Education for critical democracy'. *Journal of Education*, **171** (2), pp. 88–116, 1989.

25. Goodman, op. cit., note 6.

26. Dewey, J., *The Public and its Problems*. New York: Henry Holt, 1927.

27. Goodman, J., 'Teaching pre-service teachers a critical approach to curriculum design: a descriptive account'. *Curriculum Inquiry*, **16** (3), pp. 179–201, 1986.

28. Goodman, op. cit., note 24.

29. Goodman, J., 'Resisting the conservative agenda for education: images of a reformed elementary curriculum'. Paper presented at the annual *Journal of Curriculum Theorizing* conference, Dayton, OH, October 1992.

30. Eisner, E., *Cognition and Curriculum: A Basis for Deciding What to Teach*. New York: Longman Press, 1982.

31. Gardner, H., *Frames of Mind: The Theory of Multiple Intelligences*. New York: Basic Books, 1985.

32. Noddings, N., *Caring: A Feminine Approach to Ethics and Moral Education*. Berkeley: University of California Press, 1984.

33. Bullough and Gitlin, op. cit., note 2.

34. Finkelstein, B., 'Education and the retreat from democracy in the United States – 1979–8?' *Teachers College Record*, **86** (2), pp. 273–82 (pp. 280–81), 1984.

35. Bullough and Gitlin, op. cit., note 2.

36. Grumet, M., 'Pedagogy for patriarchy: the feminization of teaching'. *Interchange*, **12** (2/3), pp. 165–84, 1981.

37. Noddings, op. cit., note 32.

38. Grumet, op. cit., note. 36.

39. Glickman, C., 'Reflections on facilitating school improvement: issues of value'. *Journal of Curriculum and Supervision*, **6** (3), pp. 265–71, 1991.

40. Kozol, J., *Death at an early age*. New York: Bantam Books, 1968.

41. Glickman, op. cit., note 39.

42. Krall, F., 'From the inside out – personal history as educational research'. *Educational Theory*, **38** (4), pp. 467–79, 1988.

43. Schamroth, N. and Blanchard, J., 'Teachers' motivations and satisfactions in developing their own curricula'. *English Education*, **22**, pp. 99–124 (p. 99), 1990.

44. Clark, K. and Holquist, M., *Mikhail Bakhtin*. Cambridge, MA: Harvard University Press, 1984.

Chapter 5

True Stories: The Politics of Truth in Teacher Development

Henry St. Maurice, Barbara Albrecht, Nell Anderson and
Connie Milz

INTRODUCTION

During the past decade, research about teaching has been conducted from a
greater variety of approaches than ever before. This tendency toward eclecticism
has been called a trend away from searching for a Grand Strategy and towards
pursuit of a Great Conversation,[1] one in which teachers' voices have been heard
more often in scholarly discourse. Teachers are speaking out about their profession, as action researchers and in ethnographies, case studies or critiques.

During the same decade in which teachers are finding their voices among
scholars, however, they have not increased their political standing. In the name
of educational reform, most Western nations have enacted greater centralized
authority over educational policies and programmes, particularly those for
developing teaching professionals; as Clark said about teacher education in the
United States during the 1980s:

> The external changes imposed on the field had greater currency
> than any agenda being developed by the profession itself . . . . The
> vehicles to carry out the solutions fitted policy options that can be
> exercised at the state level . . . [having] an efficacious side effect to
> those who lacked confidence in teacher educators, i.e., control of
> teacher education was wrested from those who had messed it up in
> the past.[2]

By invoking such macro-political concepts as 'professionalism' or 'national
educational goals', teacher organizations and local education agencies have
abetted processes of centralization.[3-5] Even as teachers' voices are raised to
express educational ideas, or what Popkewitz called 'millennial dreams and
progressive rhetoric',[6] they are ironically becoming more enmeshed in externally
imposed rules and policies, or 'technologies that enter into and organize daily life
and its hopes and desires'.[7]

There have been numerous studies of ironies and contradictions in recent
educational policies and programmes, especially those pertaining to the education of teachers,[8-11] but there are still many questions about these trends'

micro-political effects upon teachers and schools. In particular, how do teachers articulate and respond to current research, policy and practice? As they raise their voices, how do their ideas reflect or refract those of administrators, policy-makers and the general public? In this chapter, we will discuss transactions in teacher development programmes as micro-political processes that raise issues about self and society. Three specific sites will be examined, each involving supervisory conferences and formal evaluations among administrators and teachers who have documented their descriptions, reflections and analyses. Everyday discourses and practices of teachers' professional development will be portrayed in their own words.

In presenting these vignettes of teacher development, our purpose is to show how activities that are often considered trivial can nonetheless be infused with meanings about social order. As Foucault says:

> The minute disciplines, the panopticisms of the everyday, may
> well be below the level of emergence of the great apparatuses and
> the great political struggles. But, in the genealogy of modern
> society, they have been, with the class domination that traverses
> it, the political counterpart of the juridical norms according to
> which power [has been constructed and] redistributed. Hence, no
> doubt, the importance that has been given for so long to the small
> techniques of discipline, to those apparently insignificant tricks
> that it has invented, and even to those 'sciences' that give it a
> respectable face . . . [12]

Educators, by explicitly and mutually confronting political issues in their transactions, can find ways to interpret small actions in terms of large issues, and thereby examine norms of personal truth, professional quality and public policy.

METHOD

Our methods of documentation are based on current practices of journal-keeping and action research in teacher education.[13-16] To interpret these texts, we have here drawn from sociologies of knowledge which approach discourses and practices as social constructions within particular social contexts.[17-19] By contrasting continuities and discontinuities among diverse forms of thought and action, specific ideas such as 'truth' can be investigated. By analogy, ideas of time and space may be located in reference to a single human being's 'habitat', e.g. 'here and now', or in reference to a social group's 'field', e.g. '504 Aspen Lane, 10:23 AM', thereby pointing out various orientations.[20] In comparing forms of language and action, patterns of significance or insignificance can be indicated.

The forms of teachers' language we have chosen for analysis are related to the field called 'professional development', which encompasses discourses and practices also called 'staff development', 'continuing teacher education' and 'in-

service teacher education'.[21-23] Professional development involves p
as well as courses, workshops, supervision and evaluation, although
activities figure most prominently in definitions given by practitioner:

We are the subjects of our own analyses, situated within various sc..
the midwestern United States. As teachers, administrators and teacher edu
cators jointly interested in our profession, we kept journals over the course of a
year, following models of action research that we had discussed in a summer
course.[24-27] We sought to investigate the ways in which policy issues become
imbedded in our words and deeds. We recorded and analyzed some examples of
'small techniques of discipline' within our habitats, checking them for connections to sweeping changes in our field of teaching. A theme that emerged in our
project is that simple truths can be complex, often contradictory, constructions
that have extensive effects upon individual teachers' lives and careers as well as
on the well-being of other professionals and the profession itself.

BACKGROUND: THE POLITICS OF TRUTH

These analyses therefore begin with an assumption that 'truth' is a polyvalent
concept, various versions of which are each dependent upon particular circumstances, as in, for example, the various stories in Akira Kurosawa's film *Rasho-
mon*. Truth involves each participant's particular values, through which events
are filtered and from which discourses and practices are formed. There are as
many varieties of truth as there are versions of a story; as Friedrich Nietzsche
put it, 'The different languages, set side by side, show that what matters with
words is never the truth, never an adequate expression; else there would not be so
many languages'.[28] Versions of truth are bound to cultural and political conditions which conditions shift and intermingle rapidly and subtly, disallowing
any presumptions of stability.

Polyvalent conceptions of truth mean that researchers, policy-makers and
practitioners must deal with complex sets of relations. As many contemporary
scholars point out,[29-31] since politics is the study of social relations, true stories
may be construed as political statements; according to Cleo Cherryholmes,

> If statements and not things are true or false, then truth is
> necessarily linguistic; if truth is linguistic, then it is relative to
> language use (words, concepts, statements, discourses) at a given
> time and place; therefore ideology, interests, power arrangements
> at a given time and place are implicated in the production of what
> counts as 'true'.[32]

Truth is a product of relationships among words as well as among those who use
them. It derives from auras of power and arts of persuasion as much as from rules
of evidence and rigours of proof.

Among the many commonly recognized versions of truth, two will be used here to analyse the micro-politics of professional development. The first is called 'prudence'; in this words and deeds are aligned with perceived patterns of power, much as Shakespeare's Hamlet chooses an 'antic disposition' to elude suspicion by the King on whom he seeks vengeance. The second is called 'sincerity', and here words and deeds are formed in apparent disregard of perceived patterns of power, much as characters in O'Neill's *Strange Interlude* drop masks to show their unguarded thoughts and emotions. Depending on cultural or political conditions, there may occur situations favouring one or the other version, or both versions, of truth. For example, consider the following scene: a male supervisor, after observing a female teacher's lesson for purposes of evaluation, engages in a conversation which contains pauses and interruptions typical of male–female exchanges. The supervisor might sincerely want to help the teacher to improve her work, even while the teacher is prudently avoiding saying that she cannot get a word in edgeways. In their dialogue, both employ power relations that predominate in contemporary social life. Were the roles reversed, the power relations might only be rearranged rather than eliminated, because there would be other conflicts between each one's field and habitat.

CONFLICTING VERSIONS OF TRUTH

In this chapter, our purpose is to portray some specific examples of conflicting versions of truth. Our central question then is: how could educators develop strategies to articulate and manipulate the micro-politics of truth in their encounters? In the following sections, some replies to these questions are offered. In the first section, a supervisor, 'Jean', describes a series of encounters with a teacher, 'Richard'. Next, another supervisor, 'Marie', will describe a similar situation with very different outcomes, after which 'Sue' will describe independent projects she undertook to foster her professional development as a teacher. These sections will include quotations from our journals describing actual situations, giving our own versions of some truths about our professional development.

Jean: Clinical Supervision Redux

Jean is responsible for administering reading programmes in a small school district that includes three elementary schools scattered across a wide area. She makes frequent contacts with administrators and teachers, and is directly in charge of five paraprofessionals. She must supervise and evaluate all paraprofessionals annually, according to guidelines jointly approved by the district administration and teachers' organization. Ordinarily, these procedures do not produce either overt conflicts involving her own or the paraprofessionals' development, or explicit constraints on the ways that they articulate the truths involved in observation, supervision and evaluation.

Last year, however, a unique situation emerged when Richard returned to the district after leave of absence. Before taking this leave to pursue a degree in another profession, Richard had been a secondary-level teacher and, along with his wife, a friend of Jean and her husband. When his leave of absence expired, Richard had not completed the degree and was unable to find work in that other profession. To make ends meet, he had to accept whatever open position the district offered him, which was a position as a paraprofessional under Jean's supervision. As she notes,

> To return to teaching out of need after an earlier unsuccessful experience is difficult. Added to this, Richard had been concentrating on a totally different kind of work for two years. The fact that both he and his wife had been our friends for years greatly complicated my ability to be objective, understanding and authoritative.

Richard's professional development plan – a new career – involved many conflicts on his part. For reasons of space we must focus here upon Jean's concerns, which involved her sincere doubts about Richard's fitness to be a reading teacher of children in primary grades, as well as her prudent strategies for meeting the goals set in the reading programme for each student and teacher. As she says,

> Richard's previous problems stemmed from his inability to communicate successfully with secondary students. He would consistently use vocabulary and concepts beyond their comprehension. I was greatly concerned about his ability to reach the comprehension level of kindergarten through third grade students. Would he be able to change both his methods and his ability to be understood?

A conflict between sincerity and prudence emerged for Jean early in the fall, when she first observed Richard's teaching:

> At first, Richard returned to his previous teaching methods. He used complicated vocabulary and abstract ideas inaccessible to his young students. He also asked questions without waiting for responses. Within a few minutes of the beginning of class, his students acted very confused. I realized that I needed a method of supervision that allowed me to suggest improvements without infringing on our friendship. I wanted to focus upon Richard's teaching instead of our past social contacts or our present professional situation.

As part of her own professional development, Jean was attending graduate courses, and she arranged an independent study of instructional supervision in which the text detailed a model of clinical supervision.[33] Jean thought that clinical supervision might help her address her concerns about Richard's professional development. In trying it, she was also pursuing her own growth as a supervisor:

> The Glatthorn model seemed to me extremely appropriate for this situation. The model was structured, yet it allowed for individual variation. The following four steps were used for each observation:
> **I. Pre-observation interview** – we discussed what was to be looked for and how it was to be documented, and I asked him for any questions or concerns;
>
> **II. Observation** – I wrote down what was said and done during Richard's actual teaching;
>
> **III. Post-observation interview** – we reviewed and discussed the 'script-tape' from the observation and made out an activities list and a report;
>
> **IV. Follow-up** – after an interval, I returned to collect the observation/comment form to which Richard had added comments, and we both discussed it prior to copying and filing it.

By the middle of the winter, Jean and Richard had participated in four structured observation sessions, usually followed within a day by supervisory conferences. Richard made enthusiastic responses to Jean's written suggestions, which in turn heightened her own enthusiasm about clinical supervision:

> Richard's comments concerning behaviors [sic] that facilitated or impeded learning showed his increased understanding of his new teaching situation and his own creative and beneficial abilities. With each post-observation conference, Richard and I both increased our self-confidence in our roles as well as our abilities to successfully accomplish those roles.

Jean's experience shows that, as Glatthorn states, not every supervisory interaction can or should be collegial.[34] In this instance Jean found it awkward, if not impossible, to confront collegially and sincerely the inappropriate teaching that she saw Richard doing when she first observed him. At that point she restrained her actions out of awareness of his personal situation and their prior friendship, as well as for reasons of dynamics of gender and power. A version of clinical supervision provided a buffer or, as Blumberg called it,[35] a 'sector', for manifesting a version of truth about professional development.

Within the formalities that she implemented, Jean's supervisory interactions with Richard were marked by prudence. Politically, in restricting their professional interactions to formalities outlined in a text, they enacted what Foucault called a 'dividing practice'[36] amplifying official relations within a hierarchy and diminishing unofficial collegial relations. Such practices need not be associated with oppression, however, but may in cases such as Jean's offer opportunities to confront and reconstruct relations within a hierarchy. For example, as Munro points out, prudent use of supervisory authority can be in keeping with feminist approaches to teaching and learning, in which the 'power of those in authority can be viewed not as power-over but power-with. Power emerges in shared experiences that enhance our understandings of our traditions and experiences.'[37] Jean did not approach her supervisory duties from an explicitly feminist standpoint, although she does say:

> A 'feminist' understanding of small children and their needs can be learned. Richard has become an extremely caring, patient, understanding teacher, able to communicate with young students without becoming condescending. His enthusiasm and enjoyment are contagious. He has improved the teaching atmosphere in the whole school.

In effect, Jean was able to facilitate her own development as a supervisor, and Richard's development as a teacher as well, through prudent discourse set in an apparatus of formal clinical supervision. By approaching these instances of professional development through action research, Jean was able to consider and choose methods which, as recent commentators have pointed out,[38,39] foster collegiality and experimentation. For example, Garman says that clinical supervision can involve

> a commitment of time, a commitment to looking at the ordinary with an extraordinary sensibility, a commitment to letting go of our ego and equilibrium for a while, and a commitment to certain methods and actions associated with reflection and inquiry.[40]

The politics of truth for Richard and Jean therefore demanded restrictions upon the sincerity with which each could express themselves, but within those restrictions there were ways to articulate issues that each perceived to be important for his or her own development as well as for the education of children. Such serendipity is both fragile and uncommon, as the next example will illustrate.

Marie: Clinical Supervision Awry

Marie is also a supervisor, in a larger district with many schools located in residential areas. She coordinates the delivery of instructional services to students for whom English is not a primary language. She is responsible for supervising the district's ESL (English as a second language) programme, involving 33 certified teachers and 29 paraprofessionals, in grades from pre-school and kindergarten to senior high school, as well as numerous volunteers, some of whom are themselves not yet fluent in English. Marie shares responsibility with individual principals for evaluating the performance of all participants. As a teacher who has gradually assumed these duties, she undertook a professional development plan that came to involve action research; she says:

As I progressively entered the role of supervisor and evaluator, there were several dilemmas. How was I going to start supervising and evaluating many teachers who are still my peers? How was I going to be able to adapt my evaluation style to that of the 16 principals that I was supposed to assist? How could I provide the most appropriate supervision assistance to my teachers in the various schools, and still have time for my other responsibilities of curriculum development, program [sic] management, student advocacy, etc.?

I used the district evaluation form, and followed a clinical cycle including pre-conferences and post-conferences in which we could discuss freely and openly my recorded observations and the teachers' responses to them. Because they were not part of teachers' formal evaluations, the conferences provided both me and them with genuine learning situations, as we could both question, monitor and adjust without fear of judgement.

During the past year Marie has encountered numerous situations in which clinical supervision techniques were employed. Much as Jean did, she sought ways to discuss teaching with individuals for whom personal and professional development were at issue. Often these discussions were collegial and sincere; for example, one teacher, 'Betty', had selected a transfer from classroom teaching to the ESL resource room. She was earnestly working at making the transition, but was feeling frustrated with the complex needs of the students in the new assignment as well as with not having 'her own' students as she had previously had.

Our conferences included time to vent her frustrations, yet were mostly constructive discussions of her concerns. These conferences helped her grow successfully in the new assignment. For example, in talking over her concerns we decided to rearrange her schedule so that she met students once daily for longer blocks of time, and got to know them better.

In one case, however, opportunities for sincere exchanges were constrained for professional reasons. Marie was asked by a principal to assist him in supervising 'Helen', a kindergarten teacher. She had been transferred to a class that enrolled a majority of non-native speakers of English whose language proficiency was limited at the outset of the school year. There were many aspects of this situation that troubled Marie:

The principal, 'Fred', said that Helen was unequivocally prejudiced against ESL students. He had already written her off as incompetent. His observation reports noted that she was brusque, yelled at students, and lacked the professionalism to address all students. Helen, on the other hand, claimed that Fred disliked her and that her class had been made up of students rejected from other teachers' classes. She felt that her requests for assistance went unheeded. She complained that she could not work for Fred. I felt that neither Fred nor Helen were able to work out their differences.

Nevertheless, she began observing the class and soon noticed that Helen showed much discomfort during their encounters. It soon became apparent that Helen's transfer was an implicit attempt to punish her, even to force her to resign. At one conference, according to Marie, she said 'I've been set up for failure. This is more like a pre-school class than a kindergarten class.' Marie's response was sympathetic; such administrative manoeuvres are well known to veteran teachers. The effect of this statement upon Marie's discourse with Helen was that she withdrew from formal involvement, making no written evaluations despite direct requests from administrators. She limited her contacts to making suggestions or discussing individual children's needs. As she summarizes,

> My appearance in her classroom was torture for Helen. She said
> that I was her last chance to salvage her teaching career, but my
> presence clearly caused her too much anxiety for her to teach
> effectively. I made monitoring visits that did not last more than
> ten minutes, and would leave no more than one suggestion. I kept
> my comments to specific strategies and techniques for dealing with
> cultural differences such as, 'Try doing an activity while you are
> explaining it so that ESL children can hear and see what they are
> to do' or 'Don't demand that Hmong children talk face to face with
> you, because they do not do so with adults at home.'

Marie's prudent statements differ from Jean's in that her supervisory interactions could not be directed toward joint professional development, because of Fred's minatory presence and the hierarchical power relations it represented. Helen's situation perpetuated long-standing class and gender inequities in schooling and teaching.[41] In discussing the reasons for the transfer, Marie and Helen acknowledged the administrators' inequitable actions but, unlike Jean and Richard, were unable to negotiate space within their relations for mutually agreeable exchanges. To some extent this can be attributed to patterns of socialization among all teachers, especially female primary-grade teachers.[42,43]

To a greater degree, however, Marie's reluctance to continue supervisory interchanges with Helen presents a vivid instance of the politics of truth. Faced with a sincere statement that Helen's situation was unfair, Marie prudently withdrew from a conflict that she could not resolve. She refused to proceed with a detailed cycle of clinical supervision like Jean and Richard's because she did not foresee an outcome offering either party any prospect of professional growth or personal satisfaction. Eventually the conflict was dissolved but not resolved: Helen sought and received another transfer, to a school where she and another principal have begun a cycle of clinical supervision. Marie has had no further supervisory contact with her.

Marie's story shows that, without the raw materials of mutual agreement and genuine trust, teachers cannot manufacture professional development. No educational method, especially one that takes as many diverse forms as does clinical supervision, can assure lasting beneficial effects in the absence of democratic political alignments that foster inquiry and exchange.[44,45] In their quandary, Marie and Helen dealt with the reverse side of the same coin that Jean and Richard were able to use to escape their dilemma. In the next example, a third member of our group, 'Sue', used a different method to examine options and possibilities for professional development. She began keeping a journal to examine her teaching and learning, and in so doing encountered another manifestation of the politics of truth.

Sue: Journal-keeping

Sue is a teacher of physical education in a small city district. She works in three elementary schools, and, because she is president of the teachers' organization, she has frequent interactions with teachers in other elementary schools, the junior high school and the high school. Her professional activities also include service on committees which frequently meet after school and often out of town. These duties add time constraints to a full home life on a farm, where she assumes a myriad of duties as well as driving her children to and from their after-school activities. Nonetheless, she is also a mainstay of her church and an avid runner.

When Sue began journal-keeping to meet the requirements of a course, her initial response was one of concern over the time burdens it involved: 'What will I have to give up in order to maintain a journal on a daily basis?' Once the course was completed, she volunteered to continue, as an experiment with action research and journal-keeping in her own professional development plan; as she noted in an entry:

> Professional development means different things to different
> people/teachers. I have long considered taking classes as the one
> way for me to develop professionally. With the busy schedule I
> have, this allows me to set aside time to study an area of interest.
> It also brings together teachers of like interest. Lots of 'leg-work'
> (finding others interested in the same topic as you) is completed
> for you when taking a class. During this project I was surprised at
> the number of teachers that don't agree with me. Reasons that
> they gave me were:
> - cost of the class is too high (my response: you go up the
>   pay scale);

- too much time involved (my response: you have the same 24 hours I do);

- can't find an interesting class (my response: what???)

Now I do find myself looking for other ways to develop professionally along with my peers. Some of my department members need help and I also feel that we need to deal with the area of self-concept. I personally find it hard to believe, yet I know that is one of our problems. There is a feeling of 'isolation' that physical education teachers have to learn to deal with during the teaching day. Other teachers think of us as 'down/over there' in the gymnasium/field house. I know many teachers in many areas feel this way. I remember in college talking about isolation and how to deal with it:

- get to teachers' lounge when on break

- never eat lunch at your desk

- take time to meet someone new each day

- read the local paper

- develop new interests

- talk to people in the know

Although these ideas were meant for college students getting into their first year of teaching, the idea is good for all of us: you have to make an effort to overcome isolation, no one will do it for you.

Sue's list of activities contrasts with the traditional notions of teacher isolation,[46,47] caricatured by Griffin as 'two-by-four teaching: two covers of a book by four walls of a room'.[48] As many commentators have pointed out, the 'connected' teaching that Sue advocates is part of most proposals for school reform and restructuring.[49,50]

There are, however, pitfalls along the way to making connections, not the least of which is the intensification of time demands upon teachers.[51-54] We therefore asked two questions in looking back over the past year: first, did action research and journal-keeping enable Sue to identify personal and professional truths? Next, was a truth of sincerity in her own writings constrained by a truth of prudence about the conditions under which she wrote? To these questions, Sue's reply was that, with 'the same 24 hours' as anyone else, she used a journal to focus upon her professional development without finding excessive strain.

In reply to the first question, Sue surveyed some of her colleagues about their professional development. For most of them, coursework or conferences were the readiest examples. These activities did include journal-keeping as a source of professional development for recertification credits linked to a negotiated pay-scale advancement plan. Three credits are granted for 45 clock-hours of approved work, for which the district can provide released time and financial support for conference-going. In short, Sue found that action research and journal-keeping were parts of personal, professional and institutional development plans in her district.

Both action research and journal-keeping are time-honoured and readily understood activities that can be used to connect teachers during various aspects of their professional development. Sue found a few peers who would admit to pursuing them beyond the requirements of a graduate course. Among many conditions that led to this situation, we here focus upon the politics of truth: both activities demand not only time but also a specialized discourse that demands sincere discussions of strengths and weaknesses. As Jean and Marie had, Sue encountered a dilemma that pitted her sincerely held beliefs about teaching against the prudent discourses and practices endorsed by administrators and organizations. Confronting this dilemma, she maintained her journal despite its conflicting demands.

Sue's findings are not unique: despite long traditions of teachers writing about their work, there remains much ambivalence about it. On one hand, there come from many places and times stirring chronicles of teachers uplifting students and communities; on the other, there are just as many tales of struggles lost. As Keizer says,

> I hope that I have written a thoughtful book about teaching. But thoughtful as it may be, in the end it is but an alphabet I recite in the dark . . . . I'm waiting for the day – and it will come soon – when one of my blunders leads my kids to think: And this is the guy who *wrote a book* about teaching? What a load of crap it must be! . . . . We can talk about teaching endlessly, but when we meet the student face to face, when he or she speaks to us like Job's God out of the whirlwind of paper and hurry, then like Job we realize that all our talk until this moment is dust and ashes.[55]

Journals, whether or not they are published, are ways of recording changes, not of marshalling them. Like the confessional or autobiographical genres from which they are derived, journals are used by authors to recount defeats as well as victories within their political and cultural circumstances. Generalizable concepts, as Keizer points out, are, one hopes, inferred in such works, but are no more valid there than in any other literary form. Just as brushing up on Shakespeare is not the royal road to refined taste, neither is keeping a journal a guarantee of reflective deliberation and democratic action. The politics of truth in journal-keeping, therefore, involve both sincerity about the limits of authorial experience and prudence about the specific situations in which authors write.

In action research, journals document cycles of planning and experimentation.[56,57] To the extent that a journal addresses personal, institutional, social and cultural factors, it serves as a record of conditions that affect discourses and practices. In Sue's professional development journal, she noted linkages that might otherwise have gone unnoticed: 'Problems that we had a year ago – what did we do then to solve them? What do others now suggest?' The journal genre collects such perceptions for analysis, establishing continuities where they might not be otherwise perceived.

The costs and benefits of journal-keeping are both time-related. If, like Sue, a teacher can fit a journal into his or her life, then it connects otherwise disparate moments for reflection, analysis and sharing. However, it is also possible that a journal might actually subtract time that a teacher might use for reflection, analysis or communication. The politics of truth are full of ambivalence; so journal-keeping, particularly under conditions of intensified personal and professional life, involves a delicate balance between what a teacher learns and what he or she can use, especially in connections with colleagues.

THE MICRO-POLITICS OF TRUTH IN PROFESSIONAL DEVELOPMENT

Our three stories, as told above, are all meant to show that professional development is a problematic construct. On various pretexts, teachers are asked to supervise, be supervised, attend courses and conferences, or undertake projects. Often certification, employment or compensation regulations constitute institutional frameworks within which professional development is strictly defined. Teachers sometimes operate within these frameworks towards ends that heighten a sense of efficacy, as Jean and Sue found. At other times, as Marie reported, they find much less efficacy. While many studies of professional development stress effects upon instruction,[58] many others raise questions about the effects of teacher learning upon schools,[59] as well as the communities in which they are set.[60] More teachers and teacher educators are asking political questions about their profession; for instance, as Lockwood quotes Kathleen Densmore, 'professionalism' can be said to promote 'the trivialization of teaching':

> I've seen it recently in the schools in which I work. Teachers have
> an endless amount of paperwork to manage, and an increasing
> amount of supervisory duties. The implicit message that often
> comes from school administrators is that a true professional would
> perform these tasks uncritically and not question them, and
> certainly not say that they are not part of the job description.[61]

93

In other words, professionalism is at stake in each small act, whether it is a supervisory conference, a page of writing about teaching or a lunch break with a colleague. The micro-politics of truth do not permit inaction. Whether or not they are acting or reacting, teachers define teaching as either mindless conformance to conventions of schooling and the teaching profession or thoughtful inquiry into the purposes of those conventions.

Professional development is therefore not reducible to a simple set of rules, but is better construed as a complex and ever-changing web of discourses and practices. By choice or by default, teachers' actions incorporate professional norms which give priority to some versions of truth and diminish the importance of others. Thus routine procedures have serious consequences: settling for supervision 'by the book' or random collations of courses and conferences means losing chances to ask about purposes and consequences. As Soder states,

> If teachers (including those who teach teachers) overlook or ignore
> the foundation of what they do – that is to say, the moral
> dimensions of the relationships among teachers, students, parents
> and the larger legal framework of the state, then the consequences
> involve something more than not quite making it into the camp of
> the 'real' professionals . . . . Without some sort of recourse to a
> moral dimension, to the nature of a just world, we would have
> advanced technique and knowledge, cut off from the world.[62]

The politics of truth in teachers' professional development, therefore, means asking 'What is teaching?' and 'Why teach?' as well as 'How?'. The kinds of answers that teachers make to those questions enact various forms of truth. In each situation some prudence may be called for to maintain a balance between an individual teacher's habitat and particular circumstances, such as administrative or parental accountability. Nonetheless, occasions for sincerity, like those discovered by Jean and Sue, may also be found, so that connections can be made. Micro-politics of truth, therefore, entails struggles for awareness; as Popkewitz concludes, attention must be given to 'the interrelation of ethics, morality and politics in questions about daily existence and its communicative practices'.[63,64]

CONCLUSION

Teachers are raising their voices, describing the conditions of their work, responding to calls for schooling reform and asking for empowerment and autonomy in planning their own as well as their students' learning. This trend changes but does not eliminate dilemmas that reverberate in such oft-repeated questions as 'Who shall teach?' and 'What knowledge is of most worth?'. To illustrate these dilemmas, we have offered three stories about truth, that is to say about the ways in which conceptions of truth are formed. We have not addressed questions about either how students and teachers interact, or how teachers interact with each other and with the communities that subsidize their work. Neither have we discussed how ideas of professionalism are shaped, nor how those shapes are currently changing. What we have sought to do is to show how we have encountered professional development through our action research, and to give some implications of those encounters.

In conclusion, we draw no conclusions beyond our findings that inquiry into our own professional development has enriched our awareness of teaching and heightened our appreciation of everyday transactions. In connecting with one another and with others, we have found ways to ask questions about what we do and why we do it. Through supervision, journal-keeping and action research we have examined ourselves and our profession. We were not looking for answers that would solve pedagogical or political problems in our profession, just for better questions – which, as any teacher knows, are both ends and beginnings. For any story about teachers' professional development to be true, it ought to be continued.

NOTES AND REFERENCES

1. Shulman, L., 'Paradigms and research programs in the study of teaching'. In Wittrock, M. (ed.), *Handbook of Research on Teaching.* New York: Macmillan, pp. 3–36, 1986.

2. Clark, D., 'Leadership in policy development by teacher educators: search for a more effective future'. In Gideonse, H. (ed.), *Teacher Education Policy.* Albany, NY: State University of New York Press, pp. 269–96 (p. 275), 1992.

3. Darling-Hammond, l., 'Teachers and teaching: signs of a changing profession'. In Haberman, M., Sikula, J. and Houston, W. (eds), *Handbook of Research on Teacher Education.* New York: Merrill, pp. 267–90, 1992.

4. Lawn, M. and Grace, G., *Teachers: The Culture and Politics of their Work.* London and Philadelphia: Falmer Press, 1987.

5. Kerchner, C. and Mitchell, D., *The Changing Idea of a Teachers' Union.* London and Philadelphia: Falmer Press, 1988.

6. Popkewitz, T., *A Political Sociology of Educational Reform.* New York: Teachers College Press, 1991.

7. Ibid., p. 216.

8. Britzman, D., *Practice Makes Practice: A Critical Study of Learning to Teach.* Albany, NY: State University of New York Press, 1991.

9. Lather, P., *Getting Smart: Feminist Research and Pedagogy with/in the Postmodern.* New York: Routledge, 1991.

10. Ginsburg, M., *Contradictions in Teacher Education and Society: A Critical Analysis.* London and Philadelphia: Falmer Press, 1988.

11. Zeichner, K. and Liston, D. *Teacher Education and the Social Conditions of Schooling.* New York: Routledge, 1991.

12. Foucault, M., 'Panopticism'. In Rabinow, P. (ed.), *The Foucault Reader.* 1975. Reprint. New York: Pantheon, pp. 212–13, 1984.

13. Tabachnick, B. and Zeichner, K. (eds), *Issues and Practices in Inquiry-oriented Teacher Education: Changing the Nature of Pedagogical Knowledge.* London and Philadelphia: Falmer Press, 1991.

14. Tripp, D., 'Teachers, journals and collaborative research'. In Smyth, J. (ed.), *Educating Teachers.* London and Philadelphia: Falmer Press, pp. 179–92, 1987.

15. Wood, D., 'Teaching narratives: a source for faculty development'. *Harvard Education Review,* **62** (4), pp. 535–50, 1993.

16. Woods, P., 'Action research, a field perspective'. *Journal of Education for Teaching,* **14** (2), pp. 135–50, 1988.

17. Bourdieu, P., *In Other Words: Essays Towards a Reflexive Sociology.* Stanford, CA: Stanford University Press, 1990.

18. Cherryholmes, C., *Power and Criticism: Poststructural Investigations in Education.* New York: Teachers College Press, 1988.

19. Popkewitz, op. cit., note 6.

20. Bourdieu, op. cit., note 17, pp. 191 ff.

21. Burke, P., Heideman, R. and Heideman, C. (eds), *Programming for Staff Development: Fanning the Flames.* London, New York and Philadelphia: Falmer Press, 1990.

22. Joyce, B., *Changing School Culture Through Staff Development.* Alexandria, VA: Association for Supervision and Curriculum Development, 1990.

23. Griffin, G. and Rehage, K. (eds), *Staff Development. 82nd Yearbook of the National Society for the Study of Education.* Chicago: University of Chicago Press, 1983.

24. St Maurice, H., 'A philosophical basis for staff development: a rhetorical approach'. In Burke, P., Heideman, R. and Heideman, C. (eds), *Programming for Staff: Fanning the Flame.* London: Falmer Press, pp. 10–41, 1990.

25. Smyth, J. (ed.), *Educating Teachers: Changing the Nature of Pedagogical Knowledge.* London: Falmer Press, 1987.

26. Woods, op. cit., note 16.

27. Zeichner and Liston, op. cit., note 11.

28. Nietzsche, F., 'On truth and lie in an extra-moral sense'. In Kaufmann, W. (ed.), *The Portable Nietzsche*. 1910. Reprint. New York: Viking, pp. 42–6 (p. 45), 1953.

29. Cherryholmes, op. cit., note 18.

30. Rosaldo, R., *Culture and Truth: The Remaking of Social Analysis*. Boston: Beacon Press, 1989.

31. Popkewitz, op. cit., note 6.

32. Cherryholmes, op. cit., note 18, p. 116.

33. Glatthorn, A., *Differentiated Supervision*. Alexandria, VA: Association for Supervision and Curriculum Development, 1985.

34. Ibid., p. 44.

35. Blumberg, A., *Supervisors and Teachers: A Private Cold War*. 2nd ed. Berkeley, CA: McCutchan, 1980.

36. Foucault, op. cit., note 12.

37. Munro, P., 'Supervision: what's imposition got to do with it?' *Journal of Curriculum and Supervision*, **7** (1), pp. 78–89 (p. 87), 1991.

38. Garman, N., 'Theories embedded in the events of clinical supervision: a hermeneutic approach'. *Journal of Curriculum and Supervision*, **6** (3), pp. 201–13, 1990.

39. Grimmett, P. and Crehan, P. 'Conditions which facilitate and inhibit teacher reflection in clinical supervision: collegiality re-examined'. Paper presented at the annual meeting of the American Educational Research Association, Boston, 1990.

40. Garman, op. cit., note 38, pp. 212–13.

41. Smyth, op. cit., note 25.

42. Beatty, B., 'Child gardening: the teaching of young children in American schools'. In Warren, D. (ed.), *American Teachers: Histories of a Profession at Work*. New York: Macmillan, pp. 65–98, 1989.

43. Zeichner, K. and Gore, J., 'Teacher socialization'. In Houston, W., Haberman, M. and Sikula, J. (eds), *Handbook of Research on Teacher Education*. New York: Macmillan, pp. 329–48, 1990.

44. Retallick, J., 'Clinical supervision and the structure of communication'. Paper presented at the annual meeting of the American Educational Research Association, Boston, 1990.

45. St Maurice, H., 'Clinical supervision and power: regimes of instructional management'. In Popkewitz, T. (ed.) *Critical Studies of Teacher Education*. London: Falmer Press, pp. 242–64, 1987.

46. Flinders, D., 'Teacher isolation and the new reform'. *Journal of Curriculum and Supervision*, **4** (1), pp. 17–29, 1988.

47. Zeichner and Gore, op. cit., note 43.

48. Griffin, G., 'Learning from the "new" schools: lessons for teacher education'. In Darling-Hammond, L., Griffin, G. and Wise, A. (eds), *Excellence in Teacher Education*. Washington, DC: National Education Association, p. 31, 1992.

49. Darling-Hammond, op. cit., note 3.

50. Smyth, op. cit., note 25.

51. Hargreaves, A., 'Prepare to meet thy mood: teacher time and intensification'. Paper presented at the annual meeting of the American Educational Research Association, Boston, 1990.

52. Lockwood, A., 'Rethinking professionalization'. *Focus on Change*. Madison, WI: National Center for Effective Schools, 1992.

53. Sykes, G., 'Teaching and professionalism: a cautionary perspective'. In Weis, L., Altbach, P., Kelly, G., Petrie, H. and Slaughter, S. (eds), *Crisis in Teaching*. Albany, NY: State University of New York Press, pp. 253–74, 1989.

54. Zeichner, K., 'Contradictions and tensions in the professionalization of teaching and the democratization of schools'. *Teachers College Record*, **92** (3), pp. 363–79, 1991.

55. Keizer, G., *No Place But Here: A Teacher's Vocation in a Rural Community*. New York: Penguin, p. 161, 1988.

56. Kemmis, S. and McTaggart, R., *The Action Research Planner*, 3rd ed. Victoria: Deakin University Press, 1982.

57. Tripp, op. cit., note 14.

58. Griffin and Rehage, op. cit., note 23.

59. Tiezzi, L., 'Conditions of professional development which support teacher learning'. Paper presented at the annual meeting of the American Educational Research Association, San Francisco, 1992.

60. Zeichner, op. cit., note 54.

61. Lockwood, op. cit., note 52, p. 13.

62. Soder, R., 'The ethics of the rhetoric of teacher professionalization'. *Teaching and Teacher Education*, **7** (3), pp. 295–302 (p. 300), 1991.

63. Popkewitz, op. cit., note 6, p. 243.

64. The research projects cited in this chapter were conducted under the auspices of the University of Wisconsin-Steven Point and are reproduced with permission.

PART TWO

ENQUIRING INTO CRITICAL MODES OF TEACHER DEVELOPMENT

Chapter 6

It's More Than Style: Reflective Teachers as Ethical and Political Practitioners

David Hursh

John, like the other student teachers I studied in the elementary education programme, did not aim to duplicate what he had experienced in elementary school. He questioned whether schools realized their goal of contributing to economic equality; whether schools were, as he stated, Horace Mann's 'great equalizer'. He also hoped to develop a more integrated curriculum and better relationships with his students. He was also like the other students in that he found it difficult to justify how he taught other than that it was his own *style*. When asked to discuss the basis for his teaching decisions, he stated: 'I do what is going to blend best with my *style* of teaching and me as a person . . . what kind of teaching *style* I'm going to use.' The student teachers, as I will describe below, *were* questioning educational aims and classroom practices but were finding it difficult to provide justifications that were defensible beyond their own individual styles.

In attempting to understand this contradiction between student teachers who were inclined to be more critically reflective than previous research had led me to believe yet also less sure of how to justify their teaching, I have situated their teaching practices within the larger context of discourse and institutional structures. Consequently, I will contend that education occurs within a discourse that emphasizes individual choice within a society that is viewed as natural or given. This individualistic discourse is coupled with institutional structures that prevent teachers from affecting practices beyond their own classrooms.

Therefore, I will first show how the discourse of philosophical liberalism can undermine the potential for teachers to question and reform educational goals and practices. Then I will claim that, even within such a context, student teachers still have the potential for moving beyond 'style' as a rationale for their teaching if we explicitly connect their nascent critical and ethical interests to larger ethical and political questions.

HOW REFLECTIVE TEACHING IS UNDERMINED BY THE DOMINANT EDUCATIONAL DISCOURSE *OR* HOW STYLE OVERCOMES SUBSTANCE

The philosopher William Sullivan[1] asserts that the political (and I would add educational) discourse of the United States is characterized by philosophical liberalism. Philosophical liberalism, he explains, promotes as natural individual choice, competition and an instrumental approach to institutional and social relationships. Furthermore, not only does the discourse of philosophical liberalism frame educational and political discussion; the values embedded in the discourse also influence the way in which we organize social institutions. James Donald and Stuart Hall echo this view when they write that the liberal state aims to provide the social structure through which individuals can be autonomous, competitive and free to make choices and pursue their own affairs.[2] Political activity in the liberal state becomes identified with activity aimed at securing the 'conditions for freedom so that the private ends of the individual might be met in civil society'.[3] Liberal culture emphasizes individualism and instrumentalism within a society that is assumed to be natural and competitive. Consequently, it becomes difficult to raise questions such as what would be a fair or just society, and on what occasions does the common good outweigh individual good.

This same emphasis on individualism and instrumentalism (or 'what works') is reflected in educational discourse regarding education and teaching. Teachers and student teachers, as I will show, tend to view current educational practices as natural, given, and unproblematic rather than as outcomes of the struggles between competing interest groups and concepts of education. Differences in teaching practices are viewed as merely differences in teaching *style* rather than as differences that derive from ethical and critical considerations.

How teachers talk about teaching reflects the discourse of the larger society. As poststructuralists remind us, discourse, or 'the rules and patterns of communication in which language is used', does not mirror the world but 'creates distinctions, differences, and categories that define and create the world'.[4] In education, particular discourses become dominant and accepted, thereby limiting, *but not determining*, our perceptions of the world and what we think and say.

Furthermore, discourses do not exist separately from the world but support and are supported by social practices and structures. As Kemmis and McTaggart state:

> The institutionalization of educational activities in more or less
> well-formed and characteristic *practices* depends upon the
> availability of *discourses* which can justify and/or legitimate the
> practices as educationally worthwhile, and upon the existence of
> stable *organizational forms* which nurture, protect, coordinate,

and control the emergent forms of practice . . . [emphasis in original][5]

For example, 'tracking', or the practice of sorting students into homogeneous groups, became the accepted response to the increasingly heterogeneous school population in the US in the early part of this century. The change in school population resulted from increasing immigration from the countries of eastern and southern Europe and the more rigorous enforcement of compulsory attendance laws required by modern industrial society. Tracking became an accepted organizational response for a variety of reasons, including the rise in the psychological discourse of behaviourism and the political discourse of meritocracy. These ways of talking about psychology and politics legitimized the assumption that individuals were born with predetermined abilities which could be assessed through intelligence tests. It also legitimized the belief that an individual's social standing resulted from a combination of ability and effort. As a result, sorting, tracking, and consequently narrowing students' opportunities for changing social status, were perceived as scientific and fair. Discourse, as Smith and Zantiotis remind us, comprises 'a field in which there are preferred claims of truth about the depictions of the objects and events to which the field is directed and how they are actualized'.[6]

Cherryholmes makes a similar claim when he writes that the discourse which becomes dominant in a 'historical period and geographical location determines what counts as true, important, and relevant, what gets spoken, what remains unsaid'.[7] Because current discourses and practices exist within a wider social and historical context, we should expect teacher education to reflect the currently dominant political and philosophical discourse of the society in which it is located.

But because the dominant discourse reflects particular interests whose dominance is never complete and which are neither non-contradictory nor closed to alternative interpretations, there must be a continual struggle over what counts as true and relevant. How we think and talk about society and schools is never finalized but is contested as different interests struggle for power.[8] For example, tracking was only one of several responses to the increasing diversity of student populations; other responses were and are conceivable. Now, as in the past, some educators oppose tracking, arguing that standardized tests are culturally biased and that tracking unfairly diminishes the life chances of those in the middle and lower tracks. Other approaches to diversity are possible, including developing heterogeneous classrooms with less competitive and more cooperative learning, and accounting for differences between students in our teaching and assessment. Such approaches would require that we change not only our teaching practices but also our schools' structures and the ways in which we conceptualize and discuss general and specific educational goals.

Therefore, if we are to develop reflective teachers, we need to describe the ways in which teachers' beliefs and practices are sustained and constrained by the dominant discourse, practices and organizational forms in schools and teacher education.[9] But we also need to uncover the ways in which the dominant discourses, practices and structures are contested either because of contradictions within the dominant view of teaching or because of competing views. Therefore I will begin by describing how the discourse, practices and organizational structures of teacher education reflect philosophical liberalism and thus promote reliance on individual rather than political solutions, depoliticize teaching and schooling, and naturalize or reify current practices. I will then show how what might be termed a competing concern of 'caring for students' can potentially lead to questioning the dominant view. Finally, I will propose that an ethic of caring, combined with an emerging concern for justice in education, might be used to develop educational practices in schools which would

> bestow human dignity and mutual respect in students; attend to their needs; foster an ethic of obligation that includes concern, caring, and tolerance for others; and promote critical analysis of structures in schools and how economic structures influence their lives.[10]

HOW TO ENCOURAGE REFLECTIVE TEACHING

The Liberal Discourse of Pre-service Teachers

Examples of how discourse supports and is supported by particular practices and organizational structures will be drawn from a recent ethnographic study in which eight pre-service teachers were observed and interviewed throughout their senior year in an undergraduate elementary education programme. I observed the pre-service teachers in their fall social studies methods class, their practical experience and seminar and their spring student teaching and concurrent seminar. I also interviewed the eight pre-service teachers, their university instructors, and the cooperating teachers for their practical work and student teaching.[11]

The research revealed the ways in which teacher educators and pre-service teachers tended to separate education from ethical and political concerns; they described teaching as an individual process within a setting that is reified as natural and proper. Many pre-service teachers and teacher educators described learning to teach as a matter of defining and carrying out one's individual style. As a result, different teaching methods could not be evaluated as being better or worse but were simply seen as idiosyncratic differences. They believed that no one needed to defend decisions about what or how to teach on pedagogical or political grounds. As one student responded to the question of whether any particular approach to teaching could be justified over another: 'Teaching practices are up to the individual teacher . . . you can't determine [whether] some teaching practices are better than others.'

Teachers not only had individual styles but also assumed that they should act as individuals. This was exemplified by a supervisor of student teachers (a doctoral student) who argued that schools could be improved only through individual change in one's own classroom. This supervisor frequently asserted that change can occur only within oneself and that 'behaviour is person and place specific'. Students, she claimed, would respond properly if teachers took the right tack, one based on 'love and creativity'. This approach assumes that teachers can be totally responsible for their students' success or failure and ignores the influence of other students, their own families, and the curriculum as determined by textbook publishers and curriculum and test developers at the local, state and national levels. Such an approach also emphasizes teachers' interactions with individuals and ignores the possibility that teachers could influence schooling and society beyond their own classrooms.

Because the pre-service teachers neither felt that they needed, nor were ever asked, to justify their teaching decisions in terms other than personal style, they had difficulty in resolving conflicts between what they viewed as opposing styles or personal preferences. For example, in the social studies methods class a pre-service teacher raised the question of whether, as teachers, they should promote nonsexist and nonracist attitudes if the school in which they were teaching was situated in a racist or sexist community. Their justification for reducing racism or sexism was based only on their own personal beliefs rather than on an ethical or political requirement that schools should promote justice or economic fairness. Since they also desired to respect the beliefs of others, they faced an unsolvable dilemma. If they believed that 'no teaching practice is better than others' and 'teaching practices are up to the individual teacher', then there could be no mediation between conflicting beliefs because they could not be evaluated. Education is thus not only individualized but also severed from any ethical and political context. If education is removed from a larger context, pre-service teachers come to regard the existing nature of schools as inevitable. Maxine Greene observed that few student teachers question the nature of school:

> Their schools seem to resemble natural processes; what happens in them appears to have the sanction of natural law and can no more be questioned or resisted than the law of gravity.[12]

Of course, it is not only student teachers who reify the present. One student teacher supervisor made her students read Philip Jackson's 'The Daily Grind',[13] in which Jackson compares the hidden curriculum of schools to those of other 'total institutions' such as prisons and mental institutions. After listing some of Jackson's dreary conclusions, the supervisor stated: 'This [the way classrooms are] is necessary. This is the way it has to be, but we should be aware of it.'

Teachers tend not to perceive education as, in Herbert Kliebard's words, an ongoing 'struggle',[14] but to hold a depoliticized, liberal view of education, where less than desirable outcomes – such as racial segregation – are results of temporary oversights rather than of differences in power.[15–17] They do not perceive curriculum content, classroom processes and school organization as the outcome of past and current struggles over what is to be taught, to whom, why and how.

Such perceptions should not be surprising, given that professional discourses have de-emphasized the normative and political aspects of their work, and that liberal discourse has tended to partition society into public and private realms in which the private – including education – is portrayed as a rational rather than an ethical and political activity.[18] In analysing the evolution of professionalism Popkewitz maintains that in the early 1900s professionals began to present themselves as experts in how to achieve efficiently goals which were predetermined.[19]

Separating means from ends was particularly easy to achieve in education. Because teaching has been viewed as a women's profession and women have been treated as less capable than men, teacher education and educational structures have been organized to provide teachers with few opportunities to engage in discussions and activities beyond determining how to teach the curriculum efficiently. Consequently, teachers have had decreasing control over decisions affecting their own classrooms and education as a whole.

Given the tendency to view education as a rational rather than an ethical or a political enterprise, teacher education has typically emphasized means over ends. Even within teacher education programmes where the political and ethical goals of education are likely to be included, such as the ones examined in this research, the division of teacher education into foundations and methods courses undermines the possibility of connecting ends and means.

Consequently, the organizational structure of teacher education that separates politics from practice, the structure of teaching that relegates teachers to executing education as conceptualized by others, and professional and societal discourses which emphasize efficiency over ethics support instrumental practices which leave undisturbed the existing emphasis on efficiency, meritocracy and bureaucracy. As a result, pre-service teachers tend to see themselves as fitting within an educational system that allows a narrow range of differences based on individual personalities, rather than as embodying conflicting ethical and political views of society.

Contradictions and Openings

While pre-service teachers and teacher educators tend to emphasize individual solutions and style in their approach to teaching and to perceive current practices as natural and apolitical, this understanding of teaching is not non-contradictory. Consequently, if teachers' embryonic concerns are linked to questions of discourse, structures and practices, pre-service teachers may move beyond style to become ethical and critical practitioners. For example, the student teacher supervisor referred to above who focused on 'love and creativity' in teaching objected on several occasions to what she called the dominant 'industrial model' of teaching and lamented that schools were a 'watered down version of the assembly line'. These notions came from some of her doctoral class readings which described how schools were influenced by industry's emphasis on scientific efficiency during the early twentieth century. But because she stated and, at bottom, believed that politics were irrelevant to teaching, it remained, at least throughout this study, difficult for her to embrace explanations or reforms that went beyond individual relationships.

Karen, a student teacher, expressed some of the same feelings as the supervisor described above, but because she was supported in connecting her feelings to practice and then to questioning why particular practices were or were not supported in schools, she began to develop a political and ethical analysis of schools. Like many students who enter elementary education, Karen stated that she wanted to teach because she 'cared for children'. But 'caring for children' did not remain a vague perspective; she attempted to put caring into practice. Karen wanted students to have an experience different from her own:

> When I was in grade school, if we so much as breathed wrong, you got yelled at . . . . Schools should be a place [students] don't hate coming to. They should enjoy it. They should want to come.

Then, with the encouragement of her co-operating teacher, she pushed further her thinking and practice. She said she wanted to treat students with respect and make them respect her and one another. For her this meant that they should be 'real for each other'. She stated that she and the students should value each others' opinions, be able to make mistakes, and admit it when they don't know something and ask for help. These values formed the basis for her decision to implement a language arts programme that de-emphasized worksheets and basic readers in favour of trade books and writing activities that promoted the making of meaning. She also chose to develop students' self esteem through co-operative rather than competitive learning activities.

As she attempted to put into practice her ethical beliefs, she was frustrated by the district's required curriculum and standardized methods of evaluation. These frustrations led her, again with the help of her co-operating teacher, to ask questions about the history and politics of the organization of the school and curriculum. She realized that developing a teaching approach which allowed her to 'be real' for the students would be difficult without having the power to influence how students were taught and evaluated. Over the course of her elementary education programme, Karen's original 'love' for students developed into more complex ethical and political concerns which placed students within a larger context. Her original nascent ethical concerns influenced her initial ideas about practice; her efforts to implement more meaningful language activities led her to question the purpose and structure of schooling; these, in turn, led to deeper thinking regarding ethics, practices and educational organization. Karen, who began as the most politically naïve student in the group, may have changed the most during the year, largely because of the encouragement by her co-operating teacher to question and try new methods.

Paul, like Karen and John, entered the teacher education programme critical of the emphasis on conformity in elementary schools. In his student teaching he wished to encourage questioning and independent thinking among his pupils, but because he taught in a school using a highly complex and technical curriculum package in which teachers were required to meet predetermined curriculum goals, he had little control over those goals, the teaching materials, or the classroom schedule which required students to move between several different rooms. He could make choices in how he taught but had little influence over what, when or to whom. His efforts to develop independent thinking were hindered.

Karen, Paul, and John all came to teaching with goals vaguely critical of traditional education. They were not interested in merely mimicking their co-operating teachers or in reproducing what they had experienced as students. But as teachers who were just starting, and who based their educational rationales on the concept of personal style, when their style conflicted with what already existed they were likely to acquiesce. In the example given above, when they were trying to decide in their social studies seminar whether they should promote nonracist and nonsexist attitudes and practices if the school was situated in a racist or sexist community, they were all too willing to forgo the value of reducing racism and sexism because they also valued tolerating others' beliefs, even if those beliefs were racist and sexist. And, in practice, given the constraints that they faced when student teaching, especially if combined with lack of support from their university supervisor and co-operating teachers, they tended to accept the given structure. If, as one student teacher stated, 'you can't determine [whether] some teacher practices are better than others', then how can alternatives to current practice be justified?

This lack of grounded ethical and political rationales may be central in explaining how pre-service education is frequently 'washed out' by the first year of teaching. The emphasis on instrumental rationality and technical solutions overwhelms what nurturing and critical tendencies new teachers may have. Only in Karen's case did progress occur, not because she was initially more capable or critical but because she was supported in investigating the connections between her ethical rationale, teaching practices and the organization of the school.

Repoliticizing Pedagogy

If teachers are to become reflective, to raise questions of what is to be taught, to whom, how, and for what purpose, they must treat their classroom practices as problems and analyse how their classrooms are supported or contradicted by the discourses and organizational structures of schooling. Education is political in the sense that the organization of the school and the curriculum content and practices are outcomes of contested political goals. The discourses of individualism, style and technique ignore the political and contested nature of education.

Teachers' discourses need to be analysed continually to see which of the competing concepts of society and schooling they reflect and perpetuate. Does the discourse depoliticize pedagogy by emphasizing individual choice, style and supposedly objective techniques, or does it encompass the ethical and political goals of either Deweyian progressivism, or critical theory, or Pratte's 'civil republicanism'? Does the discourse describe education as an objective or as a contested outcome of past historical and political events? Teachers, teacher educators and pre-service teachers need to work to develop alternative discourses, practices and structures.

The example above of Karen's changes suggests that an alternative might grow out of the contradictions within liberal discourse itself. Because liberal discourse has contradictory features, one of which focuses on concern for the individual child, the notion of caring might be used to develop practices that respect students' knowledge and feelings.[20] Karen's concerns for students' feelings supported her in beginning to explore alternatives to basal readers, worksheets and standardized tests. As she attempted to act on her caring, she uncovered not only the administrative and bureaucratic constraints that teachers face but also the ways in which caring is undermined by political and philosophical assumptions regarding learning and ability. She began to realize that individual actions in one's own classroom are constrained by the discourse, practices and structure of the school. The value of caring about students, which is often a primary reason given for becoming a teacher, can lead, as Nel Noddings has argued,[21] to analysing and reforming classrooms and schools.

As well as using the emancipatory potential of liberal discourse to apply the normative principles of fairness and justice to education, discourse needs to be directly contested. For example, technical, political and epistemological issues are central to the current debate between those promoting cultural literacy as the knowledge of a core body of 'objective' facts prominent in the history of the United States and western civilization (for example, E. D. Hirsch's *Cultural Literacy*) and those promoting cultural literacy as also encompassing non-western and non-majority views and the acquisition of thinking skills rather than just the banking of facts.[22,23] Such debates reflect issues such as whose knowledge is to be included in the curriculum, and whether teachers should focus on students' accumulation of facts or on understanding of concepts. In social studies, for example, teachers who hope to teach history as more a series of problems than as facts would include more social history and focus on understanding a few events rather than memorizing names and dates. Such changes would also require revising assessment methods from testing for recall to testing for understanding, using portfolios, or some other form of authentic assessment. Such changes in content, methods and evaluation would also require changes beyond the individual classroom. The debate over cultural literacy quickly becomes a debate over all aspects of the aims and methods of schools.

Such considerations require teachers to become explicit about their own ethical and political assumptions about education, curriculum and teaching. Several innovative teacher education programmes aim to link theory to practice by requiring student teachers and their co-operating teachers to conduct research on their own teaching within a 'community of learners'.[24-26] Each of these programmes attempts to relate analyses of the political, historical and cultural contexts to classroom practices. Each encourages teachers to see themselves as creators of knowledge about teaching and learning and as initiators of classroom and school reforms. If such efforts are to be successful, if teachers are to become reflective and to create successful reforms, teachers and student teachers will need to view themselves as 'reflective, foundational, political actors requiring moral judgement and commitment'.[27] Such efforts will require the uncovering of the relationship between liberal discourse and our teaching practices and the developing of new ways of teaching about and organizing schooling.

NOTES AND REFERENCES

1. Sullivan, W., *Reconstructing Public Philosophy*. Berkeley, CA: University of California Press, 1986.

2. Donald, J. and Hall, S., 'Introduction' in Donald, J. and Hall, S. (eds.), *Politics and Ideology*. Milton Keynes and Philadelphia, PA: Open University Press, 1986.

3. Held, D., *Models of Democracy*. Stanford, CA: Stanford University Press, p. 54, 1987.

4. Popkewitz, T., *A Political Sociology of Educational Reform: Power/Knowledge in Teaching, Teacher Education and Research*. New York: Teachers College Press, p. 25, 1991.

5. Kemmis, S. and McTaggart, R. (eds), *The Action Research Planner* 3rd ed. Victoria: Deakin University Press, p. 42, 1988.

6. Smith, R. and Zantiotis, A., 'Practical teacher education and the avant-garde'. In Giroux, H. and McLaren, P. (eds), *Critical Pedagogy, the State and Cultural Struggle*. Albany, NY: State University of New York Press, p. 107, 1989.

7. Cherryholmes, C., *Power and Criticism: Poststructural Investigations in Education*. New York: Teachers College Press, p. 35, 1988.

8. Henriques, J., Hollway, W., Urwin, C., Venn, C. and Walkerdine, V., *Changing the Subject: Psychology, Social Regulation and Subjectivity*. New York: Methuen, pp. 123–24, 1984.

9. Cherryholmes, op. cit., note 7, p. 93.

10. Pratte, R., *The Civic Imperative: Examining the Need for Civic Education*. New York: Teachers College Press, p. 15, 1988.

11. Hursh, D., 'Becoming teachers: pre-service teachers' understanding of school and society'. PhD Dissertation. Madison, WI: University of Wisconsin–Madison, 1988.

12. Greene, M., 'Teachers as project: choice, perspective and the public space'. Paper presented to the Summer Institute of Teaching, Teachers College, Columbia University, p. 11, 1985.

13. Jackson, P., *Life in Classrooms*. New York: Holt, Rinehart and Winston, pp. 1–38, 1968.

14. Kliebard, H., *The Struggle for the American Curriculum: 1893–1958*. London: Routledge & Kegan Paul, 1986.

15. When students receive a history of education, it is often a version of history portrayed by Cremin, L., *Tradition of American Education*, New York: Basic Books, 1977; or Ravitch, D., *The Troubled Crusade: American Education 1945–1980*, New York: Basic Books, 1984. They receive a history in which

    Despite unfortunate lapses, including slavery and McCarthyism, the fundamental openness of society and the steady improvement in the lot of minorities remain indisputable hallmarks of America's past, evidence of the fundamental soundness of American institutions. Progress could be continued through a steady application of the democratic-liberal tradition in reform – in particular of representative rather than participatory democracy. See Gintis, H., 'Communication and politics: Marxism and "the problem of liberal democracy"'. *Socialist Review*, **10**, pp. 189–232, March–June 1980.

16. Katz, M. B., *Reconstructing American Education*. Cambridge, MA: Harvard University Press, 1987.

17. Goodlad, J., *Teachers for Our Nation's Schools*. San Francisco: Jossey-Bass, 1990.

18. Giroux, H., 'Schooling and politics of ethics: beyond liberal and conservative discourses'. *Journal of Education*, **169** (2), pp. 9–23, 1987.

19. Popkewitz, T., 'Ideology and social formation in teacher education'. In Popkewitz, T. (ed.), *Critical Studies in Teacher Education*. Philadelphia: Falmer Press, 1987.

20. Gintis argues that liberal discourse is both restrictive in the way that it depoliticizes society and 'potentially revolutionary' if it can be used to 'expand that range over which person rights are to hold sway'. See Gintis, op. cit., note 14.

21. Noddings, N., *Caring: A Feminine Approach to Ethics and Moral Education*. Berkeley, CA: University of California, 1984.

22. Aronowitz, S. and Giroux, H., 'Schooling, culture and literacy in the age of broken dreams: a review of Hirsch and Bloom'. *Harvard Educational Review*, **58** (2), pp. 172–94, 1988.

23. Simonson, R. and Walker, S., *The Graywolf Annual Five: Multi-cultural Literacy*. St Paul, MN: Graywolf, 1988.

24. Cochran-Smith, M., 'Of questions, not answers: the discourse of student teachers and their school and university mentors'. Paper presented at the annual American Education Research Association Meeting, San Francisco, 1989.

25. Noffke, S. and Brennan, M., 'Action research and reflective student teaching at U.W.-Madison: issues and examples'. Paper presented at the Annual Meeting of the Association of Teacher Educators, San Diego, 1988.

26. Bullough, R. and Gitlin, A., 'Toward educative communities: teacher education and the quest for the reflective practitioner'. Paper presented at the annual meeting of the Bergamo Conference, Dayton, OH, 1989.

27. Beyer, L., *Knowing and Acting: Inquiry, Ideology and Teacher Education*. Philadelphia: Falmer Press, p. 308, 1988.

Chapter 7

Developing Voice Through Teacher Research: Implications for Educational Policy*

Peter P. Grimmett

INTRODUCTION

Curriculum is often interpreted as meaning a finely specified, sequentially prescribed body of topics and learning outcomes that all students must address. An important shift expressed in a recent innovation in British Columbia was a move away from viewing curriculum as 'ground to be covered', or something to be 'delivered', to a broader concept of curriculum that begins with a focus on the learner. The former view neglected the extent to which learning experiences are affected by students' needs, interests and choices. It also ignored the manner in which curriculum is shaped by teachers' expertise and judgements. The change could therefore be characterized by the expectation that teachers will become curriculum builders rather than curriculum deliverers. This call for the *restructuring* of schools from within as student-centred places of learning is based on constructivist[1-3] and social constructivist[4-9] views of learning and is framed around 'the need to redefine learning, to rethink the purposes of learning and the consequences for learners of different conceptualizations of learning, and to reconsider elements essential to educational reform'.[10]

Between 1990 and 1993 the British Columbia Ministry of Education decided to support teachers who came together to inquire in a focused way into issues of curriculum, teaching and student learning. These teacher research groups addressed questions that were central to the implementation of an innovative programme. This chapter will briefly describe how teachers developed their voice through teacher research and will attempt to derive important implications for educational policy.

* This chapter is based, in part, on the research project 'Teacher Development through Administrative or Collegial Processes of Instructional Consultation' (Peter P. Grimmett, Principal Investigator), funded by the Social Sciences and Humanities Research Council of Canada (Grants 410-85-0339, 410-86-2014 and 410-88-0747). It is gratefully acknowledged that this work could not have been carried out without this funding. The opinions expressed in this chapter do not necessarily reflect the policy, position or endorsement of SSHRCC.

113

The Changing Context of Education Reform

The emphasis on education reform has coincided with the ending of what Harvey has called the conditions of modernity.[11] The world in which we live has entered into a post-Enlightenment era.[12] It is a rapidly changing world characterized by two broad competing trends in society: a neo-conservative reaction and the gaining of voice by previously marginalized individuals and groups. The neo-conservative reaction welcomes the information age with the compression of time and space and the globalization of world economies that it has brought. The gaining of voice by previously marginalized groups celebrates 'grass-roots' uprisings of ordinary people against so-called experts and brings attention to the rights and interests of those who are disenfranchized in policy making and the allocation of resources.

Teachers' work context is constantly in a state of flux and frequently subject to the competing emphases of policy that, in the final analysis, may be on a collision course. Within this changing and conflictual educational context, teachers search for conditions in which to develop as professional educators. Pursuing this search, however, is problematic; it frequently involves them in a struggle. Teachers struggle because the conditions of the practical settings in which they do their work frequently prevent teachers' professionalism from obtaining its rightful recognition; these conditions also present teachers with great difficulties. These difficulties may take the form of obstacles or constraints hindering development, of temptations for teachers to do the contractual minimum,[13] or of having to contend with others who are opposed to educational changes, firmly grounded in the enhancement of student learning (as distinct from the work comfort of school practitioners), such as the ones suggested by Marshall.[14] Dealing with these difficulties requires great effort and exertion. Teachers take pains to stretch themselves dutifully to address the vexing questions and perplexing dilemmas inherent in the daily messiness of practice. In doing so, they sometimes join the fight (with themselves, with colleagues, with supervisors and curriculum policy, and with parents and students) over what is pedagogically appropriate for a particular set of students with specific learning needs in a particular set of classroom conditions and circumstances. Teachers are thus engaged in a struggle for authenticity in which they attempt to discover both their true selves as responsible professionals and the new knowledge that enables them to see possibilities in teaching that will lead to a redefinition of classroom realities and roles and an enhancement of student learning.[15] Teacher research represents a struggle for authenticity by teachers (as a previously marginalized group) who are gaining voice.

TEACHER RESEARCH

What is Teacher Research?

Teacher research – the 'systematic, intentional inquiry by teachers' into their craft – has received considerable attention of late in the works of many writers.[16–40] There are publications such as *Hands On* (the Foxfire Fund Inc., Rabun, GA), *Outlook* (the Mountain View Publishing Company, Boulder, CO), *Democratic Education* (the Institute for Democratic Education at Ohio University), and *Rethinking Schools, Working Teacher* and *Our Schools Ourselves*, published respectively by groups of teachers in Milwaukee, Vancouver (Canada) and Toronto. All these serve as outlets for teachers' accounts of their practice. In addition there have been four important reviews of teacher research.[41–44]

Teacher Research Groups in British Columbia

Since early 1991, there have been 11 Ministry-sponsored teacher research groups in operation in the province of British Columbia.[45] This was a pilot project involving approximately 120 teachers in 12 school districts. Forty seven reports were received by the Ministry of Education as part of the ongoing review of the new Primary Program.[46]

The purpose of this chapter is to examine the policy implications of the voices articulated by these teacher research groups. A detailed analysis of the teacher research group reports[47] has prompted the following themes to emerge:

- Teachers articulated how the teacher research process itself had benefited their attempted implementation of the new programme.
- Teacher research provided opportunities for engaging in professional discourse, for experiencing the phenomenon of 'teachers as learners', and for growing as persons and developing their practical grasp of the new programme.

They also addressed five specific aspects of the programme's implementation:

1. Teacher researchers were concerned with establishing a learner focus by promoting a community in which students experienced a sense of belonging.
2. They focused on making connections with students' prior knowledge and real world experiences.
3. They inquired into promoting student ownership of the learning process through structures encouraging choices.
4. They preoccupied themselves with the actual learning outcomes experienced by students in the new programme.
5. This naturally led to a concern with assessment and reporting and with ways of involving parents more vitally in the education of their children.

Teachers' voices expressed in the reports did not constitute single, fixed representations of classroom realities; rather, they articulated multiple and sometimes contradictory possibilities. In the final analysis, the teacher research process gave teachers permission to create spaces in which the experiences of their daily lives as classroom practitioners could be detailed in all their complexity. This complexity defies any attempt to unify or bring the stamp of a 'party line' to the descriptions. Accordingly, the inquiry undertaken by teachers in their respective focus groups constructed diverse and critical conclusions and recommendations about the programme's implementation. The purpose of their inquiry was to create a space where they could act and speak on their own behalf. It represented an attempt to think and investigate through a struggle of learning from practice.[48] Change, then, did not come easily. Indeed, for many teachers the implementation of the new programme was an exacting and challenging task but one in which their voices became heard and their 'exploratory impulsion – an *acute discomfort* at incomprehension . . . the rage to know'[49] (emphasis in original) was genuinely satisfied.

POLICY IMPLICATIONS OF TEACHER RESEARCH*

The utilization of teacher research groups to foster the implementation of the new programme suggests three broad implications for educational policy: teacher research enabled participants to bring the educative agenda to the fore; it provided the necessary support, stability and challenge of a community of inquirers during programme implementation; and it demonstrated important nuances between learner-focused and learner-directed teaching.

Honouring the Educative Agenda of Schools

Fenstermacher[50] distinguishes between the educative and systemic agendas of schooling.[51] The educative agenda revolves around the pursuit of moral, intellectual, and aesthetic virtues, whereas the systemic agenda is set up to ensure that the goods and services of education are distributed equitably without any possible blame being attributable to the authorities when persons or groups do not get what they need or want.[52] Given these two contrasting and competing agendas, Fenstermacher argues that educational policy is typically made to negotiate conflicts between the educative and systemic aspects of schooling. That is because policy-making essentially becomes the adjudication of relatively scarce goods and services for the purpose of optimizing (as distinct from maximizing) the impact of the educational benefits. The consequence of this is that policy tends to be directed at the systemic rather than the educative aspects of

---

* This section is taken, with slight revisions, from Grimmett, P. P., 'Teacher research and British Columbia's curricular instructional experiment: implications for educational policy'. *Journal of Education Policy*, 8 (3), pp. 219–39, 1993. Permission by the *Journal of Education Policy* to reprint this section of the article is gratefully acknowledged.

schooling. Thus policy, Fenstermacher maintains, revolves strongly around the ways in which schools are managed, because the sources of funding underwriting the educational goods and services are far removed from classroom action. This remoteness from classroom action gives policy-makers a need for data, and such a need is frequently interpreted as a requirement for testing. In this way policy-makers have essentially left the educative agenda up to teachers while constraining them with systemic responsibilities and requirements. These constraints have increased of late, causing Fenstermacher to claim that the educative agenda is now under attack from the corporate world in bed with a twentieth-century form of government mercantilism.

The support of teacher research in the province of British Columbia represents a counter-force going against this trend. Redressing the balance in favour of the educative agenda provides opportunities for students to be more adequately prepared for the demands of life in the twenty-first century that cannot be imagined and have yet to materialize. I would argue that the advent of teacher research heralds an opportunity for the balance in policy-making to be shifted back towards the educative agenda of schooling.

Engaging in teacher research around an innovation involves individuals and groups in grappling with important issues of personal beliefs and values implied by the nature of the change. There is considerable danger that, if and when the structure of a supportively challenging teacher research group is not available, such discussions could devolve into ideologically-based dogmatic disputes, thereby destroying meaningful dialogue. Understanding this fact is the first policy implication to be learned from teacher research. The implication of this is that *there must be explicit opportunities (in the form of structures and processes) for rigorous collegial discourse in the initiating and sustaining of an innovation*. Such explicit planning would provide for *more, rather than less, structures like teacher research groups in the implementation of a new programme*.

The second implication is that *any large, important innovation is likely to be* *so complex as to be beyond direct hierarchical control*.[53] Patterson, Purkey and Parker[54] discuss the complex interplay of factors impinging on school systems and conclude that a nonrational model of educational systems must replace the traditional model of a rational system. This conceptualization mirrors the structure and processes of a teacher research group in many ways. First, it acknowledges multiple and competing goals, implying that decisions are affected by many unpredictable forces both within and outside the educational system. Secondly, it recognizes the need for power sharing and collaborative decision-making. Thirdly, it makes it clear that there are many ways to improve learning as distinct from a single, correct way to teach. Not only is the change process complex in its intellectual, emotional, social, political and logistical dimensions, it is also embedded within an even more complex larger system, rather like the nature of an eddy within a surging river.

117

Such an implementation process, I would argue, dovetails with the structure and organization of teacher research groups. Teacher research enables participants to explore the complexities that Patterson *et al.* write about.[55] It provides an arena in which the intellectual, emotional, social, political and logistical dimensions of the innovation can be collaboratively understood and reframed so as to benefit the learning of students in classrooms.

However, teacher research, as it was experienced in the implementation of the Primary Program, provoked questions more than it provided teachers with answers. Given the complexity of the implementation process and the opportunity that teacher research affords for bringing the educative agenda of schools to the fore, there would appear to be a need for a policy stating that *constructively posing questions about teaching and learning* (what teacher research permits teachers to do) *represents the essence of being a professional educator and should not be construed as an organizationally disruptive act.*

Providing Support, Stability and Challenge in a Community of Inquirers

As a sports psychologist with the American Olympic luge team and as a medical practitioner dealing with the rehabilitation of chronically ill patients, Armstrong maintains that there are four factors that élite athletes and the chronically ill have in common.[56] Both groups need to be challenged; both are very prone to depression; both groups' self-esteem is frequently at risk; and, to cope with these pressures, both groups need mental skills. In other words, people with above average aspirations who are extremely challenged in situations that present a high risk to their self-esteem become very susceptible to depression. Armstrong contends that the only way people of this ilk can cope with the pressures they face is through the attainment of mental skills that enable them to deal with the many psychological agendas facing them in the daily execution of their performance.

Teachers face many of the dilemmas encountered by élite athletes and chronically ill patients. They frequently hold high aspirations for their own classroom performance; their own person is integrally part of their practice, placing their self-esteem constantly at risk; and their need for skills to help them cope with inordinate pressures created by the changing societal context is fairly evident. Like élite athletes, teachers clearly need mental skills that enable them to engage in reframing the everyday dilemmas they face in teaching and in the implementation of a new programme. However, they also need interpersonal support, stability and intellectual challenge in a community of inquirers. Teacher research provided a structure that permitted such an enabling environment to flourish. What one group focused on for students produced an important insight into an organizational phenomenon applicable to people of all ages:

> The [teacher research] process enabled teachers to explore
> children's sense of 'belonging'. The children seemed to connect *not
> belonging* to a preoccupation with problems which need to be

solved or with worry and anxiety. Consequently, they could not focus but only think of not being included or being compared. Children were clear that when one *belongs*, one gets more work done and can ask for help to facilitate greater learning. 'Belonging is to learning as soil is to a seed.' (7)[57]

The policy implication here is that this maxim, 'Belonging is to learning as soil is to a seed', addresses a very important human need in an implementation process. *Teachers need a protective culture or soil in which the seeds of ideas and principles embedded in the new programme are allowed to grow.* They need to belong to such a culture to avoid becoming consumed with anxiety by the pressures accompanying a complex, changing societal mosaic. The experiences of the teachers documented in the 47 reports suggest that, because they belonged to supportive but challenging communities of teacher inquirers, they were able to concentrate on the important focus of understanding and facilitating student learning.

For teachers not currently members of a teacher research group, however, it may be the implementation process itself (as distinct from the substance of the innovation) which generates tension and anxiety.[58] Implementing a new programme based on different principles inevitably leads teachers to raise critical questions about how students learn. It also provokes them to examine the principles on which their current practice is based. For many, such a process is somewhat unnerving because it can be expected to reveal the ambiguities and blemishes that have always existed but which may have languished unexamined for long periods of 'normal practice'. Kuhn's analysis of the process of change in scientific thinking suggests that fundamental change, which he refers to as a paradigm shift, stands in juxtaposition to long intervening periods of 'normal science'.[59] During these periods scientists operate on shared assumptions that often lead them to miss or even ignore data which contravene conventional wisdom. Consequently, they unwittingly concentrate on reinforcing the status quo. Change, therefore, may create stress not only through the introduction of new ideas but also through the surfacing of long-standing conundrums and uncertainties previously left unconsidered during a period of stability. Expressing, debating, clarifying and reaffirming or altering basic assumptions and beliefs may be both necessary and constructive but it is undeniably challenging and ultimately exhausting and, for teachers, can result in much stress and a deep-rooted longing for a return to the comfort of the status quo. Such behaviour may be, as Beairsto perceptively points out, a response as much to the process of change as to its particular substance.[60] Without disputing the call for more reflective practice, he notes that all people and all systems require the respite of conventional behaviour and 'normal' practice from time to time. It is not healthy for teachers to be entirely uncritical or complacent, but it is also impossible to imagine continuous, public, systemic critique as being sustainable for teachers without some structure that permits a reasonable degree of comfort and affirmation while encouraging a tolerance for ambiguity. Such a structure emerged in the teacher research groups that came together to study problems of practice framed around the implementation of the Primary Program.

> By sharing observations, I am forced to reflect on my methods. This reflective process is qualitatively different from my personal reflections, as others' insights force my ideas to move forward to a place I could not have reached by myself. As a result, I have made new connections and am empowered to ask a further question . . . . Teachers are always asking the question 'What more can I do?'. The group is where I can be critical of my own practice in a mutually supportive place.[61]

> We have learned that teacher research groups can create a supportive climate where teachers transform themselves as teachers and learners. We have learned that within an on-going process of reflection, teachers consciously articulate their implicit and explicit theories and knowledge about teaching. We have learned that teacher research groups provide a powerful collaborative context for teachers to think and talk together.[62]

The policy implication here is that *there is a need to create structures that provide teachers with support, stability and affirmation while simultaneously encouraging intellectual challenge and a tolerance for ambiguity. These structures would be designed to enable teachers to engage professionally in continuous, public and systemic examination and critique of substantive suggestions for change in the educational programmes of schools.* The teacher research focus groups currently in operation around the province provide a useful prototype of how such structures could be designed and of what is possible when they are in place.

Discriminating between Learner-Focused and Learner-Directed Teaching

One of the important pointers coming out of the teacher research reports[63] is the ease and regularity with which the participating teachers discriminated between learner-directed (students become the sole determinants of learning) and learner-focused (teachers and students collaboratively construct learning according to the students' needs) practice. While it was very much student-centred, learner-focused teaching was not seen as precluding certain actions on the part of teachers. Teachers were still regarded as the persons responsible for structuring the learning environment in the classroom:

> I am much more aware of the prime role the teacher has in providing a multiplicity of ways of 'drawing out' the linking and connecting abilities in children. (35)[63]

> [Teachers] need to complement student choice opportunities with
> explicit teaching of activity-language (to facilitate greater
> understanding and involvement) and more student reflection and
> self-assessment time. (13)

Teachers also viewed themselves as having powerful roles to play both in catering to individual differences and in modelling what is valued in classroom interaction:

> They [the students] affirm our beliefs about working
> collaboratively as a powerful method, but note that we must
> recognize and allow for individual differences, limitations, and
> preferences. They remind teachers of our powerful roles, in
> modelling for our students, and in helping to determine what is
> valued in the classroom. (12)

The participating teachers were very clear on what had to be done when students did not know a concept, language or set of skills that was fundamental to a child's ability to enter into a learning activity:

> We have some concerns for the social isolate (the child who is
> rarely chosen as a partner). While teachers work hard to ensure
> their inclusion, we feel that certain social skills need to be taught
> directly. (30)
> Success of spelling program [can be] put down to teachers being
> responsive to students' learning. Teacher research was the vehicle
> for teachers' responsiveness. Responsivenesss involved more than
> just listening to what the students think they need. It also
> involved teacher deduction of students' learning needs from
> analysis of their writing. (8)
> [There is a] need for the explicit teaching of concepts, e.g.,
> belonging, central to the student learning process where
> misunderstanding would take away from learning or seriously
> reinforce error. (9)

The point here is that without the explicit teaching of needed concepts and skills, students would probably not have come to some of the understandings through insight which they achieved. Providing students with substance as well as process was seen not only to be in keeping with learner-focused teaching but also to be central to it. One group explained how it balanced explicit teaching with the elicitation of student thinking:

> We were impressed by the variety of thinking processes the
> children employed when helping one another. While thinking
> strategies are directly taught in the classroom, we feel that the
> risk-free environment is important in allowing the children to
> apply these strategies naturally and frequently. The social aspect

> of the environment allows children to hear the language of others,
> to communicate their ideas and to clarify their own thinking. This
> environment permits and nurtures the individual's potential for
> growth. (30)

Essentially they taught the thinking strategies directly but concentrated on setting up a risk-free environment for students to express themselves, to listen to one another, and to clarify their thinking through discussion. Another group concluded that separating content and process in learner-focused teaching was artificial and erroneous:

> [There is a need to] ensure a balance between content and process;
> [between and among] knowledge, skills and attitudes; [between]
> mechanics and thoughtfulness. (36)

This lack of an artificial distinction between process and content and the resolute, explicit teaching of skills and concepts when students showed a need for them did not make these teachers any less student-centred in their classroom approach. On the contrary, they articulated a rigour that has sometimes been lacking in the public debate about progressive education in general and the *Year 2000* in particular.[64] They were also convinced of a relationship between teacher structuring of academic content and the emotional development of students:

> Development of academic skills has a positive impact on student
> self-esteem. (10)
> Initial learning of new concepts and skills involves a degree of
> imitation. It is difficult for learners of any age to explore in a
> vacuum. (11)

This latter point also addresses some of the teacher frustration about the implementation of a new programme. Teachers cannot experiment with new principles of learning when they have little experience of those principles in action on which to draw. When this lack of experience is not complemented by concrete examples of the principles, based on the rich action of other teachers who understand progressive ideas, many traditionally-minded teachers feel overwhelmed and confused. An important point here is that, just as the experienced teachers participating in the teacher research groups realized the students' need for direction and substance, so those responsible for overseeing the programme's implementation province-wide should also provide teachers with concrete examples that they can, at least initially, imitate as they attempt to bring about a fundamental change in their practice. These should not be viewed as practices to be transferred to teachers' classroom situations; rather, they should be viewed as beginning metaphors for reframing one's own practice. The former view is potentially limiting; the latter is transforming.

There are three policy implications here. First, it needs to be explicitly stated that *learner-focused teaching is quite different and distinct from learner-directed practice.* While learner-focused teaching allows for a good deal of student input into and, in some instances, direction of the learning process, it never abrogates the teacher's responsibility to structure the learning environment and (where necessary) to teach directly the concepts and skills that some students may lack or happen to misunderstand. At no point can learner-focused teaching be used as a justification for either the absence of teacher diagnosis and structuring or the reinforcement of student error. Lest the reader be tempted to think that this is too similar to traditional ways of teaching, a brief comparison of the conservative and progressive approaches to teaching will clarify the difference.

Learner-focused teaching departs from the conservative tradition which essentially views the educational process as a means of cultural transmission.[65] The teachers' role in the conservative tradition is either to initiate students into predetermined and distinct forms of public knowledge[66] or to re-establish a common cultural heritage that is shared by all Americans.[67] The central aim of learner-focused teaching is more consistent with the *progressive* tradition 'for students to become competent inquirers, capable of reflecting on and critically examining their everyday world and involved in a continual reconstruction of their experience'.[68] Unlike the conservative tradition with its emphasis on teacher-centred didacticism, the progressive tradition assumes that a process of inquiry revolving around students' interests gives rise to mastery of subject matter.

Learner-focused teaching is therefore very different from conservative, teacher-centred didacticism. There is an emphasis on making connections for and with students, on giving students choices, and on appreciating learning from the perspective of the learner. However, although these emphases often bring about a greater preoccupation with innovative processes and strategies, this preoccupation is never at the expense of substantive content. The second implication, then, is that *learner-focused teaching does not make an artificial distinction between content and process; there cannot be process without substantive content.*

The third policy implication has to do with the implementation of progressive educational programmes. Teachers are learners too. The principles of learning therefore apply to them as much as they do to students. Like students, not all teachers learn in the same way or at the same rate. They also construct different meanings out of the programme, depending on their prior experience and their current assumptions. Most learners who are confronted by something radically new enter a state of dissonance. Learners in a state of dissonance need concrete examples that they can imitate in their struggle to grasp a new concept, skill or practice. The policy implication here is that the Ministry and other leaders of the curricular-instructional experiment need to *provide concrete examples based on the action of experienced learner-focused teachers which less experienced and less confident teachers can initially imitate.* Without these guiding examples, many teachers who do not act on progressive or radical educational assumptions essentially flounder in a sea of confusion. Moreover, when teachers grapple with examples of learner-focused practice, they come to understand the principles of learning embedded in a new programme.

CONCLUSION

Teacher research focus groups provide the kind of cultural conditions in which individuals and groups can become familiar with and experiment around the goals and principles of the proposed change.[69,70] Teachers are not asked to demonstrate fidelity to a blueprint for programme implementation but rather are invited to examine their practice in the light of the evidence and the fundamental values supporting a change towards building a learner-focused curriculum. These cultural conditions provide not only for collegiality and experimentation but also, and most importantly, for doubt, questioning and dissent. Within the confines of a teacher research group such actions are not interpreted as recalcitrance or equivocation but are seen as the responsible exploration of concerned educators. Without this enabling environment, teachers are not free to honour the educative agenda of schools; nor are they empowered to grasp how the principles of learner-focused teaching can be enacted in their own classroom situations.

NB

Because it introduces dissonance and reveals existing flaws and inconsistencies, the implementation process generates much stress. This stress can very quickly become distress if participants in a change process lack a supportive but challenging community of inquirers in which together they construct a temporary sense of practical certainty. Teacher research groups provide this needed sense of constancy in the midst of change when teachers affirm one another through a celebration of experimental practice. A change initiative cannot be expected to proceed rationally and any attempt to control the course of events is doomed to failure. However, this does not mean that change is impossible, only that it must be approached with realism and humility. Teacher research groups provide for this realism and humility. They give teachers opportunities to clarify the intents and principles of the change. This, in turn, enables them to voice fine but critical distinctions about implementation, like the one between learner-focused and learner-directed practice.

Ultimately, the teacher research process provides support for an innovation without prescribing what the specific changes in classroom practice must be or how they are to come about. It serves as an innovative redirection of the traditional approaches to teacher development. Teacher research recognizes and encourages teachers as agents of knowing and constructors of knowledge. It is inquiry-based, frequently collaborative, and invariably generative of teachers' craft knowledge.[71] In the final analysis, it ensures that teachers' voices are heard so that any changes serve the educative and not the political-systemic agendas of schools.

NOTES AND REFERENCES

1. Bruner, J., *Actual Minds, Possible Worlds*. Cambridge, MA: Harvard University Press, 1986.

2. Newman, D., Griffith, P. and Cole, M., *The Construction Zone: Working for Cognitive Change in Schools*. Cambridge: Cambridge University Press, 1989.

3. Vygotsky, L., *Mind in Society: The Development of Higher Psychological Processes*. Cambridge, MA: Harvard University Press, 1978.

4. Chandler, S., 'Learning for what purpose? Questions when viewing classroom learning from a sociocultural curriculum perspective'. In Marshall, H. H., (ed.), *Redefining Student Learning: Roots of Educational Change*. Norwood, NJ: Ablex, pp. 33–58, 1992.

5. Collins, E. and Green, J. L., 'Learning in classroom settings: making or breaking a culture'. In Marshall, H. H., (ed.), *Redefining Student Learning: Roots of Educational Change*. Norwood, NJ: Ablex, pp. 59–85, 1992.

6. Cook-Gumperz, J. (ed.), *The Social Construction of Literacy*. Cambridge: Cambridge University Press, 1986.

7. Edwards, A. D. and Mercer, N., *Common Knowledge*. London: Methuen, 1987.

8. Santa Barbara Classroom Discourse Group, 'Constructing literacy in classrooms: literate action as social accomplishment'. In Marshall, H. H. (ed.), *Redefining Student Learning: Roots of Educational Change*. Norwood, NJ: Ablex, pp. 119–50, 1992.

9. Weade, G., 'Locating learning in the times and spaces of teaching'. In Marshall, H. H. (ed.), *Redefining Student Learning: Roots of Educational Change*. Norwood, NJ: Ablex, pp. 87–118, 1992.

10. Marshall, H. H., 'Seeing, redefining and support student learning'. In Marshall, H. H. (ed.), *Redefining Student Learning: Roots of Educational Change*. Norwood, NJ: Ablex, pp. 1–32 (p. 3), 1992.

11. Harvey, D., *The Condition of Postmodernity*. Oxford: Polity Press, 1989.

12. Polkinghorne, D., *Narrative Knowing and the Human Sciences*. Albany: State University of New York Press, 1988.

13. March, J.G., 'How we talk and how we act: administrative theory and administrative life' (In Sergiovanni, T. J. and Corbally, J. E. (eds), *Leadership and Organizational Culture*. Urbana, IL: University of Illinois Press, pp. 23–32 (pp. 27–8), 1984.) elaborates on how calculated involvement around a narrowed focus can lead to this kind of performance:

    > Long before reaching the top, an intelligent manager learns that some of the more effective ways of improving measured performance have little to do with improving product, service or technology. A system of rewards linked to precise measures is not an incentive to perform well; it is an incentive to obtain a good score.

14. Marshall, op. cit., note 10.

15. Grimmett, P. P. and Neufeld, J., 'Teacher development in a changing educational context'. In Grimmett, P. P. and Neufeld, J. (eds), *Teacher Development and the*

Struggle for Authenticity: Professional Growth and Restructuring in the Changing Context. New York: Teachers College Press, pp. 1–12, 1994.

16. Lytle, S. L. and Cochran-Smith, M., 'Learning from teacher research: a working typology'. *Teachers College Record*, **92** (1), pp. 83–103 (p. 85), 1990.

17. Bissex, G. and Bullock, R., *Seeing for Ourselves: Case Study Research by Teachers of Writing.* Portsmouth, NH: Heinemann, 1987.

18. Cole, A., 'Researcher and teacher: partners in theory building'. *Journal of Education for Teaching*, **15** (3), pp. 225–37, 1989.

19. Elbaz, F., 'Research on teachers' knowledge: the evolution of a discourse'. *Journal of Curriculum Studies*, **23** (1), pp. 1–19, 1991.

20. Elliott, J., 'Teachers as researchers: implications for supervision and for teacher education'. *Teaching and Teacher Education*, **6** (1), pp. 1–26, 1990.

21. Ellwood, C., 'Can we really look through our students' eyes? An urban teacher's perspective.' Paper presented at the annual meeting of the American Educational Research Association, Chicago, IL, 1991.

22. Gomez, M. L., 'Reflections on research for teaching: collaborative inquiry with a novice teacher'. *Journal of Education for Teaching*, **16** (1), pp. 45–56, 1990.

23. Gore, J. and Zeichner, K., 'Action research and reflective teaching in pre-service teacher education'. Paper presented at the annual meeting of the American Educational Research Association, Boston, MA, 1990.

24. Goswami, D. and Stillman, P., *Reclaiming the Classroom: Teacher Research as an Agent for Change.* Upper Montclair, NJ: Boynton/Cook, 1987.

25. Hustler, D., Cassidy, T. and Cuff, T. (eds), *Action Research in Classrooms and Schools.* London: Allen & Unwin, 1986.

26. Lampert, M. 'How do teachers manage to teach? Perspectives on problems in practice'. *Harvard Educational Review*, **55** (2), pp. 178–94, 1985.

27. McNiff, J., *Action Research: Principles and Practice.* London: Macmillan Education, 1988.

28. Miller, J., *Creating Spaces and Finding Voices: Teachers Collaborating for Empowerment.* Albany, NY: State University of New York Press, 1990.

29. Mohr, M. and MacLean, M., *Working Together: A Guide for Teacher-researchers.* Urbana, IL: National Council of Teachers of English, 1987.

30. Myers, M., 'Institutionalizing inquiry'. *National Writing Project Quarterly* **9** (3), 1987.

31. Newman, J. M., *Finding Our Own Way.* Portsmouth, NH: Heinenann, 1989.

32. Oja, S. N. and Smulyan, L., *Collaborative Action Research: A Developmental Approach*. London: Falmer Press, 1989.

33. Rorschach, E. and Whitney, R., 'Relearning to teach: peer observation as a means of professional development for teachers'. *English Education*, **18** (3), pp. 159–72, 1986.

34. Ross, D., 'Action research for pre-service teachers: a description of why and how'. *Peabody Journal of Education*, **64** (3), pp. 131–50, 1987.

35. Rudduck, J., 'Teacher research and research-based teacher education'. *Journal of Education for Teaching*, **11** (3), pp. 281–9, 1985.

36. Rudduck, J. and Hopkins, D., *Research as a Basis for Teaching: Readings from the Work of Lawrence Stenhouse*. London: Heinemann, 1985.

37. Strieb, L., *A (Philadelphia) Teacher's Journal*. Grand Forks, ND: Center for Teaching and Learning, University of North Dakota, 1985.

38. Tabachnick, B. R. and Zeichner, K. M., *Issues and Practices in Inquiry-oriented Teacher Education*. London: Falmer Press, 1991.

39. Tikunoff, W. J., Ward, B. A. and Griffin, G. A., *Interactive Research and Development on Teaching Study: Final Report*. San Francisco: Far West Regional Laboratory for Educational Research and Development, 1979.

40. Woods, P., 'Action research: a field perspective'. *Journal of Education for Teaching*, **14** (2), pp. 135–50, 1988.

41. Cochran-Smith, M. and Lytle, S. L., 'Research on teaching and teacher research: the issues that divide'. *Educational Researcher*, **19** (2), pp. 2–11, 1990.

42. Lytle and Cochran-Smith, op. cit., note 16.

43. Lytle, S. L. and Cochran-Smith, M., 'Teacher research as a way of knowing'. Unpublished paper. Philadelphia, PA: University of Pennsylvania, 1991.

44. Grimmett, P. P. and MacKinnon, A. M., 'Craft knowledge and the education of teachers'. In Grant, G. (ed.), *Review of Research in Education, Volume 18*. Washington, DC: American Educational Research Association, pp. 385–456, 1992.

45. The teacher research groups reviewed in this section were facilitated by Sharon Jeroski and Maureen Dockendorf of Horizon Research and Evaluation Affiliates, Vancouver, BC. The project was funded by the Program Evaluation and Research Branch of the British Columbia Ministry of Education. Special acknowledgement is due to the aforementioned parties and the teachers involved for the role they played in the implementation of the Primary Program and the initiation of teacher research in the province.

46. These confidential reports were made available for analysis to the Ministry's Primary Program Review Consulting Group, of which the author is a member. The

contents of this section are based in part on a preliminary analysis of these reports and have been authorized for use in this article with the proviso that the anonymity of the teachers and the confidentiality of the reports be upheld.

47. Grimmett, P. P., 'British Columbia's curricular-instructional experiment: teacher research and the implementation of the new Primary Program'. Report submitted to the Primary Program Review Consulting Group, Research and Evaluation Branch, Ministry of Education, Victoria, BC, 1993.

48. Lather, P., *Getting Smart: Feminist Research and Pedagogy with/in the Postmodern.* London: Routledge, 1991.

49. Judson, H. F., *The Search for Solutions.* New York: Holt, Rinehart and Winston, p. 5, 1980.

50. Fenstermacher, G. D., 'Where are we going? Who will lead us there?' Presidential Address to the annual meeting of the American Association of Colleges for Teacher Education, San Antonio, TX, 1992.

51. Fenstermacher (op. cit., note 50) characterizes the educative purposes of schooling as revolving around 'those activities intended to enlighten and emancipate the mind of the student, activities whose moral purpose is to impart the noblest forms of intellectual and moral virtue', (p. 3). Fenstermacher's own definition is equally compelling:

> Education . . . is the provision of means to fellow human beings enabling them to continually enlarge their knowledge, understanding, authenticity, virtue and sense of place in the past, present and future of the human race. (p. 3)

52. The systemics of schooling, according to Fenstermacher (op. cit., note 50) include such things as marks, grade levels, Carnegie units, tests, texts, grade point averages, tracks and so on. The systemics are forms and structures, processes and procedures, put in place to carry out the socializing and legitimating functions of schooling. Fenstermacher argues cogently that these have become countervailing forces to the educative purposes of schooling (p. 3).

53. I am indebted here to Beairsto (see note 60) who first brought this point about the uncontrollable complexity of educational innovation to my attention.

54. Patterson, J. L., Purkey, S. C. and Parker, J. V., *Productive School Systems for a Nonrational World.* Alexandria, VA: Association for Supervision and Curriculum Development, 1986.

55. Ibid.

56. Armstrong, H., 'Maximizing your child's athletic potential'. Address given to parents at a Vancouver, BC, high school, 1993.

57. The number in parentheses after each citation from a teacher research group report represents the internal identification system developed by the Ministry of Education

for the members of the Primary Program Review Consulting Group. Essentially, (25) stands for report 25. Only members of the Ministry's Primary Program Review Consulting Group have access to this system. It is being used here to safeguard the anonymity of the teachers and the confidentiality of the reports. No other citation details will be given.

58. This important distinction between the process and substance of change is developed in great detail by Beairsto in his chapter examining a case study of a major educational change.

59. Kuhn, T., *The Structure of Scientific Revolutions*. Chicago: University of Chicago Press, 1970.

60. Beairsto, J. A. B., 'A case study of a major educational change'. In Ruohotie, P. and Grimmett, P. (eds), *New Themes for Education in a Changing World*. Tampere, Finland: University of Tampere Press, 1994.

61. Hunter, E. and Tait, J., 'Language kids use to describe their learning: I'm smiling 'cos I've done it right'. *Research Forum*, **10**, pp. 42–5, 1992.

62. Dockendorf, M., 'Framing, valuing and reflecting on processes for teacher research groups'. *Research Forum*, **10**, pp. 15–19, 1992.

63. See note 57.

64. British Columbia Ministry of Education. *Year 2000: A framework for learning*. Victoria, BC: Queen's Printer, 1990.

65. Zeichner, K. M. and Liston, D. P., *Teacher Education and the Social Conditions of Schooling*. New York: Routledge, p. 47, 1991.

66. Hirst, P., 'Liberal education and the nature of knowledge'. In Archambault, R. D. (ed.), *Philosophical Analysis of Education*. New York: Humanities Press, 1965.

67. Hirsch, E. D., *Cultural Literacy*. New York: Vintage Books, 1988.

68. Zeichner and Liston, op. cit., note 65, p. 48.

69. Grimmett, P. P. and Crehan, E. P., 'Barry: a case study of teacher reflection in clinical supervision'. *Journal of Curriculum and Supervision*, **5** (3), pp. 214–35, 1990.

70. Grimmett, P. P., 'A cultural view of educational leadership'. In Ruohotie, P. and Grimmett, P. (eds), *New Themes for Education in a Changing World*. Tampere, Finland: University of Tampere Press, 1994.

71. Grimmett and MacKinnon, op. cit., note 44.

Chapter 8

From Critical Education to a Critical Practice of Teaching

Ronald G. Sultana

INTRODUCTION

As a teacher educator and a sociologist of education, I have been struggling for some years now to bring the insights developed by the latter field to bear on my work within universities and on that of my students, teachers-to-be.[1] This has not been an easy task for a number of inter-related reasons.

In the first place, the brand of sociology and educational theory which inspires much of my work, namely critical theory,[2] is notorious for the level of abstraction at which it works, and the often convoluted and obscure language in which it is expressed. Student-teachers trying to make connections between theory and practice find many of the readings available on the subject hard to understand, let alone to apply to the challenging situations they encounter in the classrooms.

In the second place, critical theory and education often address a meta-physical level in their insistence on the emancipatory potential of engaging with the world as it *is*, in order to imagine and bring about a world as it *could* and *should* be. The normative dimension to the task of teaching is of course crucial if one is to challenge the increasingly technocratic view that is being promoted for schooling world-wide. It does, however, raise important questions such as 'Are schools the best places to promote emancipatory rationality?' and, even more centrally in terms of the concerns of this book, 'Can teachers be expected to participate in this emancipatory venture, given their social class location and the constraints of the cultural terrain in which they must carry out their work?' In other words, how can a teacher-educator ask student-teachers to consider schools as sites for liberation, when changes in the social and bureaucratic status quo may ultimately work against the interests of this particular group of professionals?

In the third place, much that has emerged from the critical theory tradition has appealed to the individual level of consciousness-raising, and hence depends on the notion of 'conversion' to points of views which, while leading to a disposition to act truly and rightly (*phronesis*), nevertheless are short on a consideration of strategies for the mobilization of resources and people so that the desired state of affairs does in fact come about. Quite a number of students following my courses on critical education are seduced by the invitation to become reflective practitioners with a commitment to promoting justice and equality, but even the most dedicated among them are culturally, if not ideologically, incorporated in the centralized, exam-oriented bureaucratic school system that is to be found in Malta[3] as in many other countries. The heightened consciousness that critical teachers have of their role in the perpetration of symbolic violence in schools can in fact lead to an even deeper sense of frustration and despair, rather than to the transformation of people, situations and structures.

This paper will give a brief overview of the curricular, theoretical and political ways in which I have attempted to tackle the three challenges posed by critical theory to teacher educators as outlined above. In other words, the question this article will address – though, of course, not fully answer – is the following: How can critical education be taught in such a way that it is understandable, theoretically and practically appealing, and politically effective?

A. CRITICAL THEORY IS DIFFICULT

Introduction

Critical theory is difficult to read and to understand, as anybody who has tried to grapple with authors from the Frankfurt School will well appreciate. Indeed, perseverance in the decoding of that corpus of literature is only justified by the fact that critical theory has articulated with more thoroughness than any of the current critical traditions the two themes, of anti-technocratic rationality and of enlightenment, that are so crucial to the development of teacher education.[4] There have been attempts by critical educators to translate key concepts and ideas to a more accessible language, with some of these being more successful than others.[5–7] Students on teacher-training courses will not generally appreciate having to deal with texts whose theoretical sophistication does not immediately engage with real problems and issues, and where words like 'praxis', 'negative dialectics', 'ideology critique', 'reification' and 'repressive tolerance' assume an understanding of advanced philosophical and sociological knowledge.

This is not a case of replacing difficult words with simpler ones, and critical theorists themselves have rightly warned against a 'common language' approach, where the use of everyday terminology positions the reader within the ideological field that those words normally imply. I would much rather use words like 'social formation' than 'society', for instance, to emphasize the constructed and contingent nature of the social and systems relationships which predominate at a given moment. But there are other pedagogically sound ways of communicating challenging ideas which handle the theoretical/abstract level while at the same time engaging with practical instances on which that theory can be brought to bear.

The use of case-studies

One of these is the use of case-study material, where students are requested to bring to courses on critical education journal entries and descriptions of critical incidents encountered during their teaching practice placements. By looking at this material critically, and by interrogating them on their situations and activities as well as those of their students, utilizing tools and concepts provided by critical theory (and by other traditions), teachers can appreciate better the unavoidable linkage between what one does and what one thinks, and vice versa. The use of such case-studies indicates an important shift in the way that teacher training is being conceived, away from a view which encourages 'the study of academic disciplines the results of which one must then learn to apply in practice, to seeing it as the mastery of the practices pursued in a progressively more reflective and critical way'.[8]

Thus, to give an example, the practice of inter- and intra-school streaming in the Maltese educational system is confronted situationally and theoretically in terms of the vested interests that underly it, the larger purposes it serves, the presumed educational benefits accruing from it, and so on. The Habermasian distinction between knowledge and its constitutive interests, in terms of techno-cratic, hermeneutic and emancipatory rationalities, then arises from the situa-tion that (Maltese) teachers are familiar with. Similarly, a case-study of student and teacher confrontation not only raises inter-personal issues but also questions regarding power, authority and student voice. Again, the procedural principles which Habermas outlines as characteristic of the 'ideal speech situation' – truthfulness, meaningfulness, justifiability and sincerity – help students to study an incident as a problem, in terms of not only its psychological but also its structural and systemic properties.

The 'catechism'

Another tool I have developed to help students understand the implications of critical theory to their practice in schools and classrooms is based on a sixteenth-century pedagogical invention – the 'catechism'. This tool – considered by some to be the masterstroke of the Reformation, and probably the most influential pedagogic tool published by any reformer[9] – was developed by Luther in his desire to democratize theological knowledge. The catechism's method is to pinpoint specific areas considered worthy of attention and, by studying as a problem that which had hitherto been assumed to be reality, take the reader-practitioner to a plane which transcends the here and now. In this way the reader can make the link between abstract knowledge and its significance for everyday life. Building on what is, given Malta's overwhelming Christian population, a culturally appropriate tool, I developed a series of questions organized around issues related to 'preparation', 'relationships', 'pedagogy', 'control' and 'assessment', thus helping the student-teacher to focus on concerns which have developed within critical education approaches. In this way, student-teachers are encouraged to engage not only with 'what works' but also with the normative dilemmas in which their actions and decisions are embedded.[10]

This pedagogic tool has been published elsewhere,[11] but for the purpose of this paper it would be useful to outline a few questions from just one of the areas it addresses, namely what I refer to as 'relationships'. Student-teachers on teaching practice are asked to study what they are doing as a problem, by using the following questions:

1. Do you deserve the respect you are expecting from your students? In other words, are you respecting them and their rights as much as you would like them to do with regard to you?

2. Should you be open to learning from your own students? In that case, as a 'teacher-student' you enter into a horizontal (equal/dialogic) as opposed to a vertical (hierarchical/authoritarian) relationship with your 'student-teachers'. Are you aware of the implications of this to your teaching? To your pedagogy?

3. According to Friere, there must be six attitudes in a 'teacher-student' for dialogue to occur. How many of the following characterize what happens between you and your students?

    (a) *Love*: 'Dialogue cannot exist . . . in the absence of a profound love for the world and for human beings.'

    (b) *Humility*: 'Dialogue . . . is broken if I always project ignorance on to others and never perceive my own.'

    (c) *Faith*: 'Dialogue requires an intense faith in people, faith in their power to make and remake, to create and recreate, faith in their vocation to be more fully human.'

    (d) *Trust*: 'Mutual trust between the dialoguers is a logical consequence' of true dialogue.

    (e) *Hope*: 'Dialogue cannot be carried on in a climate of hopelessness. If the dialoguers expect nothing to come of their effort, their encounter will be empty, sterile, bureaucratic and tedious.'

    (f) *Critical thinking*: 'True dialogue cannot exist unless the dialoguers engage in critical thinking. The important thing is the continuing transformation of reality on behalf of the continuing humanization of people.'

B. CRITICAL THEORY AND TEACHERS

Problems of Communication

Communicating the concerns of critical theory and education in a way that is accessible to student-teachers is just one of the challenges that have to be faced in my attempt to reconstruct education as a moral and transformative enterprise. A second challenge refers not to the status of the message but to that of the group to whom it is addressed.

I have often asked myself, as I face a fresh group of students every year for my course on critical theory and education, what the chances are that they will find the course a meaningful, personally liberating and politically enlightening experience. In other words, what chance is there that my course promotes the formation of critical and autonomous educators, dedicated to the pursuit of justice in schools and other social sites?

The answer to that question necessarily goes beyond the interrogation of my abilities as a teacher. One needs also to ask whether there are structural and cultural factors which make teachers likely or unlikely candidates for transformative work in schools and classrooms. Recent sociological perspectives on teachers as a professional group have in fact tended to emphasize the limits rather than the possibilities of such an endeavour.

It has been pointed out, for instance, that teachers tend to be overwhelmingly from a middle-class background,[12,13] and that their contradictory class position in a stratified society means that they generally have little vested interest in promoting change to the status quo. In addition, when teachers enter the cultural site that is the school they find themselves locked in a pre-set structure with its routines, rituals and expectations which prove inordinately difficult to challenge. Among these constraints one can mention class size, school timetables, the education of persons who have not necessarily chosen to be at school, a hidden pedagogy, a concern with what works, and the organization of the school which means that when the teacher exercises autonomy, he or she does so within the conditions set by the institutional structure.[14]

Reflecting on such structural and cultural obstacles to the kinds of educational enterprises that have participatory democracy and the development of an active citizenry as a goal, one can hardly fault Burbules's conclusion that the relatively few teachers who do not develop in an overwhelming conservative and individualistic direction are 'more likely to quit than to remain and change the system'.[15] Moreover, as Everhart soberly points out[16], it seems to be quite unrealistic to ask teachers to challenge technocratic forms of life in schools, since more power-sharing with students will ultimately seriously challenge teachers' own roles as members of a bureaucracy.

These are important reflections which should encourage teacher educators to develop accurate bearings on the social situations of teachers and the constraints under which they work. They should not, however, lead to a counter-productive pessimism about the contribution that schools and educators can make, for in trying to draw teachers into the general struggle for more democratic forms of life we are also drawing on a group

> [whose] educational thought is still deeply influenced by classical and liberal traditions of the formation and development of the whole person . . . . These traditions enshrined notions of autonomy and of the responsibility of individuals for 'taking their rights' – at least morally and intellectually – rather than receiving them.[17]

It is true that teachers are embedded – for structural and cultural reasons – in a 'culture of individualism',[18] and that this focus often makes them blind to the social and systemic properties of their activities in schools. The same focus, however, also generates a commitment to their clients, manifesting itself in what are often unselfconscious child-centred educational experiments and approaches which keep alive 'an intuitive idea of critique, of the possibility of transcendence'.[19] Liberalism and humanism may have their limits in their inability to link the personal with the political, but they are certainly a much more suitable ground for studying the problems of everyday life than is technocracy.

A crisis situation

There remains at least one major problem in attempting to answer the question of whether teachers and schools do, in fact, represent a potential means for the organization of enlightenment. Even if we admit that there is this potential, we also have to admit that the current historical conjuncture has rendered educators vulnerable, greatly weakened as they are by one of the most severe attacks that their profession has had to endure. A growing trend towards centralized control; a greater emphasis on vocationalism and instrumentalism; the move towards treating education as a commodity; enhanced links between the corporate sector and schooling institutions, and increased de-skilling of the teaching force[20] are hardly the appropriate environment for making professional demands on teachers which require a response of heroic proportions if they are to transcend narrow and largely material concerns in order to commit themselves to the re-definition of education as a moral and liberatory activity. Crises and increasing proletarianization tend to lead to crisis-management strategies such as 'coping' and 'withdrawing'.[21,22] And yet crises carry with them another and more promising alternative, for they generate the material conditions that make mobilization and the organization of counter-offensives possible – and this not only in terms of *industrial* action in favour of better salaries and/or conditions of work but also in terms of a truly *professional* action, where teachers engage in educational and other social movements to struggle for a different form of life.

This situation of crisis, I would argue, has led many teacher educators to develop a sense of a political mission in their approach to teacher training. However, most of what is being promoted seems to me to suffer from the same weakness: a generally a-social, fragmented view of teachers' work. What we find are calls for progressive teachers to undertake 'the political and pedagogical strategies necessary to encourage oppositional behaviour in schools',[23] or to develop individual and/or group resistance within schools towards structural constraints and towards the hegemonic culture that dominates curriculum and pedagogy.[24] In the United Kingdom these kinds of resistances have been co-ordinated under the name of 'action research' which, in its best moments, helps reveal to teachers

> [the] transient and contingent status of their practice in a way
> which makes it amenable to critical transformation . . . it is
> [concerned] with establishing the conditions which would enable
> teachers to reflect critically on the contradictions between their
> educational ideas and beliefs and the institutionalized practices
> through which these ideas and beliefs are expressed.[25]

In Northern America we again find 'consciousness-raising' types of activity, whether these are addressed to experienced teachers[26] to university students,[27] or to would-be teachers on college programmes. All have the intention of helping their audiences to generate and sustain 'critical perspectives on schooling and teachers' commitments to work against the grain inside schools'.[28]

Both 'action research' and what Cochran-Smith refers to as 'collaborative resonance' (i.e. 'intensification based on the co-labor of learning communities'[29]) are an advance on previous models for promoting change, for they are neither blinkered by a sole focus on the individual to the exclusion of the social[30] nor turning a deaf ear to perspectives developed by teachers, which previously were considered to be unenlightened and unimportant.

But the exclusive focus on the local, and the fragmentary approach which does its best to utilize 'spaces' created by the predominant political forces of the time, have grave political and strategic implications, and are defensive and weak for at least two reasons. In the first place, opponents utilizing these 'micro' strategies are drawing on the ideological and political grounds provided by the wider institutional framework. In the second place, 'micro' responses which involve 'working from within' can often ironically mean 'individualized re-sponses: the very ideology [of individualism] that is embodied in Thatcherism and that socialist educators should be challenging'.[31]

Gone, in teacher development discourse, are the political strategies on the Gramscian scale, for instance, or the militancy that Castillo del Torres reports in the context of revolutionary Grenada[32], and that the likes of Wolpe and Donald promoted when they advocated the forging of alliances between educators and parents, teachers and students.[33] There have been few organized and co-ordinated responses as a reaction to the increasingly technicized views of education. There have been spates of critiques by academics, but rarely have these been translated into the effective movements that, for instance, have characterized the campaign against racism in education. Indeed, despite the obvious importance of social movements to what we do in education[34-36], the sociology of education tradition that has developed over the past three decades has failed to connect 'theory, research and practice . . . to historical movements in society and education'.[37] If anything, the language of critique that has characterized most educational theory thus far has, according to Wexler, blocked rather than facilitated educational social movements.

C. CRITICAL THEORY, MACRO RESPONSES AND TRANSFORMATION

Introduction

My way of handling the political passage from critical education to a critical practice of teaching has been to invite students following my courses to examine the relationship between challenges emerging in specific educational contexts and the larger, national battles over the definition of education. What follows is an account of how that invitation took organizational shape and became an educational movement in Malta.

The move from specific to more national and global issues in education emerged when, in the process of dialogue with and between students, the concept of 'responsible critique' demanded the development of alternative educational visions. Students recognized that it was important to carry out a sophisticated analysis of the bureaucratized and destructive social relations that prevailed in Maltese schools, of the gender and class distinctions encouraged by systems of selection and control, and of the relationship between this and a segmented labour market. They also correctly insisted, however, that their understanding of critical theory was an engagement with the world in order to *transform* it. The formation of critical teachers entailed the development of responsible citizens active in the public sphere. The key question was, therefore, how to bring together reflective minds and intentional hearts[38] so that a passion for justice could assume an organizational form.

The first activities were organized on an *ad hoc*, largely experimental basis. A group of students, many of whom had already been involved in other forms of grass-root pressure groups in green and alternative politics as well as in other movements within the Catholic Church, used the experience of their five- to six-week teaching practice to organize themselves into a critical nucleus which challenged the school's physical environment and resources, as well as the hierarchical social relations between teachers and students. Their action attracted media coverage and some changes were actually implemented in that school. The students were encouraged to report their activity during the critical education course, as a concrete example of the ability of individual social actors to make their own history through collective will formation. The next step was to adapt that model and extend it to a wider grass-root base. A core group of student-teachers, lecturers and experienced teachers began meeting, established general goals, and chose the name *Moviment Edukazzjoni Umana*[39] to reflect their key intentions. The MEU would create a forum for teachers to discuss education in Malta from a normative point of view; it would serve as a support group for those teachers who did not wish to become incorporated by the utilitarian and technocratic, examination and achievement-centred ideology of schooling in Malta; it would encourage the setting up of grass-root critical/ practical nucleii in school communities where teachers, together with students, would identify specific issues related to normative concerns such as justice, equity and caring which needed to be addressed, and develop a programme of intervention and change; it would co-ordinate these school-based projects, with each nucleus reporting to all MEU members at their monthly meeting in order to serve as a model for other teachers and to get feedback, and it would set up different action groups in favour of particular agendas.

While initially our action was ahead of our theory,[40] what we were in fact doing was what Touraine – a key author on social movement analysis – refers to in his 'sociology of action' as the intensification of conflict, the reinterpretation of social reality, and the redefinition of the self and its capacities. In contrast to the reproduction paradigm that has plagued social theory in education over the past three decades, Touraine follows the spirit of critical theory by highlighting the relative autonomy of actors, and defining the social field as a site where opponents fight over definitions and resources.[41] The interrelationship between protagonists, adversaries and the stakes – which gives rise to social movements – is a key and enduring characteristic of society, and lies 'permanently at the heart of social life . . . . These movements are not a sign of crisis or of tension in a social order; they are the outward sign of the production of society by itself'.[42]

Formal social movements are in fact the collective and organized expression of informal, but intensely personal, experiences and feelings generated in response to felt socio-cultural changes. Touraine holds the view that all contemporary social movements are in fact responding to a central concern, the desire of actors to win self-management in what is an increasingly technocratic society. Different social movements are in fact different fronts for the same battle, and constitute a major form of counter-hegemonic practice because they interpret very powerfully the attempts of 'society' to liberate itself from 'power'.[43] Touraine thus argues that in today's programmed society

> domination can no longer be challenged by a call to metasocial
> principles [e.g. order of things, divine rule, natural law, historical
> evolution, the idea of modernity]; only a direct call to personal and
> collective freedom and responsibility can foster protest
> movements.

139

Critical Education and the *Moviment Edukazzjoni Umana*

That direct call led to an expansion of the movement's membership base. Initially, recruitment took place from among the student body. The university provided a context and space, together with the rudiments of organization such as leaders and communication technology, and, through close collaboration with the Faculty of Education, it provided funds to advertise in the press, to send mail to members and to use venues for meetings. The large ecological concentrations of students whose ideological and ideational preparation was similar facilitated the recruitment of members, and the relative personal availability of students, in that they had few family commitments, made the initial task of getting the movement off the ground relatively easy. The fact that these students met other teachers during teaching practice, and that many were active in other organizations, meant that snowball recruitment was possible both with experienced members of the teaching profession and with parents. The MEU now has 200 members and, while young teachers make up the bulk, heads of schools, older and even retired teachers, as well as parents, attend the monthly meetings regularly.

The movement's actions are developed inside and outside state apparata. Nine school nucleii have developed within state schools thus far, and the focus of action for each of these has been different; one has worked on developing cross-curricular frameworks, another is trying to break down authoritarian management at school, while yet another has focused on establishing non-bureaucratic relations between teachers and students through setting up extra-curricular and cultural clubs. Action in state schools is, by definition, popular educational activity, as state schooling is practically the exclusive territory of students from working-class backgrounds. Action outside state apparata consists of monthly meetings where resolutions are taken in favour of specific agendas for action groups to work on. One action group has focused on family and school links in a working-class area in Malta. Forty couples attended a series of meetings on education, raised questions related to their children's needs, and ultimately channelled their anger and frustration into a political form by establishing a parental pressure group, independent of the movement, in order to work for getting more and better teaching resources for their village primary school, and for access to their children's teachers and classrooms.

A second action group took vocational schooling as its focus. It co-ordinated research efforts together with heads of trade schools in order to shift a discourse exclusively located within human capital theory to one which considered the educational and social implications of differential schooling in Malta. This has led to frequent meetings with trade school staff and administrators in preparation for a national conference which set out to make vocational (working-class) schooling an educational priority in Malta.

Another action group is developing skills in media and communications, hopes to produce its own newspaper on educational affairs and is planning television and radio programmes. Until these long-term goals are achieved, the action group has drawn up a roster of writers who address educational issues in the local weekly and Sunday press. Linked to this action group is an alternative theatre group, which has already produced a challenging drama on social relations in the school. The group adapted its play for street theatre, and toured different locations in Malta. A key action group started out calling itself 'Student Voice', organized research activities with students to record their experiences of schooling, and co-ordinated a national exhibition which portrayed, through student writing and drawing, the school that these students would like. This action group has used that data to draw up a charter in favour of students' rights. The charter was launched, and heads of schools and prominent personalities (including ministers), as well as teachers, students and parents, were invited to sign it. Structures were set up at a national level to ensure that the rights were safeguarded. Through its recruitment and propaganda strategies, the movement has also tapped into projects that had been started on personal initiatives by other teachers prior to the formal setting-up of the MEU.

OUTCOMES AND CONCLUSION

The implications of the MEU case-study for the development of discourses about teacher education are clear. If schools are, as Archer has so forcefully argued,[44] sites where different groups attempt to establish their agendas, then surely a key task for teacher trainers is to provide a language of critique and the political skills – if not the organizational structure – by which and through which there can be a rational, moral and purposive collective commitment in the revisioning of education.

The MEU is a leader in that enterprise through the ways in which it dramatizes social issues, through changing the value positions of those it comes into contact with, and through pressuring for structural change. The MEU does all this when it creates a space for participants – in schools and at movement activities – where they can work against the hegemonic culture in which words like 'education', 'democracy' and 'citizenship' are steeped in a technocratic rationality which 'considers education primarily in instrumental terms and interprets democracy as a system of political management rather than a distinctive form of social and moral life'.[45] Teachers and others who come into contact with the MEU's activities develop a counter-hegemonic understanding of what their activities in schools and classrooms are about, and recognize the part they can play in bringing about change.

My task within this active form of teacher development is what Touraine refers to as 'sociological intervention',[46] which involves the raising of the consciousness of movement members so that we grasp the scope of the struggle more fully. I find myself interpreting, agitating, organizing, and working as analyst or secretary by reporting and explaining the results of self-analysis such as this. Ultimately, this is my way of translating critical knowledge into action, of developing a transformative pedagogy in the specific historical conjuncture of Malta today, in order to avoid Touraine's damning accusation to us as intellectuals, when he argues that many of us

> are not self-consciously helping the blocked groups to mobilize their cultural resources for the purposes of collective self-realization . . . . We stand, fundamentally, in a relation of spectatorship to them, and not as committed interlocutors of this collectively evolving practice. We are not representing to the groups the nature of their struggles.[47]

NOTES AND REFERENCES

1. I teach students following a four-year course leading to a B.Ed. (Hons) degree. Students have a number of compulsory and optional units in educational theory, together with courses in their main and subsidiary teaching subjects, and in pedagogy and methodology. I also teach critical theory at the postgraduate level, on one-year PGCE courses and two-year M.Ed. courses.

2. As developed by the various members of the Frankfurt School, 'critical theory' has three key agendas, namely the economic analysis of contemporary developments in capitalism, the social psychological investigation of the social integration of individuals, and the cultural-theoretical analysis of the mode of operation of mass culture (Honneth, A., 'Critical theory'. In Giddens, A. and Turner, J. (eds)., *Social Theory Today*. Cambridge: Polity Press, 1987.) Critical educators have directly or indirectly engaged with the tradition developed by the Frankfurt School to tease out the implications of this to schooling. Here education is considered to involve the critical interrogation of what passes as everyday, common-sense activity so that knowledge, social forms and practices become liberatory and empowering (see Sultana, R. G., 'The challenge of critical education', *McGill Journal of Education*, **26** (2), pp. 115–28, 1991a).

3. Malta's educational systems are characterized by strong classifications of the segments, with the state sector offering academic, area and vocational schooling to students with different educational (and social class) backgrounds. The private school sector caters for about 30 per cent of all students (see Sultana, R. G., 'Social class and educational achievement in Malta'. In Sultana, R. G. (ed.), *Themes in Education: A Maltese Reader*. Msida, Malta: Mireva, 1991).

4. This point is, of course, debatable. For a defence of the critical theory tradition, in the face of the onslaught of the politically fragmenting 'postmodernisms', see Habermas, J., *The Philosophical Discourse of Modernity*. Cambridge, MA: MIT Press, 1987.

5. Simon, R. I., *Teaching Against the Grain*. Toronto: OISE Press, 1992.

6. Carr, W. and Kemmis, S., *Becoming Critical*. London: Falmer Press, 1988.

7. McLaren, P., *Life in Schools*. New York: Longman, 1989.

8. Hirst, P., 'Professional preparation and the study of educational situations'. In Sultana, R. G., (ed.), *Themes in Education: A Maltese Reader*. Msida, Malta: Mireva, p. xxi, 1991.

9. Bornkamm, H., *Luther in mid-Career 1521-1530*. London: Darton, Longman & Todd, p. 60, 1985.

10. The catechism, of course, provided the answers to the questions posed. In the case of this pedagogical tool, and in the spirit of critical theory, the questions invite the reader to explore alternatives. This does not mean, of course, that there is no agenda in the selection of the items and practices which are studied as problems. The normative stance of the author is in fact made clear in the introductory section of the tool.

11. Sultana, R. G., 'Towards a critical teaching practice: notes for the teacher educator'. *Journal of Further and Higher Education*, **14** (1), pp. 14–30, 1990.

12. Steven, R., 'Towards a class analysis of New Zealand'. *Australian and New Zealand Journal of Sociology*, **14** (2), pp. 113–29, 1978.

13. Harris, K., *Teachers and Classes*. Boston, MA and London: Routledge & Kegan Paul, 1982.

14. Sachs, J. and Smith, R., 'Constructing teacher culture'. *British Journal of Sociology of Education*, **9** (4), pp. 423–36, 1988.

15. Burbules, N. C., 'Education under siege'. *Educational Theory*, **36**, pp. 301–13 (p. 302), 1985.

16. Everhart, R. B., *Reading, Writing and Resistance*. Boston, MA: Routledge & Kegan Paul, 1983.

17. Young, R. E., *A Critical Theory of Education: Habermas and Our Children's Future*. New York and London: Teachers College Press, p. 42, 1990.

18. Hargreaves, A., 'Experience counts, theory doesn't: how teachers talk about their work'. *Socioloy of Education*, **57** (4), pp. 244–54, 1984.

19. Young, op. cit., note 17.

20. Sharp, R., 'Old and new orthodoxies: the seduction of liberalism'. In Cole, M. (ed.), *Bowles and Gintis Revisisted*. London: Falmer, 1988.

21. Merton, R. K., *Social Theory and Social Structure*. New York: Free Press, 1968.

22. Woods, P. (ed.), *Teacher Strategies*. London: Croom Helm, 1980.

23. Burbules, op. cit., note 15.

24. Kanpol, B., 'The concept of resistance: further scrutiny'. *Critical Pedagogy Networker*, **2** (1), pp. 1–4, 1989.

25. Carr, W., 'Action research: ten years on'. *Journal of Curriculum Studies*, **21** (1), pp. 85–90 (p. 86), 1989.

26. Simon, op. cit., note 5.

27. Ellsworth, E., 'Why doesn't this feel empowering? Working through the repressive myths of critical education'. *Harvard Educational Review*, **59** (3), 1989.

28. Cochran-Smith, M., 'Learning to teach against the grain'. *Harvard Educational Review*, **61** (3), pp. 279–310, 1991.

29. Ibid., p. 282.

30. Dale, R., 'Implications of the rediscovery of the hidden curriculum for the sociology of teaching'. In Gleeson, D. (ed.), *Identity and Structure: Issues in the Sociology of Education*. Driffield, North Humberside: Nafferton Books, 1977.

31. Crozier, G., 'Progressive and democratic education: is there a future?' *British Journal of Sociology of Education*, **10** (2), pp. 263–9 (p. 266), 1989.

32. Torres, C., 'Education and democracy in revolutionary Grenada'. *Access*, **5** (1), pp. 1–43, 1986.

33. Wolpe, A. M. and Donald, J. (eds), *Is There Anyone Here From Education?* London: Pluto Press, 1983.

34. Carnoy, M. and Levin, H. M., *Schooling and Work in the Democratic State*. Stanford, CA: Stanford University Press, 1985.

35. Sultana, R. G., 'Social movements and the transformation of teachers' work: case studies from New Zealand'. *Research Papers in Education*, **6** (2), pp. 133–52, 1991.

36. Sultana, R. G., 'Teacher power and the struggle for democracy: an educational movement in Malta'. *International Studies in Sociology of Education*, **2** (1), pp. 3–22, 1992.

37. Wexler, P., *Social Analysis of Education: After the New Sociology*. London: Routledge & Kegan Paul, p. 88, 1987.

38. Bell, L. and Schneidewind, N., 'Reflective minds/intentional hearts: joining humanistic education and critical theory for liberating education'. *Journal of Education*, **169** (2), pp. 55–77, 1987.

39. The word 'umana' should not translate into 'humanistic' but rather, in the Maltese language, carries connotative terms/phrases such as 'respect for the dignity and needs of the individual', 'child-centred', 'democratic' and 'participatory community', and is in opposition to a purely 'academic' form of schooling.

40. I have written a full account of the theoretical underpinnings of the activity of the MEU (see Sultana, op. cit., note 36).

41. Touraine, A., 'An introduction to the study of social movements'. *Social Research*, 4, pp. 749–87 (p. 750), 1985.

42. Touraine, A., 'The new social conflicts: crisis or transformation?' In Lemert, C. C. (ed.), *French Sociology: Rupture and Renewal since 1968*. New York: Columbia University Press, pp. 29, 31, 1981 (original French version 1977).

43. Touraine (1985), op. cit., note 41, p. 776.

44. Archer, Margaret A., *Social Origins of Educational Systems*. London: Sage, 1979.

45. Carr, op. cit., note 25, p. 36.

46. Touraine, A., *The Voice and the Eye: An Analysis of Social Movements*. Cambridge: Cambridge University Press, pp. 191ff, 1981 (original French version 1981).

47. Ibid., p. 142.

PART THREE

IMPLICATIONS OF CRITICAL CONSTRUALS FOR TEACHER DEVELOPMENT

Chapter 9

Beyond Collaboration: Critical Teacher Development in the Postmodern Age

Andy Hargreaves

INTRODUCTION

Across many (though not all) parts of the world, in countries that are restructuring and reforming their educational systems to meet the perceived needs of a postindustrial, postmodern society, politicians and administrators are beginning to acknowledge, if somewhat belatedly, that teachers are the key to effective educational change. From being at the periphery of change efforts, professional development is increasingly viewed as vital to restructuring and reform. Information about policy and practice options, and imposition of standards and expectations alone, are no longer seen as sufficient for driving and sustaining the change process. There are now few detractors from the principle that training and development of the teacher workforce is an essential accompaniment to the restructuring and reform of educational systems.

What is more a source of difference and dispute is the particular form that teachers' professional development should take. Generally, professional development literature derides short, 'one-shot deal' in-service workshops that simply raise teachers' awareness about new initiatives or expose them to new programmes or skills, on the grounds that absence of follow-up, further training or support minimizes the chances of initial or sustained impact, let alone of integrating newly learned skills into teachers' existing repertoires.[1-3] Nonetheless, these are the forms of professional development that continue to dominate in practice – largely because they are cheaper, clearer, more visibly concrete and more easily controlled than most of their competitors.[4,5] In some places, initiatives in peer coaching and mentoring between teachers have provided the structured contexts of practice, feedback and support for teachers that are needed for successful implementation.[6] The value and applicability of peer coaching strategies, however, tends to be restricted to specific training in selected skills. Such strategies are not nearly so appropriate for broad, complex, longer-term approaches to restructuring and reform in the context of multiple rather than single innovations.[7]

In a context where, for reasons I shall outline shortly, improvement and reform efforts are increasingly diverse, wide-ranging, complex and constantly changing, professional development strategies that focus in isolation on specific skill training, with or without the support of peer coaching, are therefore unlikely to yield much success. As awareness of these limitations grows, other strategies of teacher development are beginning to emerge instead: ones which seem better suited to the complexity, diversity and uncertainty of contemporary reform efforts, and which address the basic workplace cultures of teachers themselves. Paramount among these emergent strategies of teacher development is the principle of collaboration and collegiality.

This chapter looks at the strengths and limitations of collaboration as a strategy for teacher development. It evaluates collaboration not in the abstract but within a particular context, for collaboration has such diverse meanings and realizations that it can only be properly understood and evaluated *in the context of its use*. This context, I shall argue, is one of wide-ranging restructuring and reform within education, and of a rapid, uneven and conflicted transition between modern and postmodern conditions within society more generally. The chapter describes these emerging conditions of postmodernity and their implications for the collaborative project. It also outlines ways in which we may need not only to embrace particular kinds of collaboration but also to move beyond them, if we are to meet the challenges of teacher development in the postmodern age.

THE CASE FOR COLLABORATION

Collaboration has come to comprise a *metaparadigm* of educational and organizational change in the postmodern age. Paradigm shifts – profound alterations in our fundamental understandings of how the social and natural worlds are constituted, what are their central problems, how we can best inquire into them, and how we should act on the basis of this knowledge – are nothing new. Historically, conditions of rapid and radical social change have typically given rise to such paradigm shifts.[8] But the postmodern age, with its qualitative leaps in instantaneous development and dissemination of communications and information, and with the increasing pace of change that results from this, accelerates and diversifies paradigm shifts themselves. A fundamental problem of postmodernity, therefore, is one of needing to generate *metaparadigms* of understanding, analysis, development and change to interpret, analyse, synthesize and respond to the more specific paradigm shifts in technology, organizational life, intellectual thought and the like that are occurring with increasing speed within education and outside it.

One of the emergent and most promising metaparadigms of the postmodern age is that of collaboration as an articulating and integrating principle of action, planning, culture, development, organization and research. Throughout the literature on leadership, change and the working lives of teachers, the principle of collaboration is repeatedly emerging as a productive response to a world in which problems are unpredictable, solutions are unclear, and demands and expectations are intensifying. Here, collaboration commonly embodies many or all of the following principles:

Moral support

Collaboration strengthens resolve, permits vulnerabilities to be shared and aired, and carries people through those failures and frustrations that accompany change in its early stages, and that can otherwise undermine or overturn it. Such moral support may, of course, merely amount to comfort, consolation and commiseration among bombarded and vanquished teachers in the face of difficult students, poor resources, lack of leadership and loss of hope. This kind of morale boosting is the stuff of staffroom solidarity in conditions of exceptional adversity.[9,10] But moral support is also central to self-consciously caring school communities where experiments are encouraged, mistakes are forgiven and people's personal and professional concerns are properly addressed in the quest for continuous improvement.[11,12] Moral support is often regarded as one of the 'weaker ties' of collegiality among teachers – less robust than joint teaching, or collaborative action research, for instance.[13,14] While these so-called stronger aspects of collegiality are important (and, as we shall see, often neglected) we must also be careful not to rank care as inferior to critical cognition (which intellectuals who write about teaching, understandably tend to prefer!) in teachers' collaborative work. Care and the moral support that springs from it is a central human and educational value, not merely a means to or progression towards higher cognitive ends.[15] Care is also central to many women's ways of working. To derogate care, directly or by implication, is to derogate these ways of working that prevail among women teachers – the majority group in most teacher workforces.[16] Care and critical cognition are equally important and indispensable components of the collaborative enterprise.

Increased efficiency

Collaboration eliminates duplication and removes redundancy between teachers and subjects as activities are co-ordinated and responsibilities are shared in complementary ways. Together, science teachers and mathematics teachers may discover they are both teaching vectors, for instance. In isolation, it is likely that they will not. At the primary or elementary school level, collaboration can secure continuity and progression in the curriculum from year to year,[17] based less on externally imposed contents and guidelines than on principles to which communities of teachers are themselves committed, in the contexts they know best. In secondary schools, collaboration can break down subject compartmentalization, and secure consistency in expectations (homework, marking policies etc.,) co-ordination of material, and in some cases integration of learning around cross-subject themes.[18,19]

Improved effectiveness

Collaboration improves the quality of student learning by improving the quality of teachers' teaching. Collaboration encourages risk-taking, greater diversity in teaching methods, and improved senses of efficacy among teachers as self-confidence is boosted by positive encouragement and feedback. All these things impact upon and benefit student learning.[20,21] In Sarason's terms,[22] if schools are going to be better places for students to be, they have to be better places for teachers to be also. The principle of collaboration is central to constructing such a positive working community, and is consistently listed in the effective schools' literature as correlating positively with student outcomes.[23]

Reduced overload

Collaboration permits sharing of the burdens and pressures that come from intensified work demands and accelerated change, so that individual teachers and leaders do not have to shoulder them all in isolation. Leadership responsibilities can be shared and rotated.[24] Principals move more from their offices to the classroom to take on an active 'instructional' role supporting their teachers.[25] Teachers participate more in the decisions that affect them. Sometimes teachers see shutting the classroom door and working alone with their own students as a strategic defence against extraneous demands and burdensome committee work.[26,27] Some critics view what Hoyle[28] calls extended professionalism merely as a rhetorical ruse to shift more obligations and responsibilities away from administrators and on to the shoulders of teachers: a way of getting teachers to do more for less. For Apple, for instance, 'The increasing . . . intensification of the teaching act . . . [is] misrecognized as a symbol of their increased profession-alism.'[29,30] However, while this is often empirically true, it is not essentially or universally so. Moreover, what is at stake here, in the question of whether collaboration creates more or less overload, is not so much the sheer *quantity* of teachers' task and commitments but their *quality*, in other words, does teachers' work *feel* less overloaded if it is meaningful and invigorating and the teachers have high collective control and ownership of it?

Synchronized time perspectives

Collaboration narrows the differences of time perspective between administrators and teachers. When segregated into discrete and insulated roles, teachers and administrators perceive the timeframes of classroom life and teachers' work within them very differently. For administrators, at some distance from the classroom, the time taken for innovation appears to pass too slowly. They are therefore inclined to speed it up. Meanwhile, in the densely packed world of classroom tasks and commitments, time for the teacher passes all too quickly. Teachers are therefore equally inclined to slow innovation down.[31–33] Participation in common activities and communication, by contrast, can create shared and realistic expectations about timelines for change and implementation. The same principles also apply to synchronization of time perspectives and expectations between teachers and students when they become partners in the learning process. If students were involved earlier in innovation[34] instead of being the last to be informed, if at all, the customary timelines of three to five years for change to make a difference in the classroom[35, 36] might be shortened considerably.[37] Change rules are not immutable. They are a function of existing conditions, which can and should be changed.

Situated certainty

The two worst states of knowledge are ignorance and certainty. Collaboration reduces uncertainty and limits excesses of guilt that otherwise pervade teaching by setting commonly agreed boundaries around what can reasonably be achieved in any setting.[38] Collaboration also creates collective professional confidence that can help teachers resist the tendency to become dependent on false *scientific* certainties of teaching effectiveness, school effectiveness and the like, by replacing them, or debilitating occupational uncertainties, with the *situated* certainties of collected professional wisdom among particular communities of teachers.[39]

Political assertiveness

Collaboration, in its strongest forms, enables teachers to interact more confidently and assertively with their surrounding systems and with the multiplicity of reasonable and unreasonable innovations and reforms that come from them. It strengthens the confidence to adopt externally introduced innovations, the wisdom to delay them and the moral fortitude to resist them, where appropriate.[40] In that sense, it also mitigates the effects of intensification and overload mentioned earlier.

Increased capacity for reflection

Collaboration in dialogue and action provides sources of feedback and comparison that prompt teachers to reflect on their own practice. Others become mirrors for one's own practice, leading one to reflect on it and reformulate it more critically. The process of demonstration – practice – feedback – review is central to the specific and structured practice of peer coaching as a support for implementing new teaching methods.[41] Collaborative action research embraces the principles of feedback, evaluation and inquiry even more extensively as a way to bring about continuous improvements in teaching and learning.[42,43]

Organizational responsiveness

Collaboration pools the collected knowledge, expertise and capacities of the teacher workforce to enable it to respond swiftly to changing constraints and opportunities in the surrounding environment, to scan the environment proactively for forthcoming changes, and to seek out the opportunities those may offer.

Here it is often viewed as a central principle in the move towards school-based decision-making. Restructuring of the system towards site-based decision-making, it is argued, requires restructuring of the school to empower teachers and others to bring their collected expertise to the decision-making process.[44] By involving members of the school environment – parents, business, unions, communities etc. – in the collaborative process itself, the swiftness and appropriateness of schools' and teachers' responses are enhanced even further.

Opportunities to learn

Collaboration increases teachers' opportunities to learn from each other between classrooms, between departments and between schools.[45] The insulated egg-crate classrooms of traditional primary or elementary schools,[46] and the segregated, balkanized, departments of secondary schools,[47] make it difficult for teachers to learn from one another, across grade levels in primary schools, or between subjects in secondary schools. As my colleagues and I found in a recent study of secondary school work-cultures and educational change, teachers in one department who felt insecure and alone experimenting with changes like co-operative learning could be unaware that similar changes (and the sources of expertise and moral support that accompanied them) were available in other departments. Similarly, teachers facing a forthcoming provincial mandate to destream or detrack Grade 9, and unclear as to what destreamed classes would look like and what skills were required to teach them, were unaware that destreamed classes already existed in their own school in other subjects. Teachers generally underestimated the amount of change that was already going on in other classes around them. Most teachers were changing more than their colleagues thought.[48,49] We concluded that in balkanized secondary schools the organizational whole is considerably less than the sum of its parts.[50] In collaborative organizations the opposite is true. Collaboration, therefore, can be a powerful source of professional learning: a means of getting better at the job.

Continuous improvement

Collaboration encourages teachers to see change not as a task to be completed but as an unending process of continuous improvement in the asymptotic pursuit of ever greater excellence, on the one hand,[51] and emergent solutions to rapidly changing problems on the other. Because of the way it promotes shared reflection, professional learning and the pooling of collected expertise, collaboration is a central principle of organizational learning.[52,53]

CRITIQUES OF COLLABORATION

Notwithstanding its immense and very real promise as a generative principle of educational change and restructuring, collaboration carries also with it many problems and dangers. It is neither a complete nor an ultimate solution to the problem of educational change. Among the more problematic meanings and realizations of collaboration are ones where collaboration is:

- **Superficial** Collaboration can lack purpose and direction, having little clear connection with the teaching–learning process and the benefits collaboration can bring to that process. Working together can seem wasteful and pointless – collaborating for the sake of collaboration!

- **Comfortable and complacent** Collaboration can be confined to safer, less controversial areas of teachers' work - ones which avoid collaboration in classroom practice, or collaboration through systematic shared reflection, in favour of moral support and sharing of resources and ideas. This can consolidate rather than challenge existing practice and can be comfortable, cosy and complacent.[54]

- **Conformist** As my colleague Michael Fullan and I have argued elsewhere, collaboration can be conformist. It can lead to groupthink, suppressing individuality and solitude and the (sometimes disagreeable) creativity of thought which springs from them.[55]

- **Contrived** Collaboration can be administratively captured, contained and controlled in ways that make it stilted, unproductive and wasteful of teachers' energies and efforts. By making collaboration into an administrative *device*, contrived collegiality can paradoxically suppress the *desires* that teachers have to collaborate and improve among themselves,[56] and they can become gridlocked in administratively controlled procedural planning, with little time or incentive to collaborate on their own initiative.

- **Co-optative** Collaboration is sometimes used as an administrative and political ruse to secure teachers' compliance with and commitment to educational reforms decided by others. If these reforms are ethically bankrupt or suspect, such collaboration can become collaboration with the enemy (for which some people were shot in World War II !).

Collaboration can be helpful or harmful. Its meanings and realizations therefore need to be inspected repeatedly to ensure that its educational and social benefits are positive. Central to this critical inspection is an understanding of the context in which it takes place, for it is this which, in many ways, defines the purposes, consequences and limits of collaborative work.

THE CONTEXT OF COLLABORATION

There are many ways to define the context of teaching. One is in terms of the immediate situation of which teachers are consciously and subjectively aware – policy demands, class sizes, characteristics of the students, architectural restrictions of the school building, etc. These characteristics which help shape what teachers do, are particularly salient in symbolic interactionist interpretations of teaching and teacher development that link the self of the teacher to the opportunities and constraints of the surrounding situation.[57-59] The context of teaching can also be understood as a typology of context-types: an assortment of variables that interact in complex ways to influence the patterns of teachers' work. McLaughlin and Talbert, for example, on the basis of research in 16 secondary schools, delineated several contexts of teaching that are embedded within one another in a pattern of increasing inclusiveness.[60] Thus, the teacher's classroom is embedded within the subject area or department, which is embedded within the school organization, which is embedded in turn within the school system, then in the parental community and social class culture, the higher education context of admission standards and student achievement, the context of professional associations and networks, and the broad environmental context of policy initiatives, educational goals, existing norms or practice and so forth.

These interpretations of context help us to understand what factors shape patterns of teaching and teacher development. Moving beyond this, though, we also need to understand how and why the factors interact in particular ways at particular times: what configuration the context of teaching and teacher development takes *here and now*, and what forces and movements are at work in shaping it. The emergence of collaboration as a strategy of teacher development and school improvement points to important changes in the context of teaching. A central task for those taking a more critical stance towards teacher development is to understand this changing educational context, and the changing social context beyond it, for it is there that much of the meaning of collaboration will be found.

In societal terms, I want to argue that the context of collaboration can best be described in terms of a transition between modern and postmodern social conditions. This transition is neither smooth nor simple, but its broad characteristics are clearly apparent.

Modernity to Postmodernity

However we articulate it, the sociohistorical transition from *modernity* to *postmodernity* is already a familiar feature of our everyday experience. Few observers of the social world around them can be unaware of the monumental changes now taking place in the corporate world, for instance. Restructuring, downsizing, relocation and even extinction are the realities of organizational change which many corporations and their employees are having to face. Businesses are being broken up. Organizational hierarchies are being flattened as layers of bureaucracy are swept away. Leadership and the way it is exercised is undergoing extraordinary transformations. As traditional structures wither and new ones emerge, these patterns of change are sometimes celebrated in eulogies of personal empowerment or of organizational learning and development. At other times, the celebrations are but thinly-veiled euphemisms for corporate collapse, managerial ruthlessness or calculated bankruptcy. Depending on one's value standpoint, and sometimes on the situation as well, transformations in corporate life can be heroic or horrendous. Either way, their impact in the corporate world and beyond is formidable.

The social transformations we are witnessing extend far beyond the corporate world alone. Extensive changes in economic and organizational life are being accompanied by and also interrelated with equally profound changes in the organization and impact of knowledge and information, in the geopolitical reconstruction of the global map, in the restitution and reconstitution of national and cultural identities, and even in the redefinition and restructuring of human selves. With the former Czechoslovakian President and intellectual Vaclav Havel, I want to argue that these combined changes mark 'the end of the modern era'[61] – or at least the beginning of that end.

Modernity is a social condition that has been driven and sustained by Enlightenment beliefs in rational scientific progress, in the triumph of technology over nature, and in the capacity to control and improve the human condition by applying this wealth of scientific and technological understanding and expertise to social reform.[62,63] *Economically*, modernity begins with the separation of family and work through rational concentration of production in the factory system, and culminates in systems of mass production, monopoly capitalism or state socialism as ways of increasing productivity and profitability. Modernity is the era of the *smokestack society*[64], of large factories, mass labour and company towns. In modernistic economies, expansion is essential to survival. *Politically*, modernity typically concentrates control at the centre with regard to decision-making, social welfare and education and, ultimately, economic intervention and regulation as well. *Organizationally*, this is reflected in large, complex and often cumbersome bureaucracies arranged into hierarchies and segmented into specializations of expertise. In these bureaucracies, functions are differentiated rationally and careers ordered in logical progressions of rank and seniority. The *personal* dimensions of modernity have been widely commented upon. There is system and order, and often some sense of collective identity and belonging too; but the price is also a loss of spirit or magic: what Max Weber described literally as *disenchantment* in comparison with premodern existence.[65] The scale of organizational life and its rational impersonality can also lead to estrangement, alienation and lack of meaning in individual lives.

Secondary schools are the prime symbols and symptoms of modernity. Their immense scale, their patterns of specialization, their balkanized structures and bureaucratic complexity, their persistent failure to engage the emotions and motivations of many of their students and considerable numbers of their staff are just some of the ways in which the principles of modernity are expressed in the practice of secondary education.[66,67] In many respects, state secondary education has become a major part of what Taylor calls 'the malaise of modernity'.[68]

Postmodernity Most writers locate the origins of the *postmodern* condition somewhere around the 1960s.[69] Postmodernity is a social condition in which economic, political, organizational and even personal life come to be organized around very different principles from those of modernity. Philosophically and ideologically, advances in telecommunications along with broader and faster dissemination of information are placing the old ideological certainties of techno-logical conquest or socialist transformation in disrepute as people become increasingly aware of the drawbacks of these utopias, and of the alternatives to them. Even scientific certainty is losing its credibility, as supposedly *hard* findings on such things as decaffeinated coffee, global warming, breast cancer screening or even effective teaching are superseded and contradicted by new ones at an ever increasing pace.

Economically, postmodern societies witness the decline of the factory sys-tem. Postmodern economies are built around the production of smaller goods rather than larger ones, services rather than manufacturing, software more than hardware, information and images more than products and things. The changing nature of what is produced, along with the technological capacity to monitor shifts in market requirements almost instantaneously, reduce the need for stock and inventory. Units of enterprise shrink drastically in scale as a result. Flexible accumulation is now the driving economic principle as profitability becomes dependent on anticipating and responding rapidly to local and changing market demands, in order to increase the turnover time of production.[70]

Politically and organizationally the need for flexibility and responsiveness is reflected in decentralized decision-making, together with flatter decision-making structures, reduced specialization and blurring of roles and boundaries. If the organizational metaphor of modernity is the compartmentalized egg-crate, then that of postmodernity is the 'moving mosaic'.[71] Roles and functions now shift constantly in dynamic networks of collaborative responsiveness to successive and unpredictable problems and opportunities. This restructured postmodern world can create increased personal empowerment, but its lack of permanence and stability can also create crises in interpersonal relationships as these have no anchors outside themselves to guarantee their security and continuance.

The postmodern world is fast, compressed, complex and uncertain. It is already presenting immense problems and challenges for our modernistic school systems and the teachers who work within them. The compression of time and space is creating accelerated change, innovation overload and intensification in teachers' work. Ideological uncertainty is challenging the Judaeo-Christian tradition on which many school systems have been based, and raising crises of identity and purpose over what their new missions might be. Scientific uncertainty is undermining the claims of a sure knowledge base for teaching and making each successive innovation look increasingly dogmatic, arbitrary and superficial. And the search for more collaborative modes of decision-making is posing problems for the norms of teacher isolation on which teachers' work has been based, as well as problems for many school leaders who fear for their power as they worry about how far collaboration might go.

The responses of schools and teachers to the demands and contingencies of the postmodern age are often inappropriate or ineffective – leaving intact the systems and structures of the present, or retreating to comforting myths of the past. Schools and teachers either cling to bureaucratic solutions of a modernistic kind or retreat nostalgically to premodern myths of community, consensus and collaboration, where small is beautiful and friendships and allegiances tie teachers and others together in tight, protected webs of common purpose and belonging. In many respects, schools remain modernistic, and in some cases even premodern, institutions that are having to operate in a complex postmodern world.

The movement from modernity to postmodernity is more of a struggle than a transition, and an uneven, unpredictable struggle at that. The meaning of postmodernity is itself contested, and the outcome of its ongoing struggle with the forces of modernity is uncertain. Much of the future of teacher development and the meaning and impact of teacher collaboration depend on how these distinctive challenges of postmodernity are realized and resolved within our broadly modernistic school systems. The nature of this struggle and its possible outcomes can be seen especially clearly in two aspects of the postmodern condition which I call the *moving mosaic* (from Toffler[72]) and *safe simulation*.

The Moving Mosaic

One of the most central defining and determining characteristics of the postmodern, postindustrial order is a new and distinctive pattern of production, consumption and economic life. Various terms have been used to describe this emerging order: flexible accumulation[73], flexible specialization[74], and the flexible firm.[75] While these terms place different emphases on labour markets, patterns of production and the organization of enterprises respectively, the notion of flexibility is central to all of them. In response to the economic crisis of modernity, with its exhaustion of international markets and long-term debt, flexible accumulation improves profitability by reducing labour costs and increasing *turnover time* in production and consumption. This is achieved in three broad ways.

First, postmodern economies are characterized by a whole array of more flexible work technologies and labour processes. Where standardization, job demarcation and mass production characterized modern economies, flexible, postmodern work technologies break down traditional job demarcations and introduce overlaps and rotations in task assignments and job descriptions. They also facilitate rapid and easy adjustment in the size of the workforce through part-time and temporary work, contracting out, etc. Wage arrangements, too, are more flexible through the use of devices such as pay-for-performance, discretionary bonuses and merit pay.[76]

Secondly, flexible accumulation articulates and accelerates the interactions between producers and consumers. Unlike old industrial systems of mass production and consumption where standardized technologies fed standardized lifestyles, the new postindustrial economics are characterized by niche marketing targeted to specialized groups, customized production technologically tailored to individual preferences, and small batch production that allows rapid responsiveness to shifts in consumers' demand. As laser bar-codes and computer technology connect vendors and suppliers more quickly and closely, the need for stock, inventory and the labour to manage them is reduced. Through marketing and advertising, these patterns are accompanied by strategies to increase and diversify consumer desire, and to accelerate the turnover of tastes and fashions.[77] Knowledge and information in the form of advice, consultancy, tourism, speeches, spectacles and cultural events can be produced and consumed even more quickly than manufactured goods, as can the resulting economic benefits.[78]

Thirdly, flexible economies deploy new patterns of regulation and control which overcome the boundaries of geographical space. Postindustrial economies are characterized by economies not of *scale* but of *scope*.[79] Helped by instantaneous communication and computing, corporate decision-making increasingly cuts across the barriers of time and space. Operations and personnel no longer need to be concentrated for efficiency's sake in one place. Units of enterprise are becoming smaller and more manoeuvrable within the overall corporate structure. Plant location is no longer fixed by tradition and the need for large, loyal labour forces. Company towns are a thing of the past. Geographical *space* is economically flexible. Commitment to particular *places*, meanwhile, persists only as long as is warranted by local markets, favourable land values and flexible, inexpensive workforces.

Within the emerging flexible economies, units of corporate enterprise are tending to become smaller, more interconnected externally and more fluid and collaborative internally, and this is spilling over into the principles and patterns of wider organizational life. The kinds of organizations most likely to prosper in the postindustrial, postmodern world, it is widely argued, are ones characterized by flexibility, adaptability, creativity, opportunism, collaboration, continuous improvement, a positive orientation towards problem-solving and commitment to maximising their capacity to learn about their environment and themselves. Inbuilt innovativeness and routine unpredictability are the organizational oxymorons of postmodernity.[80,81]

Kanter and her colleagues provide one of the most succinct descriptions of these emergent characteristics of postmodern organizations in an account of what they call a 'tidal wave' which is becoming 'a universal model for organizations, especially large ones':

> This model describes more flexible organizations adaptable to
> change, with relatively few levels of formal hierarchy and loose
> boundaries among functions and units, sensitive and responsive to
> the environment; concerned with stakeholders of all sorts –
> employees, communities, customers, suppliers and shareholders.
> These organizations empower people to take action and be
> entrepreneurial, reward them for contributions and help them
> gain in skill and 'employability'. Overall, these are global
> organizations characterized by internal and external
> relationships, including joint ventures, alliances, consortia and
> partnership.[82]

They go on to say that global economic competition and technological change are

> hastening the evolution of an organizational model that defines
> the boundaries of organizations as fluid and permeable. It
> recognizes that influences over organizational acts come from
> many sources and directions, and through many pathways, rather
> than 'down' a 'chain of command' . . . Thus, organizational action
> in the new model needs to be viewed in terms of *clusters of activity
> sets* whose membership, composition, ownership and goals are
> constantly changing, and in which *projects* rather than *positions*
> are central. In such an image of an organization, the bonds
> between actors are more meaningful and ongoing than those of
> single market transactions but less rigid and immutable than
> those of positions in authority structures.[83]

In this view, the postmodern organization is characterized by networks, alliances, tasks and projects, rather than by relatively stable roles and responsibilities which are assigned by function and department, and regulated through hierarchical supervision.

Toffler employs the metaphor of *the moving mosaic* to describe these patterns.[84] He outlines the movement of large corporations 'from monolithic internal structures to mosaics made of scores, often hundreds of independently accounted units'[85] and asks his readers to picture

> a moving mosaic composed not on a flat, solid wall, but on many,
> shifting see-through panels, one behind the other, overlapping,
> interconnected, the colors and shapes continually blending,
> contrasting, changing. Paralleling the new ways that knowledge is
> organized in data bases, this begins to suggest the future form of
> the enterprise and of the economy itself. Instead of a power-
> concentrating hierarchy, dominated by a few central

organizations, we move toward a multidimensional mosaic form of power.[86]

This model of the moving mosaic is not an unconditionally positive one, as we shall see, but in its most favourable forms it can contribute valuably to what Senge calls *organizational learning*,[87] by offering an organizational structure 'where people continually expand their capabilities to understand complexity, clarify vision and improve shared mental models' by engaging in different tasks, acquiring different kinds of expertise, experiencing and expressing different forms of leadership, confronting uncomfortable organizational truth and searching together for shared solutions.

Secondary schools that operate like moving mosaics have more permeable departmental boundaries; membership of teachers in more than one department; less seniority, permanence and relative reward attached to the leadership position of department head; overlapping structural categories (like department and school improvement teams), as well as overlapping membership of them; and more leadership positions across and outside departments. Moreover, these organizational categories, along with leadership of and membership in them, are expected to change over time, as circumstances require.[88]

Beyond schools themselves, there are trends in staff development towards establishing professional networks where teachers are connected by electronic mail and satellite TV and can meet in smaller, interconnected sites. These networks are neither course-based in universities or school districts nor site-based in individual schools, but incorporate, extend beyond and interconnect both of these more conventional patterns.[89]

In some districts, teacher unions and federations have also started to move away from the long-standing promotion categories and formulae agreed in established collective bargaining arrangements, to establish new, more flexible categories for promotion and career development that offer greater discretion to individual schools in terms of how particular career paths and categories are defined.[90] Similarly, more than eighty schools involved in the Australian National Schools Project have agreed to suspend existing collective agreements between teachers and their employers on an experimental basis in order to discover new patterns of work organization that are more productive for students and more rewarding for teachers, and that might be replicated on a wider basis.[91,92] This is very different from beginning with baselines of established, yet increasingly outmoded, work patterns and then trying to negotiate them on a piecemeal basis.

Our visions of organizational possibility for schooling and teachers' work are beginning to extend beyond the traditional, egg-crate elementary school, the modernistic cubbyhole-like secondary school, and the smaller premodern, collaborative communities that have come to characterize a number of elementary and primary schools. While no single best model of the moving mosaic has yet emerged, and most certainly never will – for the demands of different contexts call for different structural solutions in each case – its basic principles represent some of our best hopes, organizationally, for forms of schooling and teaching in the postmodern age: flexible, responsive, proactive, efficient and effective in their uses of shared expertise and resources to meet the continuously shifting needs of students in a rapidly changing world. To build a moving mosaic is to move beyond the principle of collaboration itself to the structures which can best support it in the complex context of postmodernity.

However, if some teachers are suspicious that organizational 'flexibility' and the loosening of their roles and responsibilities may be used against them, this is not without foundation. Moving targets are notoriously hard to hit and the moving mosaic is no exception. But the appropriate response is not to preserve and protect the status quo of subjects, departments and middle management bureaucracy, to go back to the clarity, yet also the despair, of cumbersome structures and entrenched, institutionalized conflict.[93] This only stifles the organization's ability to improve, stunts its teachers' opportunities to learn from colleagues across subject boundaries, and deprives its children of a richer and continually improving education. The overall possibility of and necessity for new organizational scenarios for our secondary schools and their teachers need to be entertained very seriously even if particular versions of these scenarios should be contested.

But the problematic aspects of the moving mosaic are real, and are ones that advocates of collaboration, flexibility and the learning organization tend to overlook. While many analysts of postmodern organizations see the emergence of flatter, less hierarchical structures, and more collaborative work environments within each unit of the overall enterprise, critics have pointed to important limitations which surround such collaboration, and the forms it can take. For instance, collaboration often includes middle level workers but excludes those below them, creating collaboration, autonomy and discretion for some but subordination for the rest.[94] Management teams can collaborate without their ordinary colleagues, the innovating in-group of teachers without their more sceptical counterparts, teaching staff without support staff, or members of the school without parents in the community. The parameters of collaboration and site-based decision-making may also be confirmed by the information which management chooses to make available to its employees. Menzies points to a case-study of one company where

> the information provided is often of the company's selection – for instance, reams of statistics on sales forecasts and defects per million logged in other . . . plants around the world, but no forecasts touching on the organization of work and the future of jobs in the plant. Workers complained: 'They keep everybody in the dark'. Management's reply: 'We tell them as much as we think will be beneficial to them and healthy without raising hopes or fears'.[95]

In this respect, the demands of flexible economies may foster more self-management within individual units of enterprise, but in ways that are para-doxical. Workers (or at least some workers) at site level may be able to exercise greater discretion over how things are produced, but the more controversial aspects of the production process, along with decisions about what is to be produced, tend to remain the prerogative of an inaccessible and unaccountable centre which coordinates all the separate units. And should these units prove to be unproductive or uncooperative, they can be closed down and reopened else-where, at any time, by exploiting the flexible uses of space in the global economy.[96]

Educationally, the impact of the moving mosaic as the manipulative mosaic can be seen most clearly in the emergence of school-based financing, school-based staff development, and the self-managing school, where the principles of postmo-dern organization have perhaps made their strongest inroads into the sys-tem.[97,98] Based on developments in the field of corporate management, school-based management also promises autonomy, empowerment, collaboration, flex-ibility, responsiveness and release from the grip of meddling bureaucracy. In early experiments, when schools are typically granted the latitude to innovate, self-managing schools can exemplify some of the more positive aspects of these principles rather well. But when developed across entire systems, in a context where self-management or local management is accompanied by retention of central control over what is produced (through stringent controls over curricu-lum and assessment), then school-based management is no longer an avenue of empowerment but a conduit for blame.[99] This is especially true where the curriculum and assessment requirements that are imposed connect poorly with the needs and interests of students who are socially and educationally at risk and may actively contribute to their educational failure. In this respect school-based management, like corporate self-management, is unlikely to deliver on its promises of teacher empowerment and cultures of collaboration unless the sphere of decision-making is broad, and issues of curriculum, assessment and educational purpose leave ample scope for teacher self-determination.[100,101] Renihan and Renihan put it best:

> Empowerment is, in its own right, a compelling force in its
> potential to achieve organizational excellence (but) above all it is
> imperative that we recognize what empowerment is *not* . . .
> Empowerment is *not* kidding teachers into thinking preplanned
> initiatives were their ideas. (That is entrapment.) Empowerment
> is *not* holding out rewards emanating from positive power. (That is
> enticement.) Empowerment is *not* insisting that participation is
> mandated from above. (That is enforcement.) Empowerment is *not*
> increasing the responsibility and scope of the job in trivial areas.
> (That is enlargement.) Empowerment is *not* merely concluding
> that enlarged job expectations just go with the territory. (That is
> enslavement.) Empowerment is, rather, giving teachers and

students a share in important organizational decisions, giving
them opportunities to shape organizational goals, purposely
providing forums for staff input, acting on staff input, and giving
real leadership opportunities in school-specific situations that
really matter.[102]

Flexible organizational structures which resemble the metaphor of the moving mosaic are urgently needed in our schools, particularly at the secondary level, to enable schools and teachers to be more responsive to the changing educational needs of students who live in a complex, fast-paced and technologically sophisticated society. But the moving mosaic can easily become the manipulative mosaic, with teachers and schools having responsibility without power as the centre retains control over the essentials of curriculum and testing, over the basic products or outcomes which teachers must turn out. Much of the future will be settled by the way in which this emerging context of organizational flexibility is determined and defined.

Safe Simulation

Moral frameworks of purpose and a keen awareness of, as well as a willingness to engage with, the organizational and political realities of schooling are essential if teacher collaboration is to be rigorous and robust – not cosy and complacent, contrived and controlled or safely restricted to administrivia and inessentials. This is especially important in a postmodern world in which aesthetics can be elevated above ethics and the way that things *appear* is often accorded priority over how they actually *are*.

A World of Images   Teachers now live and work in a world where images are everywhere – where reality tries to live up to, becomes suffused with, and may be indistinguishable from its images. While this profusion can give rise to experiences that are exciting, engaging and entertaining, it can also make it difficult to generate serious and sustained moral discourse, public debate and considered judgement about purposes and values. Glossy school brochures and colour-coded staff development booklets may bear little relation to what actually goes on in schools or within the staff development practices of school systems. In his book *America*, Baudrillard has encapsulated the potentially trivializing effects of the ubiquitous image in a provocative though also characteristically overstated 'cameo' description of what he calls 'Reagan's smile'.

> And that smile everyone gives you as they pass, that friendly
> contraction of the jaws triggered by human warmth. It is the
> eternal smile of communication, the smile through which the child
> becomes aware of the presence of others, or struggles desperately
> with the problem of their presence . . . they certainly do smile at
> you here [in America] though neither from courtesy, nor from an
> effort to charm. This smile signifies only the need to smile. It is a

bit like the Cheshire Cat's grin: it continues to float on faces long after all emotion has disappeared . . . The smile of immunity, the smile of advertising: 'This country is good. I am good. We are the best!' It is also Reagan's smile – the culmination of the self-satisfaction of the entire American nation – which is on the way to becoming the sole principle of government . . . Smile and others will smile back. Smile to show how transparent, how candid you are. Smile if you have nothing to say. Most of all, do not hide the fact that you have nothing to say, nor your total indifference to others. Let this emptiness, this profound indifference shine out spontaneously in your smile . . . Americans may have no identity, but they do have wonderful teeth.

And it works. With this smile, Reagan obtains a much wider consensus than any that could be achieved by a Kennedy with mere reason or political intelligence . . . the whole American population comes together in this toothpaste effect. No idea – not even the nation's moral values in their entirety – could ever have produced such a result. Reagan's credibility is exactly equal to his transparency and the nullity of the smile.[103]

Where people are surrounded by a plethora of images, this can create dramatic spectacles but also moral and political superficiality, aesthetic attractiveness but also ethical emptiness. In many ways, contemporary images disguise and deflect more unseemly realities, but when technologically generated images are as profuse and pervasive as they are in postmodern society, the relationship between image and reality becomes even more complex than this. Baudrillard captures this complexity in his discussion of 'the successive phases of the image'[104] where

- it is the reflection of basic reality
- it masks and perverts a basic reality
- it masks the *absence* of a basic reality
- it bears no relation to any reality whatsoever
- it is its own pure *simulacrum*

In his last phase, Baudrillard argues, the image is 'no longer in the order of appearance at all, but of simulation'.[105] It becomes hard to tell what is simulated and what is 'real'. For example, technologically complex images have led to increasingly pervasive and popular trends in museums, aquaria, etc. towards creating sophisticated simulations or hyper-realities[106] of Victorian villages, 'frontier' gold mines, or entire ecosystems in which dolphins, birds or butterflies appear to be completely at home. Travelling to Disneyworld's Epcot Centre and seeing robots which look like humans and which, in many respects, are more perfectly human than humans themselves, one cannot help but marvel at the technological triumph of all this. It can be extremely pleasurable to immerse oneself in the self-confirming, simulated world which this contrived imagery has created.

Simulation and Reality   There is more to simulations than this, though. In what they portray, and how they portray it, postmodern simulations also convey moral messages about history, nature and human relationships which are implicit and seductive, rather than explicit and open to debate. This is true, we will see, not just in entertainment but also for certain kinds of 'simulated' behaviour in organizations and workplaces, including those of teachers.

What does it mean to simulate something? According to Baudrillard 'To dissimulate is to feign not to have what one has. To simulate is to feign to have what one hasn't . . . Simulation threatens the difference between "true" and "false", between "real" and "imaginary" '.[107] Simulations can have powerful effects on our senses and constructions of reality.

My point here can best be illustrated by referring to the changing character of killer whale and dolphin pools and how they are presented to the public. In many modernistic 'dolphinaria', constructed in the 1970s or thereabouts, a concrete pool painted in garish blue, with clear, sweeping lines and expansive vistas, contains the dolphins which are made to bounce coloured balls, jump through hoops, and somersault over sticks by their youthful, brightly dressed trainers. Here nature is visibly subjugated, tamed and arguably even improved by the triumph of human technology.

In the postmodern dolphinarium at Chicago Shedd Aquarium, however, the pool is surrounded on three sides by huge windows so the audience looks out onto and feels an inclusive part of what it might imagine to be the ocean, even though it is only Lake Michigan, in which a dolphin could never live. The vast oceanarium, of which the dolphin pool is a part, consists of a sophisticated reconstruction of the Pacific Northwest. The dolphins still do somersaults, slap their tails, and open their jaws on command, but now their quietly-spoken, 'ecologically correct' trainers in their gender-neutral wet-suits assure us that all this behaviour is 'natural', that they tell the dolphins not *what* to do, only *when* to do it. More than this, they say, making the dolphins open their jaws on command makes it less stressful when they need to have their teeth checked, just as cuddling the dolphins out of the water makes it easier to administer injections when they are sick – all in the interest of their health and natural development, of course.

The dolphins are doing the same captive dolphin tricks, but the simulated imagery gives their behaviour a very different meaning. This *simulation* of nature, its order and goodness, is achieved only by *dissimulating* not only the capture, control and containment of the animals which make the experience possible but also the suppression of the spontaneous, dangerous, unpredictable and possibly even unentertaining behaviour in which these animals might indulge if left to their own desires.

This postmodern phenomenon of safe simulation has a significance that extends far beyond the theatrical worlds of zoos, museums and theme parks.

Changing approaches to the in-service training and development of teachers have some disconcerting parallels with changing approaches to the training of dolphins! This is most evident in those activities in classrooms and staffrooms which involve creating cultures of cooperation and collaboration among students, teachers or both.

Co-operative learning   One example can be seen in the meteoric rise in North America of what has come to be called co-operative learning. Though there are several leading advocates of co-operative learning with different and often highly contested philosophies, it normally includes a range of specific classroom tasks with names like 'Jigsaw' or 'Think-Pair-Scheme', designed to build active, co-operative learning and involvement among students. There is also a somewhat specialized language of principles and procedures (such as five kinds of 'positive interdependencies') which teachers are asked to master in order to understand it fully and implement it effectively.[108] Co-operative learning involves students not just working *in* groups, but *as* groups, often in specific roles (for instance, as 'encouragers'). Because active group work is uncommon in most classrooms, co-operative learning undoubtedly offers valuable additions to teachers' repertoires of classroom strategies, especially when they are applied with flexibility and discretion. Indeed, I use many such strategies in my own teaching. However, advocates typically make a stronger case for co-operative learning than this.

For writers like Kagan[109] co-operative learning is not just another string to the teacher's bow, a useful addition to the repertoire. It responds to and compensates for a supposed 'socialization void' among many young people, especially culturally and socially disadvantaged ones, in their family and community relationships. Co-operative learning therefore supplies not only improved cognitive learning but also much needed social skills. Its designated tasks and roles and the specialized language which surrounds them are seen to address and fill up the void which many children are said to encounter in their homes and on the streets outside their schools.

However, researchers such as Rudduck[110] and Quicke[111] have demonstrated that many students from working-class and ethnic minority backgrounds do *not* lack the social skills of co-operation or experience a socialization void. Indeed, the cultures of their class and community already supply them with rich, if rather rough and ready, forms of association and assistance of an informal, spontaneous nature. In schools, these things often appear as 'cheating' - a form of co-operation that is unwanted and illegitimate in the school atmosphere of competitive achievement and hierarchical grading.

In this way, the insertion of co-operative learning into classroom teaching and learning can be read as a response not to a socialization void in home and community but to a void created by the school itself, with its disciplinary processes, and grading and assessment practices, that have already driven more dangerous, spontaneous, desire-laden forms of student collaboration out of the classroom and made them illegitimate. Co-operative learning is then inserted and inscribed as a contrived and controlled set of collaborative structures, practices and behaviours with its own special language. It becomes its own self-contained and self-affirming system – a safe simulation of the more spontaneous forms of student collaboration which the school and its teachers have already eradicated.

Contrived Collegiality Similar *safe simulations* of collaboration occur among teachers. These take the form of what I have elsewhere described as *contrived collegiality*.[112,113] Contrived collegiality occurs when spontaneous, dangerous and difficult-to-control forms of teacher collaboration are discouraged or usurped by administrators who capture, contain and contrive it through such things as compulsory co-operation, required collaborative planning, and processes of collaboration to implement non-negotiable programmes and curricula whose viability and practicality are not open to discussion. The point here is *not* that contrived collegiality is a manipulative, underhand way of tricking passive teachers into complying with administrative agendas, for I have documented elsewhere that teachers are very quick to see through such contrivances.[114,115] Rather, the administratively simulated image of collaboration becomes its own self-sustaining reality, with its own symbolic importance and legitimacy. In this sense, the major problem that contrived collegiality raises for teachers and their work is not that it is controlling and manipulative but that it is superficial and wasteful of their efforts and energies. It is not just that simulated collaboration is an imaginary front for 'real' collaboration. Rather, as simulations become more sophisticated and complex, the boundaries and distinctions between simulation and reality themselves begin to dissolve. It is no longer clear what is simulated and what is not.

As we move into the postmodern age, a key challenge for schools, administrators and teachers is whether they can live with or even actively encourage full-blown co-operative classrooms, collaborative staffrooms and self-managing schools that are charged with spontaneity, unpredictability, danger and desire; or whether they will opt for self-sustaining or be drawn into safe simulations of these things that are controlled, contrived and ultimately superficial in character.

BEYOND COLLABORATION

For teacher development and school reforms alike, committing to certain kinds of collaboration and becoming critical about others is important. But what has also become clear is the need to move beyond the principle of collaboration to moral principles that should guide it, and structures that can best support it, in the distinctive conditions of the postmodern age. I want to close this chapter by identifying some problems and justifying several ways in which we might move productively beyond collaboration without also abandoning it.

1. One of the spectres of the postmodern age is that it may become confusing and chaotic. Decentralized decision-making and the plurality and diversity of different voices can create a cacophony of fragmented and dissonant perspectives and desires.[116] Instead of a wealth and plurality of insight and perception, we can become trapped within an autistic culture of miscommunication and misunderstanding, a culture with no hope of consensus, community or common ground. School-based collaboration, for example, can be decentralized to such an extent that it becomes chaotic. Leaving the development of missions and visions to the complete discretion of each individual school and its teachers definitely runs this risk. Free-market systems of site-based management and parental choice of school institutionalize the problem even more deeply.[117]

2. The postmodern age can also be one where bureaucratic forces of regulation and control are reinstated behind postmodern façades of accessibility and diversity. Collaboration can be controlled and contrived. As in the corporate sphere, despite the existence of participatory decision-making at site-level, overall co-ordination of the terms and conditions of collaboration can be overly determined at the centre.[118] The *process* of collaboration can become bounded by and separated from decisions about its *products*.

3. An important challenge for school improvement and restructuring and the principles of collaboration contained within it is to articulate, listen to and bring together different voices in the educational and social community, and also to establish guiding ethical principles around which these voices and their purposes can cohere. Without an ethical discourse about or ethical principles underpinning collaboration and restructuring, contrived collegiality, for instance, can induce teachers' compliance with imposed curricula that are élitist and ethnocentric in nature, such as the British national curriculum with its emphasis on British history and British literature,[119] and thereby prejudice the achievements of those cultural and ethnic minorities which may be estranged from such curricular contents.[120] Similarly, where the form and focus of collaboration are entirely discretionary, teachers in secondary schools may, as McLaughlin has found,[121] collaborate over issues of academics and curriculum development in middle-class communities, and over very different preoccupations with young people and their social adjustment in more socially deprived ones. These different emphases may be read as pragmatic responses to the educational and social demands of each particular context, but they can also be seen as ways of perpetuating imbalances and inequities between those contexts.

4. Collaboration should not be confined to teachers and other educators themselves. What Michael Fullan and I have elsewhere advocated as interactive professionalism among teachers[122] can often become incestuous professionalism that excludes others. Zeichner has pointed to the 'almost total lack of attention to community empowerment in the mainstream educational literature advocating

teacher leadership and restructuring'.[123] Teachers are usually weak at explaining innovation to students and weaker still at involving them in its development.[124] If they restructure their strategies of assessment, they usually do so in ways that maintain students as objects of, rather than partners in, assessment.[125] Parents are often ignored or merely instructed late about the efforts their children's schools are making to restructure, yet schools which involve parents early in the restructuring process, even when its outcomes are still uncertain, are more likely to gain sympathy and support from the community rather than the anxiety and suspicion that usually surrounds change efforts.[126] So while collaboration and empowerment will mean more discretion for teachers in some domains, as they work more closely with students and parents, it should mean considerably less discretion in others.

5. Collaboration and restructuring need to be located within an ethical discourse and political parameters that guide individual schools, teachers and their communities in the quest to improve within their own settings. Not all educational purposes that teachers or communities pursue through the collaborative process may be appropriate. The ethical principles that guide collaborative efforts are, of course, contestable and should be open to public debate in order to set agreed system-wide goals and frameworks (though not specific and detailed contents) which guide the educational systems in which teachers work. Some subject teachers may otherwise be self-interestedly protective about maintaining their own subject domains, together with the socially and academically advantaged, university-bound students most likely to benefit from them. Zeichner points to the parallel danger that even where communities are involved in the collaborative process, 'what communities assert for their schools may be in conflict with principles of a democratic society, repressing particular points of view, or discriminating against certain groups of people'.[127] The defence of creationism and the imposition of Judaeo-Christian values on multi-faith communities are examples of this. Overall, argues Zeichner,

> Although we need to encourage and support a process of
> democratic deliberation within schools that includes parents and
> students as well as administrators and teachers, we need some
> way of making determinations about the 'goodness' of the choices
> that emerge from these deliberations . . . [that they] . . . do not
> violate certain moral standards, such as social justice and equity.

6. Collaboration will therefore not always be smooth and easy but will place interests, careers and identities in jeopardy and create conflict. Indeed, as Louis and Miles argue, if there is no such conflict, the changes being attempted are probably superficial.[128] Conflict is a necessary part of change,[129] and is also desirable as a way of generating and working through critical dialogue about educational and social purposes and the current structures and interests which prevent their realization.[130] Teachers and leaders need to be prepared for the best

171

way to value and work through such conflict in constructive ways for the sake of educational improvement.

7. There needs to be honest acknowledgement of the fact that the possibilities for establishing more vibrant and vigorous teacher cultures are seriously limited by the existing structures in which many teachers work. If teachers are to interact more flexibly, learn from each other more extensively, and improve their own expertise continuously, then new structures may need to be created pre-emptively which make this more possible. Respecting the teacher's voice should not mean romanticizing it: validating everything that a teacher says simply because a teacher has said it. As I noted earlier, teachers' hopes and fears are deeply embedded within and to some extent limited by the historically ingrained structures within which they work – many of which are the very source of the problems of underachievement and inequity which change efforts are otherwise trying to address. Teachers can be expected to be committed voluntarily to change, collaboration and improved education for their students. But such voluntary commitments are, in most cases, unlikely to extend to reshaping or abandoning the basic structures in which teachers' own interests and identities have been formed. Yet the interests of student equity and achievement may demand that these structures be changed, with or without teachers' collaborative involvement. The future of educational restructuring may, in this sense, need to embrace the principles of teacher collaboration and empowerment, without necessarily accepting or endorsing all teachers' existing conceptions of these things.

NOTES AND REFERENCES

1. Fullan, M., *The New Meaning of Educational Change*. New York: Teachers College Press, 1991.

2. Fullan, M. and Hargreaves, A., *What's Worth Fighting For?: Working Together for your School*. Toronto: Ontario Public School Teachers' Federation; Milton Keynes: Open University Press; Andover, MA: The Network, North East Lab, USA; Melbourne: Australian Council for Educational Administration, 1991.

3. Joyce, B. and Showers, B., *Student Achievement Through Staff Development*. New York: Longman, 1988.

4. Little, J. W., 'District policy choices and teachers' professional development opportunities'. *Educational Evaluation and Policy Analysis*, **11**, pp. 165–79, 1989.

5. Little, J. W., 'Teachers' professional development in a climate of educational reform'. *Educational Evaluation and Policy Analysis*, **15** (2), pp. 129–52, 1993.

6. Joyce and Showers, op. cit., note 3.

7. Little, op. cit., note 5.

8. Kuhn, T., *The Structure of Scientific Revolutions*. Chicago: University of Chicago Press, 1962.

9. Woods, P., 'Teaching for survival'. In Woods, P. and Hammersley, M. (eds), *School Experience*. London: Croom Helm, 1977.

10. Hammersley, M., 'Staffroom news'. In Hargreaves, A. and Woods, P. (eds), *Classrooms and Staffrooms*. Milton Keynes: Open University Press, 1984.

11. Nias, J., Southworth, G. and Yeomans, R., *Staff Relationships in the Primary School*. London: Cassell, 1989.

12. Nias, J., Southworth, G. and Campbell, P., *Whole School Curriculum Development in the Primary School*. London: Falmer Press, 1992.

13. Little, J. W., 'The persistence of privacy: autonomy and initiative in teachers' professional relations'. *Teachers College Record*, **91** (4), pp. 509–36, 1990.

14. Fullan and Hargreaves, op. cit., note 2.

15. Noddings, N., *The Challenge to Care in Schools*. New York: Teachers College Press, 1992.

16. Acker, S., 'Women teachers working together'. Unpublished manuscript. Toronto: Ontario Institute for Studies in Education, 1993.

17. Campbell, R. J., *Developing the Primary Curriculum*. London: Cassell, 1985.

18. Hargreaves, A. and Macmillan, R., 'Balkanized secondary schools and the malaise of modernity'. In Siskin, L. and Little, J. (eds), *Perspectives on Departments*. New York: Teachers College Press (forthcoming).

19. Sizer, T., *Horace's School: Redesigning the American High School*. Boston: Houghton-Mifflin, 1992.

20. Ashton, P. and Webb, R., *Making a Difference: Teachers' Sense of Efficacy and Student Achievement*. New York: Longman, 1986.

21. Rosenholtz, S., *Teachers' Workplace*. New York: Longman, 1989.

22. Sarason, S., *The Predictable Failure of Educational Reform*. San Francisco: Jossey-Bass, 1990.

23. Mortimore, P., Sammons, P., Stoll, L. *et al.*, *School Matters: The Junior Years*. Berkeley, CA: University of California, 1988.

24. Barth, R., *Improving Schools from Within*. San Francisco: Jossey-Bass, 1990.

25. Greenfield, W., *Instructional Leadership: Concepts, Issues and Controversies*. Boston, MA: Allyn and Bacon, 1987.

26. Flinders, D. J., 'Teachers' isolation and the new reform'. *Journal of Curriculum and Supervision*, **4** (1), pp. 17–29, 1988.

27. McTaggart, R., 'Bureaucratic rationality and the self-educating profession: the problem of teacher privatism'. *Journal of Curriculum Studies*, **21** (4), pp. 345–61, 1989.

28. Hoyle, E., 'The study of schools as organizations'. In MacHugh, R. and Morgan, C. (eds), *Management in Education*, Reader 1. London: Ward Lock, 1975.

29. Apple, M., *Teachers and Texts*. New York: Routledge & Kegan Paul, p. 45, 1989.

30. Robertson, S., *Teachers' Labour and Post-Fordism: An Exploratory Analysis*. Deakin: Deakin University Press (forthcoming).

31. Hargreaves, A., *Curriculum and Assessment Reform*. Milton Keynes: Open University Press, 1989.

32. Hargreaves, A., *Changing Teachers, Changing Times: Teachers' Work and Culture in the Postmodern Age*. London: Cassell; New York: Teachers College Press; Toronto: OISE Press, 1994.

33. Werner, W., 'Program implementation and experienced time'. *Alberta Journal of Educational Research*, **XXXIV** (2), pp. 90–108, 1988.

34. Rudduck, J., *Innovation and Change*. Milton Keynes: Open University Press; Toronto: OISE Press, 1990.

35. Fullan, op. cit., note 1.

36. Huberman, M. and Miles, M., *Innovation Up Close*. New York: Plenum, 1984.

37. Hargreaves, A., Leithwood, K., Gérin-Lajoie, D., Cousins, B. and Thiessen, D., *Years of Transition: Times for Change*. Toronto: Queen's Printer, 1993.

38. Hargreaves, A. and Dawe, R., 'Paths of professional development: contrived collegiality, collaborative culture and the case of peer coaching'. *Teaching and Teacher Education*, **6** (3), pp. 227–41, 1990.

39. Rosenholtz, op. cit., note 21.

40. Reicken, T., 'School improvement and the culture of the schools'. Unpublished PhD thesis, University of British Columbia, Vancouver, 1989.

41. Joyce and Showers, op. cit., note 3.

42. Lytle, S. and Cochran-Smith, M., 'Learning from teacher-research: a working typology'. *Teachers College Record*, **92** (1), pp. 83–103, 1990.

43. Elliott, J., *Action Research for Educational Change*. Milton Keynes: Open University Press, 1991.

44. Murphy, J., *Restructuring Schools: Capturing the Phenomena.* New York: Teachers College Press, 1992.

45. Woods, P. (ed.), *Working for Teacher Development.* Dereham, Norfolk: Peter Francis Publishers, 1989.

46. Lortie, D., *Schoolteacher.* Chicago: University of Chicago Press, 1975.

47. Hargreaves and Macmillan, op. cit., note 18.

48. Richardson, V., 'How and why teachers change'. In Conley, S. C. and Cooper, B. S. (eds), *The School as a Work Environment: Implications for Reform.* Needham, MA: Allyn and Bacon, 1991.

49. Huberman, M., *The Lives of Teachers.* London: Cassell; New York: Teachers College Press, 1993.

50. Hargreaves, A., Davis, J., Fullan, M., Wignall, R., Stager, M. and Macmillan, R., *Secondary School Work Cultures and Educational Change.* Final report of a project funded by the OISE Transfer Grant. Toronto: Ontario Institute for Studies in Education, 1992.

51. Rosenholtz, op. cit., note 21.

52. Senge, P., *The Fifth Discipline.* New York: Doubleday, 1990.

53. Fullan, M., *Change Forces; Probing the Depths of Educational Reform.* New York: Falmer Press, 1993.

54. Little, op. cit., note 13.

55. Fullan and Hargreaves, op. cit., note 2.

56. Hargreaves, op. cit., note 32.

57. Woods, op. cit., note 9.

58. Becker, H., 'The career of the Chicago public school teacher'. *American Journal of Sociology,* **57**, March 1952.

59. Nias, J., *Primary Teachers Talking.* London: Routledge, 1989.

60. McLaughlin, M. W. and Talbert, J. E., *Contexts that Matter for Teaching and Learning.* Stanford: Centre for Research on the Context of Secondary School Teaching, p. 17, 1993.

61. Havel, V., 'The end of the modern era'. *New York Times,* 1 March 1992.

62. Habermas, J., *The Philosophical Discourse of Modernity.* Cambridge: Polity Press, 1987.

63. Turner, B. S., 'Periodization and politics in the postmodern'. In Turner, B. S., *Theories of Modernity and Postmodernity*. London: Sage Publications, 1990.

64. Toffler, A., *Powershift*. New York: Bantam Books, 1990.

65. Weber, M., *General Economic History*. 1968. Reprint. New Brunswick and London: Transaction Books, 1981.

66. Hargreaves, D., *The Challenge for the Comprehensive School*. London: Routledge & Kegan Paul, 1982.

67. Powell, A., Farrar, E. and Cohen, D., *The Shopping Mall High School: Winners and Losers in the Educational Marketplace*. Boston, Houghton & Mifflin, 1985.

68. Taylor, C., *The Malaise of Modernity*. Concord, Ontario: House of Anansi Press, 1991.

69. Harvey, D., *The Condition of Postmodernity*. Oxford: Basil Blackwell, 1989.

70. Ibid.

71. Toffler, op. cit., note 64.

72. Ibid.

73. Harvey, op. cit., note 69.

74. Piore, M. and Sabel, M., *The Second Industrial Divide*. New York: Basic Books, 1984.

75. Atkinson, J., 'Flexibility: planning for an uncertain future'. *Manpower Policy and Practice*, **1**, pp. 12–25, Summer 1985.

76. MacDonald, M., 'Post-Fordism and the flexibility debate'. *Studies in Political Economy*, **36**, pp. 177–201, 1991.

77. Harvey, op. cit., note 69.

78. Ibid.

79. Ibid.

80. Leinberger, P. and Tucker, B., *The New Individualists: The Generation after the Organization Man*. New York: Harper Collins, 1991.

81. Taylor, op. cit., note 68.

82. Kanter, R. M., Stein, B. A. and Jick, T. D., *The Challenge of Organizational Change*. New York: The Free Press, p. 3, 1992.

83. Ibid.

84.   Toffler, op. cit., note 64.

85.   Ibid., p. 215.

86.   Ibid., p. 216.

87.   Senge, op. cit., note 52.

88.   Hargreaves, *et al.*, op. cit., note 50.

89.   Lieberman, A. and McLaughlin, M., 'Network for educational change: powerful and problematic'. *Phi Delta Kappan*, **73** (9), pp. 673–7, 1992.

90.   Buenger, C., *Cincinnati Business Committee Task Force on Public Schools*. Cincinnati, OH: Cincinnati Business Committee, 1991.

91.   Tonkin, D., 'The Australian National Schools Project: some early issues'. Paper presented to OCED experts' meeting on Rethinking Schooling: Changing Patterns of Work Organization, Perth, Australia, 1992.

92.   Chadbourne, R., *The National Schools Project in Western Australia*. Perth: International Institute for Policy and Administrative Studies, 1992.

93.   Robertson, op. cit., note 30.

94.   Menzies, H., *Fast Forward and Out of Control: How Technology Controls Our Lives*. Toronto: Macmillan, 1989.

95.   Ibid., p. 151.

96.   Harvey, op. cit., note 69.

97.   Caldwell, B. J. and Spinks, J., *The Self-Managing School*. New York: Falmer Press, 1988.

98.   Caldwell, B. J. and Spinks, J., *Leading the Self-Managing School*. New York: Falmer Press, 1988.

99.   Hargreaves, A., and Reynolds, D., 'Decomprehensivization'. In Hargreaves, A. and Reynolds, D., *Educational Policies: Controversies and Critiques*. New York: Falmer Press, 1989.

100.   Hargreaves, op. cit., note 31.

101.   Troyna, B., *Racism and Education*. Milton Keynes: Open University Press, 1993.

102.   Renihan, F. I. and Renihan, P., 'Educational leadership: a renaissance metaphor'. *Education Canada*, **11**, p. 11, 1992.

103.   Baudrillard, J., *America*. London and New York: Verso Press, p. 34, 1988.

104. Baudrillard, J., *Simulations*. Columbia University, New York: Semiotext, 1983.

105. Ibid., p. 13.

106. Eco, U., *Travels in Hyperreality*. San Diego, CA: Harcourt Brace Jovanovich, 1990.

107. Baudrillard, op. cit., note 104, p. 5.

108. Johnson, D. W. and Johnson, R. T., 'Social skills for successful group work'. *Educational Leadership*, **47** (4), pp. 29–33, 1989/90.

109. Kagan, S., 'Constructive controversy'. *Cooperative Learning*, **10** (3), pp. 20–26, 1990.

110. Rudduck, op. cit., note 34.

111. Quicke, J., 'Personal and social education: a triangulated evaluation of an innovation'. *Educational Review*, **38** (3), pp. 217–28, 1986.

112. Hargreaves, A., 'Contrived collegiality: the micropolitics of teacher collaboration'. In Blase, J. (ed.), *The Politics of Life in Schools*. London: Sage, 1991.

113. Hargreaves, op. cit., note 32.

114. Hargreaves, op. cit., note 112.

115. Hargreaves, op. cit., note 32.

116. Ibid.

117. Smyth, J. (ed.), *A Socially Critical View of the Self-Managing School*. New York: Falmer Press, 1993.

118. Menzies, op. cit., note 94.

119. Goodson, I. F., 'Nations at risk and national curriculum: ideology and identity'. In *Politics of Education Association Yearbook*. Taylor & Francis Ltd, pp. 219–52, 1990.

120. Blair, M., 'Black teachers, black students and education markets'. Paper presented to International Sociology of Education Conference, University of Sheffield, 1993.

121. McLaughlin, M., 'What matters most in teachers' workplace context?' In McLaughlin, M. and Little, J. W. (eds), *Cultures and Contexts of Teaching*. New York: Teachers College Press, 1992.

122. Fullan and Hargreaves, op. cit., note 2.

123. Zeichner, K. M., 'Contradictions and tensions in the professionalization of teaching and the democratization of schools'. *Teachers College Record*, **92** (3), pp. 363–79 (p. 368), 1991.

124. Ruddock, op. cit., note 34.

125. Hargreaves *et al.*, op. cit., note 37.

126. Ainley, J., 'Parents and the transition years'. In Hargreaves, A., Gérin-Lajoie, D. and Thiessen D., *Years of Transition, Times for Change: A Review and Analysis of Pilot Projects Investigating Issues in the Transition Years*. Toronto: Queen's Printer, pp. 293–316, 1993.

127. Zeichner, op. cit., note 123.

128. Louis, K. and Miles, M. B., *Improving the Urban High School: What Works and Why*. New York: Teachers College Press, 1990.

129. Lieberman, A., Darling-Hammond, L. and Zuckerman, D., *Early Lessons in Restructuring Schools*. New York: National Centre for Restructuring Education, Schools and Teaching (NCREST), 1991.

130. Little, op. cit., note 5.

Chapter 10

Mentor and Mentoring: Did Homer Have It Right?

Marilyn Cochran-Smith and Cynthia L. Paris

More than a dozen recent articles on professional development, pre-service teacher education and state-mandated teacher induction mention that the term 'mentoring' is taken from Homer's epic poem *The Odyssey*.[1-4] As we may recall from our high school English classes, Homer's character Mentor, an old friend of Odysseus, was 'entrusted [with] his whole household when he sailed [for Troy] ... with orders to keep everything intact'[5] and especially to look after Telemachus, Odysseus' son. Many of the articles that point out the origin of the term imply that Homer had it right about modern-day mentoring when he described the guidance with which Mentor provided Telemachus, and thus imply that we ought to preserve the essence of the ancient relationship when we design mentoring programmes in school and university settings.[6,7]

Before we work to preserve the classical relationship, let us look more closely at the mentoring that goes on in *The Odyssey*. To begin with, Homer tells us nothing about what transpired between Mentor and the child Telemachus during the 20-odd years that Odysseus was away from Ithaca. When the poem begins, we know only that a horde of suitors are squandering the wealth and occupying the house of the former king, and although Telemachus is disconsolate, he has done nothing about the situation. It is not until Athene, Odysseus' long-time champion, visits Telemachus that he begins to take action. Disguised as the old man Mentor, Athene spends time encouraging and inspiring Telemachus, but she spends much more time dispensing precise instructions about what to do, and at one critical point stops giving directions altogether and simply does the job herself, magically assuming Telemachus' own form and voice while he sleeps.

It is Athene, then, who is the leading mentor in *The Odyssey*. She appears to Telemachus throughout the poem – usually in Mentor's form – giving authoritative instructions and, when necessary, taking over and doing herself what she fears Telemachus will not be able to do. Athene-as-divine-mentor, who intervenes through commandments, apparitions and ventriloquism, works extraordinarily well in Homer's epic tale of men, gods and magic. With Athene's help

Telemachus matures in courage and wisdom and rightfully deserves his measure of credit for the bloody (but just) conclusion of the tale when Odysseus is restored to the throne.

Contrary to recent articles and to prevailing practice, however, Homer's 'Mentor', who persuades, directly instructs, and takes over when necessary, is quite unsuitable as an image for working with new and beginning teachers. The very mortal, un-magic and female profession of teaching requires another vision of mentoring. In this chapter we offer an alternative by exploring three of the central characteristics of mentoring – source and status of knowledge for teaching, role relationships of mentor and mentee, and orientation to social and school reform. We contrast this alternative vision with prevailing practice, arguing that mentoring has the greatest potential to contribute to reform in teacher education and in the teaching profession when it is based on teachers' ways of knowing, women's ways of collaborating, and school and social change agendas.

MENTORING BEGINNING TEACHERS: PREVAILING PRACTICE

The prevailing view of mentoring is explicit in state and school district guidelines for teacher induction programmes,[8–11] in descriptions of pre-service teacher preparation and new teacher induction programmes that employ mentors,[12–16] and in syntheses of effective mentoring practices published by professional organizations.[17–19] Drawing largely on business and industry definitions of mentoring, these documents presume that the mentoring relationship is hierarchically structured and that its major goal is the beginner's effective job performance and smooth socialization into the culture of the workplace.

Although the details of mentoring practice differ significantly from one site to another, criteria for selecting mentors and establishing their responsibilities are similar across sites. Mentors are selected for their demonstrated excellence in classroom teaching.[20–23] With few exceptions, they are expected to keep their knowledge of students 'fresh' and their ties to classroom teaching strong and recent.[24–26]

These criteria would seem to suggest that it is *teachers'* knowledge of classrooms, students and teaching that is to be valued and utilized in mentoring relationships – that teachers who have spent their professional lives working inside schools have essential knowledge, unique perspectives and critical skills to share with beginning teachers. However, in actual mentoring practice, there is a curious paradox at work – in order to become official mentors, and *prior* to their work with beginners, experienced teachers are commonly trained in university researchers' knowledge and language for classroom instruction and in university-generated models of clinical supervision and of the needs of new teachers.[27,28] The university domination of mentors' training makes it clear that it is researchers' rather than teachers' knowledge and skills that are essential for

182

the beginning teacher. The competent beginner is defined as one who is learning to make sound professional decisions using the concepts, strategies and language of university-generated research on teaching and management,[29–33] and similarly the competent mentor is defined as one who is able to provide systematic feedback, demonstration and coaching in these same areas.

We use descriptions of mentoring in the state-wide induction programmes of our home states (Pennsylvania and New Jersey, respectively) to provide some detail about the concept of mentoring that underlines prevailing practice for first- and second-year teachers. In New Jersey, for example, mentoring was first embedded in The Provisional Teacher Program, the state's alternative certification procedure that bypasses traditional pre-service preparation. Since 1992, however, alternative-route teachers and all other new teachers have been issued provisional certificates and assigned to a Professional Support Team which includes a mentor, the building principal, a college faculty member and a curriculum specialist. In Pennsylvania, in order to qualify for permanent certification, beginners are required to participate in an induction programme, the centrepiece of which is a structured relationship with a mentor. In Pennsylvania the mentor's role is defined as a 'personal relationship' in which 'instruction and guidance' are provided so that the beginner achieves 'a practical, working command of what is known about how to teach effectively'.[34] The mentor's role in New Jersey is defined by a list of activities including orienting the beginner to district and school 'policies, procedures, and expectations', providing 'feedback, coaching, and support', modelling 'effective teaching techniques', and providing 'informal support and consultation'.[35] In both states, the interactions between mentors and beginners are expected to be sensitive, non-judgemental and supportive, and it is specified that they are intended to focus on the beginners' classroom performance.

State-wide mentoring programmes for beginning teachers share many of the characteristics of mentoring for pre-service teachers. Although mentors for student teachers have traditionally been selected expediently, poorly trained and only marginally connected to the teacher education programme,[36] the situation is changing. Experienced co-operating teachers are increasingly taken seriously as mentors for student teachers and invited to play larger roles in restructured pre-service programmes. In many of these instances, however, co-operating teachers are selected for the congruity of their practice with that advocated by the teacher-education institution,[37] and they are trained prior to their work as mentors in the knowledge base generated and developed by those who work outside schools. Training programmes mostly emphasize effective teaching strategies[38–42] and clinical supervision/conferencing.[43–45]

Like mentors in induction programmes, then, what mentors in pre-service programmes are expected to do is help beginners implement 'best practice' and adopt the language and culture of the local site as quickly as possible.[46] When mentoring is seen in this way, however, it serves to reproduce rather than to

183

reconsider curriculum, pedagogy and the structural arrangements of schooling – arrangements in which inequities based on race, culture and gender are deeply embedded. It also disempowers teachers by devaluing the professional knowledge and theory that are grounded in practice and relegating teachers to the role of receivers rather than producers of knowledge. In the remainder of this chapter we posit an alternative vision of mentoring, one that stretches the boundaries of both the classical model and prevailing practice.

UNDERSTANDING MENTORING: THREE CHARACTERISTICS

We consider mentoring according to three central characteristics: source and status of knowledge for teaching, role relationships of mentor and mentee, and orientation to social and school reform. We describe each in turn, contrasting prevailing practice with practice based on an alternative vision.

Source and Status of Knowledge for Teaching: From Knowledge Base to Teachers' Way of Knowing

How about some inclusive language?

The mentoring literature allows that part of a mentor's knowledge is her 'disposition for inquiry'[47] and her ability to 'reflect' on her own work.[48,49] In practice, however, many mentoring programmes controvert an epistemology based on the experience of teaching and pre-empt teachers' knowledge by a university-certified 'knowledge base'. What we wish to argue here is that mentoring will not reach its potential as a strategy for reform in teaching and teacher education until it is based on an epistemology that includes teachers' ways of knowing and acting about teaching. This does not mean that mentors should *never* suggest strategies for instruction and management derived from the university-certified knowledge base or that they should *not* provide beginners with information about school and school district norms and procedures. We are suggesting, however, that the content of interactions among mentors and beginners needs to be much richer and more substantive than that.[50]

Teachers' way of knowing[51,52] include how teachers treat the data of school life as diverse texts to be connected and interpreted, how they see the events in their classrooms, how they think through issues and raise questions, and how they interpret children's actions. These ways of knowing also include the questions that teachers consider unanswerable, the kinds of information they consider problematic, where they look for evidence to document and explore particular issues, and which bodies of knowledge they bring to bear on particular situations. If teaching is regarded as an intellectual activity and teachers are among those who have the authority to generate knowledge about teaching, then a central task involved in mentoring is supporting beginners as they learn to be knowers.

This means learning to be not only critical consumers and interpreters of other people's knowledge but also knowledge-makers who formulate analytical frameworks, pose problems of practice and develop conjoined ways of collecting and connecting evidence in order to make decisions about teaching.

A recent analysis of the developmental and socio-historical foundations of mentoring by Gallimore, Tharp and John-Steiner[53,54] is particularly useful for thinking about the kinds of mentoring contexts that would make teachers' ways of knowing central. They base their argument on the premise that all higher-order psychological functions have their origins in everyday social settings that give children, apprentices and other mentees opportunities to participate with mentors in goal-directed activities. Cautioning that mentors have minimal effects on apprentices' learning when their *only* purpose is to mentor and their *only* joint activity the process of mentoring itself, they argue that mentors must participate *with* mentees in social activities that have meaningful products as their goals. Their work suggests that what are needed in mentoring programmes are contexts in which mentors work with one another and with beginners in order to accomplish joint work, not just in order to mentor or be mentored.

We think that the productive work in which mentors and beginning teachers can best engage is the collaborative construction of knowledge about teaching. This is obviously not an easy process to illustrate. But it is possible, as the following excerpt from a weekly school-site meeting of three student teachers, their three experienced teacher mentors and a university supervisor suggests.[55] It is important to note that this interaction is *not* based on transmission of the knowledge base in which one teacher (the mentor) tells another teacher (the beginner) what is positive and negative about what happens in some set of classroom events and then prescribes the management and instructional strategies that might be applied to make the situation more effective. Nor, however, does the interaction feature a more experienced teacher offering moral support to a less experienced one, helping her to define problem areas for further observation, or prompting her to reflect on what happens in particular classroom episodes. Rather than focusing on the interactions of two teachers, one transmitting knowledge and one receiving it, and centring on 'the lesson' as the unit of analysis, the mentoring interaction below is located within the context of an intellectual community where everybody is engaged in the real work of learning about teaching. The unit of analysis is not the lesson but rather particular incidents and cases over time that relate conceptually and thematically to the more abstract principles being constructed.[56]

> **Third Grade Mentor**   I was thinking about a boy we had –
> Darryl. He was in fourth grade and was still not writing and was
> drawing pictures that were very complicated and detailed. . . .
> [His] pictures were so incredibly detailed.

Fourth Grade Mentor   Yes, what Darryl actually did by fourth grade in art was what writers do with their words. He was trying to add the past and the present in his drawings. What would happen was he would begin with the drawing and add another layer on top and another layer on top. . . . [But] he was not able to make that shift and do it in words, put that kind of thought on paper.

Fourth Grade Beginner   Also with the third and fourth graders, the picture is very important to them too. When I've read with them and there is a picture, I've had situations that maybe the picture might be of what's to come and not what they've read already so that when [just] the picture is there they say, 'Wait a minute, where's the mother?' . . . [The picture seems to] give them an extra thing to think about . . . and I think it helps them give the story a stronger foundation in their minds.

Third Grade Mentor   I think of Clarence years ago, this little boy whom I thought was brilliant, but [that] didn't show up on the test and [he] came from a really deprived background, and he wrote very stilted kinds of stories, and he hated to draw. . . . The summer between second and third grade [was important] . . . September, the first day of school, he came to me and said he had a drawing book that he had taken out and must have kept all summer from the library, how to draw things. He said, 'I worked with this book all summer and now I can draw.' He worked all summer to draw and his pictures were big and detailed, and [then] also his writing [changed]. There really was a connection.

Fourth Grade Mentor   I used to feel at first when kids wanted to trace that I shouldn't let them do it and if the kids wanted to copy stories when I first taught third and fourth grade, I didn't want them to do it. But for some kids they've lost that connection and the only way to let that back in is to allow that to happen. So drawing books even when they trace first [are important] . . . The tracing is helpful to them because it re-establishes the ability to do it. Also copying stories – two years ago, when Timmy was in our room as a third grader, he . . . just couldn't write more than a couple of words. [But] he was really interested in the insects and the animals we had in our room and I gave him a book to copy. . . . He copied it, and then he copied a couple of other books and then he wrote a story on watching the insects. And then he started. He never got to that point where he was so wonderfully fluent, but [copying] broke the barrier for him.

In this excerpt, just a thin slice from a 90-minute conversation, mentors worked with one another and with beginners toward a conjoined product – a general explanation about children as users of language and visual symbols and their relationship to classroom learning opportunities that support growth and development in these areas. Over the course of this lengthy conversation, participants weighed their explanations at the same time as they weighed the usefulness of various practices. As they collaborated in this discussion, the teachers not only constructed meanings for the actions of particular children but also constructed meanings for the ways these were connected to one another. Mentors clearly had more to say than beginners, but this is not surprising nor undesirable when we think of mentoring as the joint work of more and less experienced teachers rather than as the delivery of knowledge from one to another.

It is also important to note that the joint product in the above example is not the translation of theory to practice, and even less the correct application of general procedures to specific classroom situations. Rather, the product is conjoined understanding – the joint building of an explanation based on closely observed children across classrooms and time periods. In this discussion the knowledge of experienced teachers rather than of a university-certified knowledge base is privileged. The teachers draw on their experiences over the course of many years spent observing children in the process of learning how to express their stories artistically and in written words. They describe children's learning from rich historical perspectives – how certain children struggled in kindergarten or first grade to break into print and how they fared toward the end of their elementary school years. They mention their uncertainties about which literacy practices were most helpful for young children, and they reflect on how their practices changed over time. They try out explanations that seem to fit several cases, but they always ground these in specific instances of practice.

When mentors and beginners engage in interactions where teachers' knowledge is privileged and where the joint product is understanding some particular aspect of teaching, a significant by-product of the interactions is disclosure to beginners of experienced teachers' ways of knowing. In other words, joint authentic work among mentors and beginners reveals mentors' ways of thinking. Hence their conversations function as vehicles for disclosure: they make explicit and visible the usually implicit and invisible ways of knowing of experienced teachers[57] and provide beginners with a window on what Dewey called their 'habits of mind'.[58] This does not mean that when mentoring focuses on teachers' knowledge it can teach beginners to interpret teaching situations in the ways that experienced teachers do, or prompt them to raise and explore the kinds of questions experienced teachers consider. But it does mean that within the social context of joint collaborative work, where mentors carry much of the burden for reflection and inquiry, beginners have opportunities to learn *ways to learn* from teaching.

Role Relationships of Mentors and Mentees: From Expert-Novice to Collaborators

An epistemology that favours research-based knowledge for teaching affords higher status and power to those who possess that knowledge and lower status to those who must depend upon others to transmit it.[59] Commonly the role relationships of mentor and beginner follow along these lines: expert status is bestowed on the mentor who has been trained in the knowledge of the academy, while the beginner is regarded as a novice in need of that knowledge. This status differential is often played out in dyadic tutorial relationships in which the mentor coaches the beginner in effective teaching strategies, initiates her into the standard practices and norms of a particular school culture and offers emotional support. In each of these roles the mentor provides and the beginner receives. Even in programmes based on a clinical supervision model of mentoring, where there are formalized mechanisms for the beginner to identify her own goals and evaluate her own classroom performance, the role of the beginner is largely to be the object of other people's activity rather than a participant in some kind of joint work.

It is clear from the literature cited in many recent articles on teacher mentoring, that a hierarchical image of mentor-mentee role relationships is drawn from research on adult male development, specifically career paths in male-dominated professions. A particularly productive line of analysis has demonstrated the positive effects of a paternalistic mentoring relationship wherein a younger male mentee 'admires' and 'emulates' an older male mentor who functions as a model for imitation and a source of sage advice as the younger man moves up the career ladder.[60] Not surprisingly, it has been pointed out that this male career model may be quite inappropriate in a profession dominated by women and characterized by a flat career path.[61] Our own experience working over many years with new and experienced teachers, most of whom are women, suggests that they often resist the masculine business image of mentor. In fact, when experienced teachers are cast in helping roles with their colleagues (beginners or otherwise), they tend to shun distinguishing titles or other indications that they hold greater knowledge, status, or power than others, and they often face resistance or resentment from their colleagues.[62,63]

From a masculine perspective on mentoring that assumes a hierarchical relationship, the solution to this problem is to alter the culture of the profession by formalizing selection criteria and training programmes and hence certifying officially both that mentors hold sanctioned knowledge and that their differentiated leadership roles are justified. When this happens in schools, however, the more powerful informal culture of equity tends to diminish, deny or obscure the mentor's role through status and resource reduction.[64] One possible conclusion here is that there is something wrong with (women) teachers or with the way in which they approach the task of mentoring. However, when a feminist perspective on collaboration and a social constructivist view of knowledge are assumed, it is possible to reach another more constructive conclusion.

From a feminist perspective on knowledge, power, and joint work, a non-hierarchical view of mentoring that is both more complex and more elusive than the male model follows. While acknowledging asymmetry in their relationships, women find it possible at the same time to position themselves differently in relation both to each other and to the knowledge that is the focus of their work together. In her sensitive exploration of relationships in women's lives, Bateson suggests that women often construct relationships that are asymmetrical in terms of the knowledge or experience each brings but at the same time symmetrical in the ways they interact with one another through collaboration and 'mutual discovery' enriched by 'many dimensions of difference'.[65] Bateson attempts to capture these relationships with language but at the same time rejects all the existing terms that describe asymmetry because they 'imply hierarchy and have curious undertones of exploitation or dominance'.[66] She eventually concludes that there *are* no words that convey both symmetry and asymmetry at once.

Mentoring relationships that assume both asymmetry *and* equal participation in conjoined work not only offer an alternative to the strictly hierarchical positioning of participants but also create social contexts uniquely suited to the construction and critique of knowledge about teaching. Dewey's argument against a transmission model of teaching[67] suggests a way to think about the relationship of mentors who have a wealth of professional knowledge and beginners who have a relatively small but growing accumulation of knowledge. Dewey does not suggest that the teacher deny her knowledge or 'stand off and look on'. He argues instead that 'the alternative to furnishing ready-made subject matter and listening to the accuracy with which it is reproduced is not quiescence, but participation [and] sharing in an activity'.[68]

In some versions of mentoring, the mentor or coach seems to be expected to deliver ready-made knowledge and then evaluate how closely the beginner has reproduced it. In the alternative version of mentoring for which we are arguing, the roles of both mentor and beginner revolve around shared activity where, as Dewey reminds us, 'the teacher is learner and the learner is, without knowing it, a teacher'.[69] This shared activity is possible when beginners and mentors work together to understand teaching, learning and schooling. In many instances the medium for this work is talk, but it is not the discourse of instruction or the didactic talk that women frequently experience as silencing or pre-empting.[70] It is instead 'real talk', characterized by the 'absence of domination' and the presence of 'reciprocity and cooperating'. As the examples throughout this chapter suggest, this kind of talk 'draws on the analytic abilities' of each participant[71] and honours the knowledge that each one brings to the discourse.

189

One community composed of mentors for student teachers and for first- and second-year teachers explored the way to create mentoring relationships that drew on their own knowledge but did not disempower beginners or interfere with beginners' own processes of coming to know. In the following excerpt from a weekly dialogue, group members focused on when to 'be directive' – telling beginners what they wanted or appeared to need to know, when to support them in constructing their own understandings, and how to achieve a balance between the two.

Although taken in chronological order, the comments that follow appear at times to be contradictory and/or vacillating. They are. However, they also accurately represent the work over time of a group of mentors struggling to construct ways to position themselves in relation to beginners and to knowledge itself.

> **Pre-school Mentor (working with a new teacher)** The problem that I'm encountering is when I go and speak with her I don't want to come out and tell her what to do. It's not that I don't want to be direct, but I'm trying to get her to bring things out of herself.

> **English Teacher Mentor (working with a second-year alternative route teacher)** He felt he needed to be told what to do with classroom management issues – when he felt he just didn't know what to do – when he was groping his way through trying this and trying that and trying to be stern and that wasn't working. He just needed somebody to say, 'Here's a strategy. Here's how to do it. Go forth and try it. I'll come see how it looks and we'll talk about it'.

> **Maths Teacher Mentor (working with a first-year teacher)** We've all grappled with the idea of, 'Why am I better? Where do I come off telling him [or her] what to do?' However, if you're . . . in that position [of knowing that you need to tell], I think you have to take responsibility and do it when it is necessary.

> **English Teacher Mentor (working with a second-year alternative route teacher)** But part of the metamorphosis [of the beginner] that we were talking about earlier [involves] not necessarily giving the beginner *our* way of thinking about it or *our* way of doing it but helping the beginner come to his or her *own* understandings.

As they talked to each other and to the beginners with whom they were paired, these mentors explored some of the ways in which they could use their professional knowledge to support beginners who also needed to construct their own understandings. Members of this group had very different prior experiences working in mentor-like roles. Despite their different experiences, all of the mentors seemed to want to construct relationships with one another and with beginners that were asymmetrical but not hierarchical. Their ongoing struggle with the mentoring relationship reflects the fact that there are no models or language for asymmetrical, non-hierarchical helping relationships in the culture of the teaching profession, although there is a need for them.

Social Orientation: From Occupational Socialization to School and Social Reform

Mentoring beginning teachers has been widely acknowledged as part of an answer to the policy problem of occupational induction,[72,73] or socializing newcomers into membership in the society of teachers. Zeichner and Gore have synthesized the research on occupational socialization out of three distinct intellectual traditions.[74] Rooted in logical positivism, the functionalist tradition explains how the socialization of new teachers accomplishes continuity and conjunction in the teaching profession, reproducing 'the status quo, social order, consensus, social integration, solidarity, need satisfaction, and actuality'.[75] From this perspective, the existing social order of schools and other external forces are assumed to determine the perspectives of beginning teachers who are more or less passive and malleable recipients of existing culture rather than active and interacting agents in its construction.[76] Challenging the assumptions of functionalist sociology, the interpretive tradition of research in teacher socialization seeks to 'understand the fundamental nature of the social world at the level of subjective experience'.[77] From this perspective, the existing order of schools is assumed to be influenced by the actions and interactions of individuals who make strategic choices and take autonomous actions that can result in change.[78]

As Zeichner and Gore point out, however, neither the functionalist nor the interpretive research tradition challenges the status quo. Both assume that socialization is fundamentally a unifying process whereby an individual learns roles and procedures that allow him or her (more or less actively) to settle into the existing culture of the profession. The critical tradition, on the other hand, begins with the assumption that the realities of schooling are both socially constructed and socially maintained and thus has the goal of 'social transformation' and 'increasing justice, equality, freedom, and human dignity'.[79] From this perspective, teacher socialization is recognized as a process of contradictions,[80] of beginning teachers' search for voice and identity amidst cultural myths and normative discourses,[81] and possibly of their struggle to teach against the grain of institutional habit and outside expertise.[82]

Although the approaches identified by Zeichner and Gore are traditions in *research* on occupational induction, they also provide a useful lens for exploring the *practice* of induction, particularly the social orientations implicit in mentoring programmes for beginners. It is interesting, for example, that descriptions of mentoring almost never include roles such as change agent, reformer, restructurer, curriculum creator, critical action researcher or teacher researcher, or activities such as praxis, production (as opposed to reproduction), emancipation, knowledge generation, interrogation of assumptions, development of critical pedagogy, and challenging standard practices and policies. These omissions are also evident in descriptions of the selection of mentors for student teachers. As Goodlad's recent survey of pre-service programmes nationwide reveals,[83] only five per cent of student and faculty respondents ever even alluded to the idea that the teacher could be an agent for change when they were questioned about the roles of teachers in schools, and no programme respondents indicated that they intentionally placed student teachers in centres of school renewal or reform.[84,85]

It is not surprising, then, that the view of teacher socialization implicit in many mentoring programmes – the 'hidden curriculum' of mentoring[86] – is functionalist[87] and relatively narrow. Almost by definition, mentoring is intended to help beginners ease as smoothly as possible into the prevailing system. Almost by definition, mentors are selected for their past records of successful work within the constraints of the system. Little has thoughtfully pointed out that the mentoring phenomenon is somewhat puzzling in the teaching profession – it appears to be based on disjunction with past practice in that it attempts to formalize teacher leadership in a profession without precedents for its legitimation or for the legitimation of teacher knowledge as an epistemology.[88] We would suggest, however, that the puzzle is partially explained when we realize that prevailing mentoring practice actually makes for very little disjunction with past traditions – role relationships remain hierarchical, university-generated knowledge is privileged, and, even though it passes through teachers as conduits,[89] a transmission model of teacher learning operates. Hence, even when mentoring is offered as a ladder to increased leadership for experienced teachers, and even when mentors and beginners are encouraged to reflect on their practices, mentoring is fundamentally a conservative activity that maintains the existing institutional, social and cultural arrangements of schools and schooling and eases the beginner into the prevailing norms of the local and larger professional culture.

Part of an alternative vision of mentoring is an altered social orientation, away from a narrow kind of occupational socialization into the prevailing system and toward a more emancipatory socialization into school and social reform. If beginning teachers are to be involved in efforts to rethink and reform school and classroom practice, however, they need opportunities to work and learn with mentors who are also involved in these efforts. In the excerpts that follow, a group of mentors and beginners from several different schools focus on issues of race, class and gender, and try to make visible some of the ways in which these factors structured their experiences as teachers and students.[90] The most striking aspect of this conversation is that beginners and mentors alike do not assume that the prevailing structures of school and society are inevitable or natural. Instead they struggle to raise difficult questions about their work as raced, classed and gendered persons, the ways in which they are positioned as teachers in relation to the positions of their students, and the ways in which stereotyped images may be unintentionally reproduced in school and classroom practice.[91]

Third Grade Mentor (School 1) I'm speaking as a [white] teacher . . . and also as a parent of an active biracial boy . . . I think we [unintentionally] set up a 'feminine' environment for compliant, quiet children – the stereotypical feminine environment, because we [elementary teachers] are women predominantly. And active kids [may] have difficulty with it. Mostly it's boys . . . And when it's a white boy we don't seem to say it's the problem with the structure, we say it's a problem with the child . . . [but] when it's a black child we back off. And . . . we're afraid of being called racist. And yet I don't think that we've looked at the structure. We haven't looked at who is invited into the process of the classroom successfully.

Fourth Grade Beginner (School 1) Why do we do that? Is it because of some kind of prejudice that is maybe more common than I would like to believe in a community [of teachers and student teachers] like this? Or is it because we're more unfamiliar [with black children]? I'm saying 'we' because the majority of people in here are white women. Are we more unfamiliar than we want to be with black kids' backgrounds, [with] where they come from, [with the] kinds of structures they have at home? I don't understand why we behave that way.

Fourth Grade Beginner (School 1) [In our school] there is a great respect and appreciation for diversity [but] . . . I really don't think the kids are [actually] very diverse in their class and race. Yet there's a lot of talk about the diversity of the school, and people seem to want to believe that it is a very diverse environment. And I think it *is* successful in getting the kids to really appreciate the diversity that is there, but I keep wondering if that's not because the diversity is not that great [in the first place] that they end up having such success.

Kindergarten Mentor (School 4)   I have a kindergarten class that's in a . . . white working-class area. . . . But we [also provide] service for children from [the children's home], who are children taken from their families because the mothers are put in jail or are on drugs, and these children [happen] to be Hispanic and black. There's also, of course, a class difference. But the class differences are not what's obvious to my children and to their parents . . . Their behaviour is far far different from the norms of the community. I worry about the stereotypical attitudes that my children are forming about these other children who are different in race. . . . I have a lot of questions, and I have a lot of fears.

Second Grade Beginner (School 6)   [As an Asian-American] what I have is a brief question about an underlying assumption within our discussion . . . as we talk about the differences between black and white children, or black and white teachers, it's often phrased or termed as race [differences], but as we talk about the differences between Asian children and white children, or an Indian girl or Korean boy and white children, it seems [we say] cultural differences. And I think that between black and whites there are cultural differences too.

Kindergarten Beginner (School 3) (addressing Kindergarten Mentor, School 4)   I can't imagine that whoever decided to send those kids to your school [from the children's home] wouldn't have thought it out more thoroughly. . . . I wonder how many times people realize what it is to be a minority [like me], what it is to be different. They have no sensitivity. I just can't understand that. . . . And it just sounds like the stereotype is just going to be continued on and on and on.

These excerpts from a much longer conversation suggest that it *is* possible for the interactions of beginners and mentors to have a critical rather than a functional stance or orientation to the existing social and institutional arrangements of schooling. This means that it is possible for beginners and mentors to work together as collaborators to construct and reconstruct their understandings of teaching, learning and schooling. It is possible for the phenomenon of mentoring to include: reconsideration of school and classroom labels, categories and policies; examination of the stereotypes and assumptions underlying teachers' own practices and the organizational contexts of schooling; and attempts to make visible and then grapple with whose interests are served by the current structures of schooling.[92–94]

CONCLUSION

Our analysis suggests that the prevailing view of the work of teacher mentors is not unlike the task of the original Mentor – to help beginners to acquire the skills and materials, in Homer's words, to 'keep the household intact'. As we know, however, Homer's Mentor, who was supposedly selected for his wisdom and experience, was overtaken by Athene whenever she wanted to convey instructions, and throughout the tale her divine knowledge and words pre-empted his. Teacher mentors are similarly pre-empted – they are supposedly selected for their classroom experience and for their school-based knowledge of teaching and learning, but they are subsequently given words and practices generated largely by university-based researchers.

As Little has rightly argued,[95] the history and culture of the teaching profession exert a powerful conservative influence on any innovative practice. It may be true that new positions such as 'teacher mentor' help to professionalize teaching by permitting teachers to participate officially in the socialization of beginners and by creating leadership roles in a career characterized by a flat profile. It is not necessarily true, however, that these new positions challenge the current structures of schooling. In fact, when the conservative effects of the profession are compounded by a reproductive image of mentoring, its reforming potential is particularly limited.

What we have tried to suggest throughout this chapter is that prevailing mentoring practice is limited by its focus on a university-certified knowledge base as opposed to teachers' ways of knowing, on hierarchical role relationships as opposed to asymmetrical collaboration, and on occupational socialization into current best practice as opposed to school reform and social justice agendas. Bounded by the classical image, mentoring reproduces rather than advances or alters the social life of schools. We need alternative visions of mentoring, visions that stretch the boundaries of both the classical model and prevailing practice. We need images that are more humanistic in respect for individual knowledge and experience and more transformative in activity, relationships and goals, images that call into question both the prevailing epistemology of teaching and many of the cultural norms of schooling. We have found some of these images in the work of learning communities wherein beginners and mentors collaborate to analyse and question theories and practices of teaching. Their work reveals what is possible when the goal of mentoring is transformed – not keeping the household intact but helping to build a new household.

NOTES AND REFERENCES

1. Anderson, E. M. and Shannon, A. L., 'Toward a conceptualization of mentoring'. *Journal of Teacher Education*, **39**, pp. 38–60, 1988.

2. Galvez-Hjornevik, C., 'Mentoring among teachers: a review of the literature'. *Journal of Teacher Education*, **3** (1), pp. 6–11, 1986.

3. Healy, C. C. and Welchert, A. J., 'Mentoring relations: a definition to advance research and practice'. *Educational Researcher*, **19** (9), pp. 17–21, 1990.

4. Gallimore, R., Tharp, R. G. and John-Steiner, V., 'Developmental and socio-historical foundations of mentoring'. Manuscript.

5. Homer, *The Odyssey*. Translated by E. V. Rieu. New York: Penguin Books, p. 43, 1946.

6. Clawson, J. G., 'Mentoring in managerial careers'. In Derr, C. B. (ed.), *Work, Family and the Career*. New York: Praeger, pp. 144–65, 1980.

7. Gehrke, N. J., 'On preserving the essence of mentoring as one form of teacher leadership'. *Journal of Teacher Education*, **XXXIX** (1), pp. 43–5, 1988.

8. New Jersey State Department of Education, *Provisional Teacher Program: Implementation Guidelines*. Trenton, NJ: The Department, 1991.

9. Morey, A. T. and Murphy, D. C., 'Models of new teacher induction programs'. In Far West Labs, *Designing Programs for New Teachers: The California Experience*. San Francisco: Far West Laboratory for Educational Research and Development, pp. 61–84, 1990.

10. Pennsylvania Department of Education, *Guidelines for Induction*. Harrisburg, PA: The Department, 1987.

11. Toledo Public Schools and Toledo Federation of Teachers, *The Toledo Plan: Intern, Intervention, Evaluation*. Toledo, OH: The Organizations, 1988.

12. Borko, H., 'Clinical teacher education: the induction years'. In Hoffman, J. V. and Edwards, S. A. (eds), *Reality and Reform in Clinical Teacher Education*. New York: Random House, pp. 45–63, 1986.

13. Hoffman, J. V., Edwards, S. A., O'Neal, S., Barnes, S. and Paulissen, M., 'A study of state mandated beginning teacher programs'. *Journal of Teacher Education*, **37** (1), pp. 16–21, 1986.

14. McNergney, R., Lloyd, J., Mintz, S. and Moore, J., 'Training for pedagogical decision-making'. *Journal of Teacher Education*, **39** (5), pp. 37–43, 1988.

15. Varrah, L. J., Theune, W. S. and Parker, P., 'Beginning teachers: sink or swim?' *Journal of Teacher Education*, **37** (1), pp. 30–4, 1986.

16. Winitzky, N. and Arends, R., 'Translating research into practice: the effects of various forms of training and clinical experiences on pre-service students' knowledge, skills and reflectiveness'. *Journal of Teacher Education*, **42** (1), pp. 52–65, 1991.

17. Bey, T., and Holmes, C. T. (eds), *Mentoring: Developing Successful New Teachers*. Reston, VA: Association of Teacher education, (introduction by Teresa Bey), 1990.

18. Gordon, S., *How to Help Beginning Teachers Succeed*. Alexandria, VA: ASCD, 1991.

19. Huling-Austin, L., Odell, S. J., Ishler, P., Kay, R. S., Edelfeldt, R. A., *Assisting the Beginning Teacher*. Reston, VA: ATE, 1989.

20. Bird, T., *The Mentor's Dilemma*. San Francisco: Far West Laboratory for Educational Research and Development, 1986.

21. Galvez-Hjornevik, op. cit., note 2.

22. McNergney *et al*, op. cit., note 14.

23. Zimpher, N. L. and Reiger, S. R., 'Mentoring teachers: what are the issues?'. *Theory into Practice*, **XXVII** (3), pp. 175–82, 1989.

24. Lowney, R. G., *Mentor Teachers: The California Model*. Bloomington, IN: Phi Delta Kappan, 1986.

25. Toledo Public Schools and Toledo Federation of Teachers, op. cit., note 11.

26. Zimpher, N. L. and Grossman, J. E., 'Collegial support by teacher mentors and peer consultants'. In Glickman, C. (ed.), *Supervision in Transition*. Alexandria, VA: ASCD, 1992.

27. Huling-Austin *et al.*, op. cit., note 19.

28. Veenman, S., 'Perceived problems of beginning teachers'. *Review of Educational Research*, **54** (2), pp. 143–78, 1984.

29. Dill, D. D., (ed.), *What Teachers Need to Know: The Knowledge, Skills and Values Essential to Good Teaching*. San Francisco: Jossey-Bass, 1990.

30. Good, T. L., 'Building the knowledge base of teaching'. In Dill, D. D. (ed.), *What Teachers Need to Know: The Knowledge, Skills and Values Essential to Good Teaching*. San Francisco: Jossey-Bass, 1990.

31. Brophy, J. and Good, T. L., 'Teacher behavior and student achievement'. In Wittrock, M. C., (ed.), *Handbook of Research on Teaching*, 3rd ed. New York: Macmillan, pp. 328–75, 1986.

32. Reynolds, M. C., *Knowledge Base for the Beginning Teacher*. Oxford: Pergamon Press, 1989.

33. Rosenshine, B., 'Unsolved issues in teaching content: a critique of a lesson on federalist paper No. 10'. *Teaching and Teacher Education*, **2** (4), pp. 301–8, 1986.

34. Pennsylvania Department of Education, op. cit., note 10, p. 3.

35. New Jersey State Department of Education, op. cit., note 8, p. 4.

36. Lanier, J. E., 'Research on teacher education'. In Wittrock, M. C. (ed.), *Handbook of Research on Teaching*, 3rd ed. New York: Macmillan, pp. 527–69, 1986.

37. Cochran-Smith, M., 'Reinventing student teaching'. *Journal of Teacher Education*, **42** (2), pp. 104–18, 1991.

38. Borko, op. cit., note 12.

39. McNergney *et al.*, op. cit., note 14.

40. Morey and Murphy, op. cit., note 9.

41. Winitzky and Arends, op. cit., note 16.

42. Zimpher, N. L., 'A design for the professional development of teacher leaders'. *Journal of Teacher Education*, **39** (1), pp. 53–60, 1988.

43. Gordon, op. cit., note 18.

44. Odell, S. J., 'Developing support programs for beginning teachers'. In op. cit., note 19, pp. 19–38.

45. Winitzky and Arends, op. cit., note 16.

46. Wunner, K. E., 'Great expectations: an analysis of the induction of new teachers'. Unpublished dissertation, University of Pennsylvania, 1991.

47. Zimpher, op. cit., note 42.

48. Morey and Murphy, op. cit., note 9.

49. Shulman, J. H, and Corbett, J. A., *The Mentor Teacher Casebook*. San Francisco: Far West Laboratory for Educational Research, 1987.

50. Others argue that critical but missing parts of the discourse of mentoring are subject-matter knowledge or academic content (Feiman-Nemser, S. and Parker, M., 'Mentoring in context: a comparison of two US programmes for beginning teachers', National Center for Research on Teacher Learning Special Report. East Lansing: Michigan State University, 1992. Feiman-Nemser, S. and Buchmann, M., 'Pitfalls of experience in teacher preparation', *Teachers College Record*, **87** (1), pp. 53–65, 1985; Shulman, J. and Bernhardt, V., 'Role of experienced educators in assisting new teachers'. In Far West Lab, *Designing Programs for New Teachers: The California Experience*. San Fransisco: Far West Laboratory for Educational Research and Development, pp. 40–50, 1990) as well as diversity of student populations. Feiman-Nemser and Parker suggest that subject matter, which in one sense is the *sine qua non* of teaching, is seldom a part of beginners' and mentors' interactions and is instead either ignored or assumed. We agree wholeheartedly with this emphasis as we do with Shulman and Bernhardt who call for greater attention to issues of race and ethnicity and ways of working with increasingly culturally diverse student populations. Although we take a different tack, like Feiman-Nemser and Shulman and Bernhardt we are arguing here for an enlarged vision of the content that is central in mentoring and for a deepened view of what counts as the knowledge

necessary for successful entry into the teaching profession.

51. Cochran-Smith, M. and Lytle, S., *Inside/Outside: Teacher Research and Knowledge*. New York: Teachers College Press, 1993.

52. Lytle, S. and Cochran-Smith, M., 'Teacher research as a way of knowing'. *Harvard Educational Review*, **62** (4), pp. 447–74, 1992.

53. Gallimore, Tharp and John-Steiner, op. cit., note 4.

54. Tharp, R. G. and Gallimore, R., *Rousing Minds to Life: Teaching, Learning and Schooling in Social Context*. Cambridge: Cambridge University Press, 1988.

55. The examples used in this paper, reproduced with permission, are drawn from data sources at two research sites where mentoring is being explored as part of larger studies of pre-service and in-service teacher education: Project START, a fifth-year pre-service programme in elementary education at the University of Pennsylvania, and Rider University's undergraduate programmes in early childhood/elementary teaching, and graduate programmes in curriculum, instruction and supervision. The first, situated within a graduate school at a large research university, is explicitly designed to challenge current educational practice by placing student teachers with mentors who are involved in school and classroom reform. It features a year of student teaching with the same mentor as well as school-site student teacher/teacher mentor research group meetings and monthly university seminars. The second, situated in a small liberal arts university in New Jersey, an alternative route state, features the placement of undergraduate student teachers with experienced mentors who concurrently may elect to take a graduate course in mentoring and supervision. This programme is intended to challenge the common assumption that the mentoring relationship is one of expert-novice knowledge transmission and instead tries to develop mentoring relationships that are deliberately collaborative and teachers' knowledge-based.

56. Cochran-Smith ('Colour blindness and basket making are not the answers', *American Educational Research Journal*, forthcoming) has provided a critique of 'the lesson' as the unit of analysis for learning about and improving teaching at the pre-service level.

57. Cochran-Smith, M., 'Of questions, not answers: the discourse of student teachers and their school and university mentors'. Paper presented to American Educational Research Association, San Francisco, 1989.

58. Dewey, J., 'The relation of theory to practice in education'. *The Third NSSE Yearbook* (Part 1). Chicago, IL: University of Chicago Press, 1904.

59. Gray, W. A. and Gray, M., 'Synthesis of research on mentoring beginning teachers'. *Educational Leadership*, **43** (3), pp. 37–43, 1985.

60. Galvez-Hjornevik, op. cit., note 2.

61. Lowney, op. cit., note 24.

62. Little, J. W., 'The mentor phenomenon and the social organization of teaching'. *Review of Research in Education*, **16**, pp. 297–352, 1990.

63. Zimpher and Grossman, op. cit., note 26.

64. Little, op. cit., note 63.

65. Bateson, M. C., *Composing a Life*. New York: Penguin, p. 102, 1990.

66. Ibid.

67. Dewey, J., *Democracy in Education*. New York: The Free Press, 1916.

68. Ibid., p. 160.

69. Ibid.

70. Belenky, M. F., Clinchy, B. M., Goldberger, N. R. and Tarule, J. M., *Women's Ways of Knowing*. New York: Basic Books, 1986.

71. Ibid., p. 146.

72. Little, op. cit., note 63.

73. Zimpher and Grossman, op. cit., note 26.

74. Zeichner, K. M. and Gore, J. M., 'Teacher socialization'. In Houston, R. W. (ed.), *Handbook of Research on Teacher Education*. New York: Macmillan, 1990.

75. Ibid., p. 330.

76. Hoy, W. and Woolfolk, A., 'Socialization of teachers'. *American Educational Research Journal*, **27** (2), 1990.

77. Zeichner and Gore, op. cit., note 75, p. 330.

78. Lacey, C., *The Socialization of Teachers*. London: Methuen, 1977.

79. Zeichner and Gore, op. cit., note 75, p. 331.

80. Ginsburg, M., *Contradictions in Teacher Education and Society: A Critical Analysis*. London: Falmer Press, 1988.

81. Britzman, D., *Practice Makes Practice*. New York: State University of New York Press, pp. 61–115, 221–43, 1991.

82. Cochran-Smith, M., 'Learning to teach against the grain'. *Harvard Educational Review*, **61** (3), pp. 279–310, 1991.

83. Goodlad, J. I., 'Studying the education of educators: from conception to findings'. *Phi Delta Kappan*, **71** (9), pp. 698–701, 1990.

84. Edmundsen, P. J., 'A normative look at the curriculum in teacher education'. *Phi Delta Kappan*, **71** (9), pp. 717–22, 1990.

85. This situation has been changing somewhat since Goodlad's survey with the creation of professional development schools where prospective teachers complete their student teaching (Holmes Group, *Tomorrow's Schools*. East Lansing, MI: The Group, 1990; Lanier, op. cit., note 36) and with the development of innovative programmes where participation in reform and teacher inquiry are criteria for the selection of co-operating teachers (Cochran-Smith, op. cit., note 37).

86. Ginsburg, op. cit., note 81.

87. Zeichner and Gore, op. cit., note 75.

88. Little, op. cit., note 63.

89. Paris, C., *Teacher Agency and Curriculum Making in Classrooms*. New York: Teachers College Press, 1993.

90. It is important to note that this conversation occurred in the spring of a school year during which mentors and beginners together had read and discussed a number of articles exploring race and gender issues (e.g. Delpit, L. 'The silenced dialogue: power and pedagogy in educating other people's children'. *Harvard Educational Review*, **58** (3) pp. 280–98, 1988; Ogbu, J., *Minority Education and Caste*. New York: Academic Press, 1978; Heath, S.B. 'What no bedtime story means: narrative skills at home and school'. In *Language in Society*, **11** (1), pp. 49–76, 1982; Laird, S., 'Reforming "women's true profession": a case for feminist pedagogy in teacher education'. *Harvard Educational Review*, **58** (4) pp. 449–63, 1988) and participated in several seminars at their school sites and at the university that approached these issues from different angles.

91. This example is a series of excerpts lifted from a number of different points in time in a two-hour conversation. It is intended to give a rich and accurate sense of the contour of the questions and concerns that were raised by beginners and mentors, but it does not provide verbatim information nor a real-time picture of the flow of the conversation.

92. Beyer, L., 'Critical theory and the art of teaching'. *Journal of Curriculum and Supervision*, **1** (3), pp. 221–32, 1986.

93. Carr, W. and Kemmis, S., *Becoming Critical: Education, Knowledge and Action Research*. London: Falmer Press, 1986.

94. Smyth, W. J., *A Rationale for Teachers' Critical Pedagogy: A Handbook*. Victoria, Australia: Deakin University Press, 1987.

95. Little, op. cit., note 63.

Chapter 11

Connecting Action Research to Genuine Teacher Development

Jennifer M. Gore and Kenneth M. Zeichner

TEACHER DEVELOPMENT: THE ISSUES

A current emphasis of educational reform in many countries, including the United States and Australia, is the need to improve schooling by improving the status, power and working conditions of teachers. This emphasis on teachers as the most important actors in educational reform has come after belated recognition by at least some educational reformers and administrators of the futility of attempting to improve schools primarily through greater external prescription of school processes and outcomes.[1]

We have worked hard as teacher educators to prepare student teachers to be active agents in their own professional development and in determining the direction of schools, and to support the efforts of teachers who were already engaged in doing so. We do not want to minimize the importance of continuing to struggle in support of teachers' efforts to gain more control or their work, and to make schools places where teacher learning is as much valued as student learning. However, our aim in this chapter is not to convince readers of the priority that we believe should be accorded teacher development, teacher learning and teacher empowerment. Rather, we want to raise some of the difficult issues of teacher development which are rarely discussed in public forums and yet which continue to undermine the authenticity and social value of such efforts.

Despite all the rhetoric to the contrary, we still see in the educational research establishment, which has attempted to articulate a 'knowledge base' for teaching, a general disregard for the craft knowledge of good teachers.[2] For example, in the most recent edition of the American Educational Research Association's *Handbook of Research on Teaching*,[3] which is supposed to be a compilation of the state of the art of our knowledge about teaching, there are 35 chapters and over a thousand pages on various aspects of teaching, such as teaching mathematics, teaching social studies, classroom organization and management, and so on. Not a single chapter is written by a classroom teacher, and there are few, if any, references to *anything* written by a classroom teacher. The same is true for most publications about research on teaching controlled by university academics.[4] Also, in spite of everything in the professional literature about the importance of improving the working conditions of teachers and supporting their efforts to play more meaningful roles in determining the content and contexts of their work, and of building more collaborative professional environments within schools,[5] we see efforts (often under the banner of teacher empowerment) which maintain the teachers' subservient position to those outside the classroom with regard to the core aspects of their work and which deny them any say about the contextual conditions of their work such as time and resources.[6]

An examination of the ways in which the concepts of reflection and the reflective practitioner have been integrated into pre-service teacher education programmes clearly illustrates our concerns. Put briefly, the potential for genuine teacher development through 'reflection' has been undermined by:

1. a focus on helping teachers better reproduce practices suggested by university-sponsored research, and neglect of the theories and expertise embedded in teachers' own practices;
2. a means-end thinking which limits the substance of teachers' reflections to technical questions of teaching techniques and internal classroom organization and a neglect of questions of curriculum and educational purposes;
3. neglect of the social and institutional context in which teaching takes place;
4. a focus on helping teachers reflect individually.

All of these practices help create a situation where there is merely the illusion of teacher development.[7,8]

Even when teacher development is a real concern and not a charade, however, we are concerned when teacher development and teacher empowerment become ends in themselves unconnected to any broader purposes or to questions of equity and social justice. In its extreme form we see a glorification of *anything* that a teacher does or says, such as the common assumption, in the reflective inquiry movement in teacher education, that teaching is necessarily better merely because teachers are more deliberate and intentional about their actions. This view ignores the fact that greater intentionality by teachers may help, in some cases, further to solidify and justify teaching practices that are harmful to students.[9] One consequence of this extreme reaction to oppressive forms of staff development and educational reform is that questions related to the broader purposes of education in a democratic society sometimes get lost.

While educational actions by teachers within schools cannot solve societal problems by themselves, they can contribute their share to the building of more decent and just societies. The most important point here is that teaching cannot be neutral, and neither can teacher development. Those of us who claim to be concerned about teacher development must act with greater political clarity about whose interests we are furthering in our work because, like it or not, we are taking a stand through our actions and words. In the next section of this chapter we examine the potential of action research for contributing to genuine teacher development which is connected to the promotion of greater educational equity and social justice; looking at both its promise as a strategy for teacher empowerment and its pitfalls.

ACTION RESEARCH: POTENTIAL AND PITFALLS

Examining the Emancipatory Potential of Action Research

In the last two decades the terms 'teacher research', and 'reflective practice' have become slogans for educational reform all over the world. On the surface this international movement can be seen as a reaction against a view of teachers as technicians who merely carry out what others outside the classroom want them to do, a rejection of top-down forms of reform that involve teachers merely as passive participants. It involves a recognition that teachers must play active roles in formulating the purposes and ends of their work as well as the means. These slogans also signify a recognition that the generation of knowledge about good teaching practice and good schools is not the exclusive property of universities and research and development centres. There is a recognition that teachers too have theories that can contribute to the knowledge that informs the work of practitioner communities.[10] With action research there is a clear recognition of teachers as knowledge producers and of the need for teaching to be put back into the hands of teachers.

There is also a concern, within at least some traditions of action research (e.g., socially-critical or emancipatory action research),[11] with focusing teachers' reflections both inwardly at their own practices and outwardly towards the social conditions which influence those practices. Here there is a concern for both personal renewal and social reconstruction through action research,[12] a view that is consistent with the democratic impulse that was associated with the origins of the action research movement in the US and Europe in the early part of this century.[13,14] There is also a concern, within certain segments of the action research movement, about the importance of collaborative aspects of school-based inquiry to both personal renewal and social transformation.[15]

Action research thus provides a methodology which potentially makes possible genuine teacher development which promotes greater educational equity and social justice. Specifically, the 'body' of work known as emancipatory action research, grounded in particular political and theoretical traditions, has provided specific guidance for the practice of socially critical (or social reconstructionist)[16] teacher education. As such it is unique and admirable. At the same time, however, we acknowledge that action research within pre-service or in-service teacher education programmes is not without its dangers. In Foucault's analyses of power and knowledge and their relationships in discourse,[17] we confront the possibility that emancipatory action research can become reinscribed in the very politics of truth it opposes. This chapter is therefore not intended as merely a celebration or legitimation of action research. Rather, heeding Foucault's reminder that 'everything is dangerous',[18] we want to attempt to identify some of the specific practices through which action research can have effects of domination, despite the emancipatory intentions of those of us who are involved in it.

Examining the Dangers of 'Emancipatory' Action Research

As Noffke has demonstrated elsewhere, action research has always been imbued with a tension between democracy and social engineering.[19] In teacher education and teacher development the particular manifestation of this tension has been linked with discourses of critical social science and teacher professionalism, and with its institutional location.[20] As with our discussion of teacher development, our focus is on the regulative side of the tension and the 'silences' of the action research discourse.

Emancipatory Action Research and Critical Social Science   Action research, as a methodology for social scientific research and social change, has historically been linked to a language of 'democracy' and 'transformation'. With contemporary origins in the social work of Kurt Lewin and others, action research was employed to give community members a greater say in, and sense of control over, improving their own lives. Those responsible for the recent resurgence of interest in action research as a methodology for the improvement of *educational* practice and situations draw especially upon the Critical Theory of the Frankfurt School in justifying their political and theoretical basis.[21]

While the 'power' of emancipatory action research can be seen to lie in its connection to critical social science (this is what separates this form of action research from other discourses/practices which employ similar 'techniques' or claim the same label), we want to argue that it is precisely these connections which contribute to its potential 'dangers'. Critical social science, as a modernist discourse of enlightenment, tends to function through abstract and universalized conceptions of democracy, notions of knowledge's control over power, and a belief in the intellectual's centrality to social transformation.

Critical social science distinguishes itself through its aim for emancipation but, perhaps in the name of optimism and simplicity, tends towards rather universalized notions of oppression and emancipation.[22] The form of action research under discussion here thus tends to be presented in ways which *assume* emancipatory rather than regulative effects. We want to emphasize that there is nothing inherent to action research that makes it emancipatory. As evidence, consider how smoothly action research has been appropriated into other traditions of teacher education.[23,24] The claim that such appropriations are 'not real action research' does little more than demonstrate a will to knowledge and a desire for control over the boundaries of action research discourse. 'Action research', the term given to a particular set of practices, never did exist outside its practice. Attempts to separate claims of what is action research from how it functions, ironically, deny what *is*.

Universalized notions of emancipation and oppression also function to legislate particular notions of the appropriate content for emancipatory action research. Class, gender and race formations (and often only one of these) have tended to become *the* issues for all contexts. Given the feminist criticism that much critical social science is inscribed within a patriarchal discourse which devalues women's perspectives on the social world,[25] the appropriate content for action research is further proscribed. Thus, although action research is said to proceed from the particular concerns of those who are to conduct it, there has been a tendency to prescribe a moral basis which is generalized rather than specific to particular contexts. While one does not have to look far or listen long to find all kinds of injustices in society, we would argue, unlike many advocates of critical social science, that we can only 'know' which injustices to address within specific contexts and local manifestations. Particularly in a field like education where there is so much complexity and diversity, local identification of relevant issues and inequities seems more appropriate than the single-issue politics and universalized notions of need characterizing much critical social science.

In the relationship of action research to critical social science there is also a rather uncritical belief in the value of action research as a means toward social transformation. While some would see 'action' as the goal of action research, it can be argued that action research aims for knowledge – knowledge which can help to control power. This view of the power–knowledge relation, in which, as Foucault puts it, knowledge functions as 'revenge' to power, goes with a traditional concept of power which shows little hesitation in identifying *the* social formations to be resisted and reconstructed.[26] For Foucault, however, the potential for truth's control of power is limited. In his view, power is circulating everywhere, is exercised rather than possessed, and is not necessarily repressive. Power passes through multiple points and turns on multiple axes, and so the production of knowledge through action research has no necessary impact on social conditions or practices. Given the complexities of power, many action research attempts will be limited in their effects and can even have effects which counter those intended.

Emancipatory action research also takes from critical social science the attribution to the 'intellectual' of a major role in the processes of social transformation. Through consciousness raising, revealing the distortions of everyday life, the critical intellectual is to lead the masses, functioning as the agent of their emancipation. While action research would appear to diminish the role of the intellectual in its call for collaborative and participatory approaches, the authority of persons who initiate the action research cannot be underestimated, especially in the context of teacher education (a point to which we will return shortly).

Shaped as it is through critical social science, one of the specific practices through which emancipatory action research in teacher education can have unintended effects of domination is seen in the tendency to direct students' research topics – knowing what they need to know, knowing the needy targets of all action research initiatives, in other words, those who have been oppressed by the gender, class and race formations of society. Furthermore, within emancipatory action research in teacher education there has been a gesture toward individualizing, providing each student with the opportunity to conduct his or her own research according to his or her own interests. Even when we do not direct topics, however, there is an effect of integrating or normalizing all students into a rather singular notion of what counts as socially critical knowledge (a particular rationality). This 'integration' occurs through the ways in which the assignment is structured, the emphasis that is placed on reflection, the emphasis on particular social formations, and so on. The point here is not to suggest that this kind of rationality is somehow necessarily evil. Our concern is that those of us who use action research in teacher education should be aware of its effects; for example, that we are aware of the way it normalizes even as we claim to individualize.

The practice of assessing students' work poses another problem for emancipatory action research. As has been discussed by other teacher educators, the contradictions of assessing students' action research reports are blatant, functioning to normalize and integrate further.[27] Perhaps less obvious are the problems with setting action research as an assignment which students are to complete, often without sufficient support from them to develop the intellectual and methodological attitudes and skills that would facilitate their work. In our experience, action research too often becomes so consuming of the course within which it is required that there is little time for such educative work as might complement that task, for example discussing pertinent readings and exploring the literature of the relevant field.

From a Foucauldian perspective it can also be argued that this kind of use of emancipatory action research has effects of self-regulation and self-surveillance, functioning in a way that requires students to confess. Such 'technologies of the self' are all part of what Foucault refers to as 'modern disciplinary society'. No longer governed by monarchical or sovereign rule, modern society functions through mechanisms that require individuals to police themselves. The process of conducting action research, especially within pre-service teacher education, requires students to participate in constructing themselves as particular kinds of subjects.

Emancipatory action research and teacher professionalism With the integration of action research into programmes of teacher education, emancipatory action research becomes entangled with the discourse of teacher professionalism. Although many would argue that action research provides a voice for teachers and is a way of validating their personal, professional and political knowledge (acknowledging that they are professionals capable of producing their own research), there is a sense in which the 'scientific' mask of action research, of social scientific research generally, can be seen to devalue what teachers know and the ways in which they have traditionally practised their work. This scientific aura, and general credibility of, action research in teacher education circles is linked to its nomenclature as 'research' in a field which has needed to improve its research profile (having historically focused on teaching), its emphasis on 'action' in a field which values practice, and its connections with the 'respectable' disciplinary field of sociology and professional field of social work.

Brought into the field of teacher education, the advocacy of action research in relation to teacher professionalization can function to serve the interests of teacher educators rather than the interests of teachers.[28-30] Action research has clearly appealed to those in teacher education who have wanted to appear more scientific. Such appeal helps to account for the now wide adoption of 'action research' (though rarely with emancipatory intent) across the range of teacher education traditions in North America.[31] Through such links to teacher professionalization, the dramatic effects of action research are diminished (even in emancipatory form) as it becomes enmeshed with attempts to regulate the development of teachers. Moreover, contextualized within teacher education, the regulative effects become more pronounced as the patriarchal language of justice and democracy imposes itself on a still predominantly female cohort of student teachers.[32]

Some of the specific practices through which regulative effects can occur include the intensification of teachers' work that emerges from the expectation that they will, or, the perceived obligation to conduct research as part of their role as extended professionals.[33] Student teachers socialized into such a rhetoric of emancipatory action research might also find their energies diverted from the school's primary academic mission.[34] How frequently is action research conducted by teachers except in places where special institutional and/or social *and* ideological support is provided?

Despite the rhetoric of valuing teachers as researchers, our experience is that the action research reports produced by student teachers or teachers are not widely circulated in teacher education programmes or broader educational circles.[35] Not using students' knowledge productions probably undermines our efforts to convince students of the value of action research, further diminishing democratic or emancipatory intentions.[36] Caught within the same system that values more highly the kind of 'academic' knowledge production in which we are engaging as we write this chapter, such oversights can contribute to the very 'disempowerment' of teachers that emancipatory action research aims to correct.

As with critical social science, the specific practices through which teachers are implored to act 'professionally' through the conduct of research can operate to involve them further in their own regulation and subjectification. For whom is action research conducted?

Emancipatory action research in teacher education Our last point becomes even more crucial when emancipatory action research is examined historically within the context of institutionalized teacher education. Emancipatory action research discourse (like much critical educational discourse)[37,38] has tended to neglect the historical context in which practices like action research have been inserted. Pedagogy within educational institutions has always functioned, in part, to regulate groups of people. The authority of the teacher or teacher educator cannot be escaped. Linked to the human sciences, institutionalized pedagogy normalizes, classifies, labels and distributes individuals.[39] Emancipatory action research, as a course requirement, struggles to maintain any emancipatory effect within such a context. Action research, even of the emancipatory kind, can become just another assignment, just another technique for sorting students.

Furthermore, when action research is conducted by student teachers it is frequently in the context of a temporary placement in the artificial environment of someone else's classroom. Despite sincere, and sometimes successful, attempts of some co-operating teachers to share their classrooms, the rooms are still seen (often emotionally as well as legally) as 'theirs', and intellectual responsibility for what occurs in the classroom will always be limited.[40] Student teachers' action research within such contexts is always constrained. As a manifestation of this institutionalization of action research, we have found students yet again participating in their own subjectification, turning themselves into the kinds of subjects they think we want them to be, telling us what we want to hear in their socially critical action research projects.[41]

TOWARDS GENUINE TEACHER DEVELOPMENT

The examination of the dangers of action research in which we have engaged here can easily lead to a paralysing pessimism. If emancipatory action research in teacher education is fraught with such regulative effects, why use it at all? First, we do not want to argue that we should try to do away with all will to knowledge, teacher authority, or technologies of self. Foucault's point is that these will always exist. The aim of such a critique is to examine specific effects of current discourses and to alter discursive and institutional practices which need not be as they are towards more contextually appropriate ends.

Secondly, if power exits only in action, as Foucault argues, attention is drawn to local and specific practices.[42] Metatheoretical narratives, like Critical Theory and Feminism, have not fully achieved their political goals in part because of their assumptions of unity and sameness across contexts.[43] Focusing more locally does not deny the existence of massive inequalities with respect to educational opportunities and outcomes for students through gender, race, class, religion and other distinctions. Nor does a local focus paralyse the commitments of teacher educators who seek a more just, humane and equitable world. Rather, our analysis urges a greater humility and tentativeness about our accomplishments, ongoing reflexivity about ways to alter what we do, and a more local focus for our actions even as they pertain to the more universal concerns that guide our political and pedagogical work.

For emancipatory action research to be more reflexive than it currently is in pre-service and in-service teacher education, we believe it needs to: be embedded in a programme context which has emancipatory goals – it cannot stand alone; occur within the context of the establishment of research communities in schools whereby teachers and student teachers can work together on projects relevant to their situations; proceed through metapedagogical techniques whereby teacher educators make use of their authority and the uniqueness of the teacher education environment to spend time reflectively addressing the emancipatory action research processes in which they are engaged.[44] Moreover, these reflections about the use of action research as a strategy for teacher education must be located within discussions of the purposes of education in a democratic society. When we use action research as a vehicle for teacher reflection in our teacher education programmes, we must be concerned with how our use of action research contributes toward or hinders the realization of greater educational equity and social justice.

While there are no examples portrayed in the literature of action research in teacher education programmes which exemplify all of these criteria, there are clearly some programmes of work at different institutions which reflect attention to some of them. The University of Pennsylvania's efforts to establish teacher research communities composed of university faculty, teachers and student teachers is one example of such a programme.[45] The self-reflectivity of action research facilitators such as Noffke & Brennan, Robottom, and Trubek,[46-48] who assess the reality of action research in relation to its democratic goals, is another example. These efforts, in conjunction with ongoing debates among practitioners and academics, demonstrate that action research remains a vital source in the continuing search for genuine teacher development which contributes to greater educational equity and social justice.

NOTES AND REFERENCES

1. Darling-Hammond, L. and Berry, B., *The Evolution of Teacher Policy*. Washington, DC: Rank Corporation, 1988.

2. Lytle, S. and Cochran-Smith, M., 'Learning from teacher research: a working typology'. *Teachers' College Record*, **92** (1), pp. 83–103, 1990.

3. Wittrock, M., *Handbook of Research on Teaching*. 3rd ed. New York: Macmillan, 1986.

4. Grimmett, P. and MacKinnon, A., 'Craft knowledge and the education of teachers'. In Grant, G. (ed.), *Review of Research in Education, 18*. Washington, DC: American Educational Research Association, pp. 385–486, 1992.

5. Lieberman, A. (ed.), *Building a Professional Culture in Schools*. New York: Teachers College Press, 1989.

6. Zeichner, K., 'Connecting genuine teacher development to the struggle for social justice'. *Journal of Education for Teaching*, **19**(1), pp. 5–20, 1993.

7. Zeichner, K., 'Conceptions of reflective teaching in contemporary US teacher education programs'. In Valli, L. (ed.), *Reflective Teacher Education: Cases and Critiques*. Albany: State University of New York Press, 1992.

8. Zeichner, op. cit., note 6.

9. Ellwood, C., 'Teacher research: for whom?' Paper presented at the annual meeting of the American Educational Research Association, San Francisco, 1992.

10. Cochran-Smith, M. and Lytle, S,, 'Communities for teacher research: fringe or forefront'. *American Journal of Education*, **100** (3), pp. 298–324, 1992.

11. See Kemmis & McTaggart (op. cit., note 15) and Tripp, D. 'Socially critical action research'. *Theory into Practice*, **29** (3), pp. 158–66, 1990.

12. Zeichner, K., 'Educational reform and teacher knowledge: personal renewal and social reconstruction through teacher research'. In Hollingsworth, S. and Sockett, H. (eds), *Teacher Research and Educational Reform*. Chicago: University of Chicago Press, forthcoming.

13. Altrichter, H. and Gstettner, P., 'Action research: a closed chapter in the history of German Social Science?' *Educational Action Research*, **1** (3), pp. 329–60, 1993.

14. Noffke, S., 'Action research: a multidimensional analysis'. Unpublished doctoral dissertation. Madison, WI: University of Wisconsin-Madison, 1989.

15. Kemmis, S. and McTaggart, R., *The Action Research Planner*. Geelong, Victoria: Deakin University Press, 1988.

16. Liston, D. and Zeichner, K., *Teacher Education and the Social Conditions of Schooling*. New York: Routledge, 1991.

17. Foucault, M., 'Afterword: the subject and power'. In Dreyfus, H. L. and Rabinow, P. (eds), *Michel Foucault: Beyond Structuralism and Hermeneutics*, 2nd ed. Chicago: University of Chicago Press, pp. 208–26 (p. 221), 1983.

18. Ibid.

19. Noffke, op. cit., note 14.

20. Gore, J. M., 'On silent regulation: emancipatory action research in pre-service teacher education'. *Curriculum Perspectives*, **11** (4), pp. 47–51, 1991.

21. Young, R., *A Critical Theory of Education: Habermas and Our Children's Future*. New York and London: Teachers College Press, 1990.

22. Ladwig, J.G., 'For whom is critical theory critical?' *Review of Education*, **14** (1), pp. 61–8, 1992.

23. Kemmis, S., 'Action research and the politics of reflection'. In Boud, D., Keogh, R., and Walker, D., (eds), *Reflection: Turning Experience into Learning*. London: Kogan Page, pp. 139–63, 1985.

24. Zeichner, K. and Tabachnick, B. R., 'Reflections on reflective teaching'. In Tabachnick, B. R. and Zeichner, K. (eds), *Issues and Practices in Inquiry-oriented Teacher Education*. London: Falmer Press, pp. 1–21, 1991.

25. Luke, C., 'Feminist politics in radical pedagogy'. In Luke, C. and Gore, J. (eds), *Feminisms and Critical Pedagogy*. New York and London: Routledge, 1992.

26. Foucault, op. cit., note 17.

27. Noffke, S. and Brennan, M., 'Action research and reflective student teaching at the University of Wisconsin-Madison'. In Tabachnick, B. R. and Zeichner, K. (eds), *Issues and Practices in Inquiry-oriented Teacher Education*. London: Falmer Press, pp. 186–201, 1991.

28. Gitlin, A., 'Power and method'. Paper presented at the Twelfth Conference on Curriculum Theory and Classroom Practice, Dayton, OH, 1990.

29. Labaree, D. F., 'Power, knowledge and the rationalization of teaching: a genealogy of the movement to professionalize teaching'. *Harvard Educational Review*, **62** (2), pp. 123–54, 1992.

30. Ladwig, J. G., 'Is collaborative research exploitative?' *Educational Theory*, **41** (2), pp. 111–20, 1990.

31. Arnold, G., 'Strengthening student teachers' reflective/critical thinking skills through collaborative research'. Paper presented at the annual conference of the Eastern Educational Research Association, Hilton Head, SC, 1992.

32. McCarthy, C., 'Teacher training contradictions'. *Education and Society*, **4** (2), pp. 3–15, 1986.

33. Apple, M., *Teachers and Texts*. New York: Routledge, 1986.

34. Zeichner, K., 'Contradictions and tensions in the professionalization of teaching and the democratization of schools'. *Teachers College Record*, **92** (3), pp. 363–79, 1991.

35. This is beginning to change somewhat now with the initiation of several new journals which will include the action research studies of teachers. These include *Educational Action Research*, a new international journal sponsored by the Classroom Action Research Network, and *Teaching and Change*, a new journal sponsored by the National Education Association, the largest teacher union in the US.

36. Gore, J. M. and Zeicher, K. M., 'Action research and reflective teaching in pre-service teacher education: a case study from the United States'. *Teaching and Teacher Education*, **7** (2), pp. 119–36, 1991.

37. Bernstein, B., *The Structuring of Pedagogic Discourse*. London and New York: Routledge, 1990.

38. Gore, J. M., *The Struggle for Pedagogies: Critical and Feminist Discourses as Regimes of Truth*. New York and London: Routledge, 1993.

39. Hunter, I., *Culture and Government: The Emergence of Literary Education*. London: Macmillan, 1988.

40. Dewey, J., 'The relation of theory and practice in education'. In Borrowman, M., (ed.), *A Documentary History of Teacher Education in the US*. New York: Teachers College Bureau of Publications, pp. 140–71, 1904/65.

41. See Gore and Zeichner (op.cit., note 36) for a discussion of the tensions and difficulties which are often associated with trying to facilitate action research in pre-service teacher education which considers the social and political aspects of teaching practice and institutional as well as individual change. While it is important for students to maintain ownership over their inquiries, they are often disinclined toward this kind of social and political analysis of teaching practice. How to facilitate attention to these aspects of teaching in action research while maintaining student teachers' control over their research, and at the same time avoiding the 'impression management' that is frequently associated with student/teacher educator encounters, is a problem of great complexity.

42. Foucault, M., 'Truth and power'. In Gordon, C. (ed.), *Power/Knowledge: Selected Interviews and Other Writings 1972–1977*. New York: Pantheon Books, pp. 63–77, 1980.

43. Gore, op. cit., note 38.

44. John Elliott (*Action Research for Educational Change*. Milton Keynes and Philadelphia: Open University Press 1991) has referred to these inquiries of teacher educators as 'second order' action research.

45. Cochran-Smith, M., 'Learning to teach against the grain'. *Harvard Educational Review*, **61**, pp. 279– 310, 1991.

46. Noffke and Brennan, op. cit., note 27.

47. Robottom, I., 'A research-based course in science education'. In Nias, J. and Groundwater-Smith, S. (eds), *The Enquiring Teacher: Supporting and Sustaining Teacher Research*. London: Falmer Press, pp. 106–20, 1988.

48. Trubek, J., 'Learning from ourselves: doing teacher research with student teachers'. Paper presented at the first annual meeting of the Madison Area Action Research Network, Middleton, WI, 1993.

Chapter 12

Teaching as a Profession of Values

Jon Nixon

PROFESSIONALISM AFTER THE EARTHQUAKE

I start with an observation – and also with a question. The observation, though by now commonplace, has been memorably stated by Eric Hobsbawm 'Human societies, and the relations of people within them, have undergone a sort of economic, technological and sociological earthquake within the lifetime of people who have barely got beyond middle age.'[1] The question, for those who teach or support the work of teachers, follows Hobsbawm's observation: 'What might teacher professionalism mean after the earthquake?'

In responding to that question, this chapter explores the nature of these economic, technological and sociological changes and the ways in which the teaching profession has tended to react to them. Reliance on traditional notions of professional autonomy has, I shall argue, proved an inadequate bulwark and helped to create a situation in which teachers as an occupational group have become politically outmanoeuvred and their status reduced to that of semi-professionals. What is required is an alternative version of professionalism based on a very different notion of autonomy and articulated in terms of educational values and their relation to practice.

This alternative version is discussed with reference to a particular research project, 'Expectations in the Early Years of Secondary Schooling – and Beyond', one of the principal aims of which has been to explore precisely that relation.[2]

PROFESSIONALISM UNDER THREAT

Teachers in the UK have been getting a bad press of late, so much so that, in 1991, even the *Guardian* newspaper came out against them and, as part of its editorial, questioned not only the quality but also the very existence of teacher professionalism.

> The sad fact is that teaching is poorly regarded not just to an
> uncompromising outside world, but within the profession itself.
> Career development for a teacher means getting out of teaching.
> Pedagogic skills are valued lower than the administrative talents

> that get a teacher out of the classroom and into the prized
> management jobs. . . . Teaching does not yet behave like a
> profession.[3]

British newspaper editors are not best placed to offer advice on professional standards. Nevertheless, the public esteem and self-respect of teachers is undoubtedly at a low ebb and it is worth asking how this has come about – and why. In fairness, teachers have never been held in particularly high regard and their development as professionals has always been, at best, a minor policy consideration. However, the current situation – characterized on the one hand by far-reaching educational 'reforms', and on the other by widespread demoralization among the occupational groups charged with responsibility for implementing these same 'reforms' – requires a renewed effort of analysis.

Any such analysis must acknowledge the immense social and economic changes within which professional groups generally are trying to redefine their roles. These changes are difficult to grasp, because they remain part of something that is still very much in the making:

> a shift to the new 'information technologies' . . . decline of the old
> manufacturing base and the growth of the 'sunrise', computer-
> based industries; . . . a greater emphasis on choice and product
> differentiation, on marketing, packaging and design . . . ; a decline
> in the proportion of the skilled, male manual working class, the
> rise of the service and white collar classes and the 'feminisation' of
> the workforce; an economy dominated by the multinationals . . . ;
> the 'globalisation' of the new financial markets, linked by the
> communications revolution; and new forms of the spatial
> organisation of social processes.[4]

The shifts and transformations which Stuart Hall sees as characterizing the 'new times' rely not on the methods of mass production but on an economic order that requires new kinds of flexibility and specialization with regard to consumer choice. What we are living through is not just the easily observable shift from factory to office and from shop-floor to shop, but rather the redefinition – and reconstitution – of society around the shibboleth of consumer choice and the particular notion of individualism that underpins it.

That notion, as Raymond Williams argued, has been shaped both by the experience of increased geographical and social mobility and by the privatization of individual and family life; so that, as he put it, that life is a kind of 'shell which you can take with you . . . to places that previous generations could never imagine visiting'.[5] The shell is more than just a set of personal or familial possessions: more, even, than a lifestyle. It is a moral system in miniature. For, as Zygmunt Bauman has noted, 'ethics has become a matter of individual discretion, risk-taking, chronic uncertainty and never-placated qualms'[6] – and so, by the same reckoning, has knowledge itself.[7]

Criticisms

Within this changing context teachers as an occupational group have proved to be vulnerable on two counts. One set of charges frequently brought against them is that they have failed to keep up with the pace of social and economic change; that, as a consequence, they are failing to equip pupils with the appropriate skills and attitudes for productive participation in a modern technological society; and that they are, therefore, inevitably contributing to – or, at the very least, failing to arrest – the economic decline in which the country finds itself. What we need is enterprise – and teachers are failing to deliver it!

At the same time teachers are criticized for a supposed moral decline in the nation's youth. If only (so the argument runs) pupils were disciplined in schools and teachers taught them right from wrong (as of course they always used to), then the crime rate would drop, industrial action would be virtually unheard of and the nation would generally do as it is told. Slovenliness, left-wing bias, anti-authoritarianism are, according to this account, all charges to be levelled against teachers and to be used as a simple and ready-made explanation of Britain's supposed moral ills. What we need is to get 'back to basics' – and teachers are preventing us from doing so!

The fact that on several counts these two sets of charges cancel one another out would seem not to matter. Why shouldn't teachers be criticized as, on the one hand, economic stick-in-the-muds and, on the other, morally dangerous progress-ives? The point is that things are on the move and that teachers – individually and collectively – are surely (so it is said) failing to take proper account of these movements.

Responses

There are several ways in which the teaching profession has sought to counter these charges. One is simply to deny them: 'We are doing a grand job – just leave us to get on with it.' While this is an increasingly difficult position to maintain, it still exerts a residual influence. One of the reasons for this continuing influence is that it fronts a wide variety of professional opinion. It offers both an excuse for the self-satisfied and a cover for those who are still trying to pursue a radical agenda.

Another way of countering the charges is to acknowledge the need for change while stalling on at least some of its implications: 'We are changing – it's just that it takes time for these changes to have an impact on classroom practice.' This is a common response among those who are responsible for the professional development of teachers. It is conciliatory in tone, but again it covers a range of opinion – from those who never really intend to change to those for whom a change is a reflective process involving the interplay of both principle and practice.

Both responses are understandable. Neither, however, engages explicitly with the central value issue that is implicit in the charge brought against the teaching profession: whether it exists to endorse or to help understand the processes of social and economic change. Are we, as teachers and as teacher educators, reacting as if coerced – or responding as if our professional deliberations really mattered?

VERSIONS OF PROFESSIONALISM

A third response to the charge of professional failure addresses precisely that issue. It sets out to question the assumptions upon which the charge is made and says in effect: 'We are thinking about what we are doing and about the changes that are happening around us – our professionalism is dependent upon our capacity to do just that.' Any such response runs the risk of being dismissed as a general unwillingness to move with the times, and on occasion it may indeed be little more than that. Sometimes, however, it represents a genuine attempt to exercise an altogether different kind of choice from that which is celebrated within, and formed by, a consumer society: the choice, that is, as to whether or not to stop and think critically about the nature and future course of that society.

Teachers' Autonomy

Until recently the possibility of this kind of choice has – in theory, though rarely in practice – been held open by a notion of autonomy which was central to the dominant version of teacher professionalism. With that version, as Gerald Grace points out,[8] teachers 'had fought off the impositions of payment by results in the nineteenth century and they had also fought off accusations of indoctrination and political bias in the 1920s'. It might reasonably be expected, therefore, that they would successfully fight off the reassertion of explicit state control by similar means. After all, 'the whole historical consciousness and experience of organised teachers suggested that in the face of central state initiatives this version of professionalism would be their best defence.'

Central to this version of teacher professionalism was a sense of loyalty between teachers and of collaboration across schools. Professional organizations and teachers' unions played an important part in maintaining the linkage upon which this sense of loyalty relied. Undoubtedly it involved an element of exclusivity, but it was based upon shared values and a common concern for equalizing opportunities. As a version of professionalism it seemed strong and grounded – and sensitive to the particular tensions and strains that characterized British society well into the 1970s. However, it did not reckon with the imposition of a policy framework which constitutes a direct attack upon these notions of autonomy and loyalty. Teacher professionalism within England and Wales[9] – in the context of the 1988 Education Reform Act in general and its stipulations regarding the statutory curriculum in particular – would seem to have little if anything to do with curriculum and pedagogical autonomy. Insofar as the teacher can be seen as fulfilling a professional role, he or she might be more appropriately characterized 'as an operative rather than as a decision-maker, as someone whose role is merely to implement the judgements of others and not to act on his or her own'.[10]

Teachers as Semi-professionals

This revised version of the teacher as a semi-professional operative is firmly premised on a dissolution of the old loyalties: through, for example, the introduction of open enrolment, together with financial inducements offered by central government to schools opting out of local authority control. Co-ordinated planning across schools – in order to ensure a balanced student intake, a fair allocation of resources and the provision of shared facilities – has thereby become more difficult to achieve. Every aspect of recent legislation, as John Elliott has argued, 'plays its part in prompting competition rather than collaboration'[11] – with the result that schools now have to operate in the competitive free-for-all of the market place. And the market assumes 'that my purposes, my development, must always be at the expense of someone else's'; it makes of 'every interaction and relationship a "zero-sum" game: my success depends upon your defeat'.[12] Partnership, collegiality and the traditions of professional collaboration are more difficult to sustain within a system that is constructed around the purposeful promotion of social stratification.[13] Moreover, such a system is also more difficult to challenge because of its appearance of technical rationality and managerial efficiency. Whether it is employing the terminology of performance indicators, professional competencies or criteria for school inspection, its cumulative effect is the same: to produce what Richard Rorty has called a 'local final vocabulary'[14] which in this case grossly oversimplifies the complexity of schools and classrooms.

Insofar as increased public confidence is the aim, it is being bought at the expense of any genuinely public debate as to what constitutes quality in education. Organized around endless lists and league tables – statutory and non-statutory pre-specifications of outcome – the system keeps teachers and students perpetually on the run-around. Assessment, it would seem, has taken over from development as the prime curriculum task of the teacher and from learning as the prime curriculum experience of the student – and all this from a government committed by its own White Paper[15] to ushering in 'a new century of excellence'!

Teachers cannot reclaim their autonomy simply by proclaiming it. They need to reconceptualize it. What teachers – across the entire range of educational institutions – ought to be doing is rethinking their notions of professionalism, not in terms of the old categories of autonomy and status, but in such a way as to carve out a very different kind of category: namely the irreducible core of educational values that articulates their professional practice. From this perspective, as Hugh Sockett puts it, professionalism must 'be viewed as an aspiration which requires constant reworking rather than be seen as a comparative status to be achieved'[16] – and the reworking is, of course, all in the practice.

A PROFESSION OF VALUES

The assumption that there is a necessary relation between educational values and the practice of teaching is now something of a commonplace. It is an important assumption because it challenges the simplistic view that professional values are invariably derived from bodies of theoretical knowledge and then simply applied to particular professions. Such a view, as Wilfred Carr has argued, is inappropriate to a professional field of practice such as education in which 'teachers develop professionally by reflecting critically on their own tacit practical knowledge rather than by applying theoretical knowledge produced by academic experts'.[17]

Values are important not because they provide logical explanations, but because they are asserted and require assent. They affect action by satisfying our sense of what feels right or awakening our sense of what is morally offensive. The affective nature of values – the way they cling to feelings and associations – accounts for their resilience and for the continuing influence they exert across generations. Values take us, as individuals and groups, back to our roots for the purpose of reclaiming what is morally alive in our communal pasts; they trace old loyalties but point also to new possibilities for realizing our own moral agency and for supporting that of others. They can, and do, lead to the exclusivity of tribal and ethnic nationalisms, but they are also expressed in innumerable acts of altruism and self-sacrifice. 'The history of cultures and social formations', as John Fekete reminds us, 'is unintelligible except in relation to a history of value orientations, value ideas, goods values, value responses, and value judgements, and their objectivisations, interplay, and transformations.' [18]

The assumed relationship between values and practice stands in need, then, of considerable qualification and refinement. For values within the field of education are not uncomplicatedly embedded in whatever it is that professionals do when they are practising their profession. The values implicit in that practice have to be actively sought out and acknowledged. From this perspective teaching is a profession only insofar as the educational values it espouses in theory are professed in – and through – its practice. The prime task for teachers as professionals, therefore, is to work out their educational values, not in isolation and abstraction but in collaboration with colleagues and amid the complexities of school life.

The 'Expectations' Project

The 'Expectations in the Early Years of Secondary Schooling – and Beyond' project has set out with a principal aim of understanding what exactly this task entails. Fifteen secondary schools in England and Wales were studied, using evidence drawn mainly from student and teacher interviews but also from school and classroom observations and relevant documentary evidence. The focus of the

220

research has been on the early years of secondary schooling, but continuity across the years of compulsory schooling – and beyond – has been a major theme.[19]

Each of the populations served by these schools is facing a unique combination of social and cultural problems compounded by changing patterns of local employment and unemployment. In these localities schools are often seen as offering few opportunities, and learning tends, therefore, to be accorded scant respect either by the students themselves or by the communities from which they are drawn. Each of the schools, in other words, is having to work out its core educational values within a context of continuing struggle, but has the advantage of a strong sense of corporate purpose and professional identity.

Common Themes These core educational values coalesce around a number of common themes:

- **The centrality of learning** All the schools see themselves as centrally concerned with learning and with students as learners.

- **Student self-determination** They also emphasize the importance of students taking responsibility for their own learning and achieving agency and self-determination through that process of engagement.

- **Supportive relationships** Each of the schools is concerned to develop mutually supportive relationships between students and between students and teachers and considers such relationships as a necessary condition of learning.

- **Breadth of achievement** The schools recognize and build on student achievements across a wide range of activities and situations without necessarily subjecting these achievements to the routines of formal assessment.

Although distinct, these themes share a common concern with learning – learning as process, that is, not as a body of received knowledge or a set of acquired skills. Within that process, self-determination and mutuality of support should not be conceived as either the extrinsic rewards or the prior conditions of learning. They are its intrinsic goods.

Starting Points for Action and Change This complex interplay of value-laden themes has given rise to different starting points for action and change across the various school settings:

- acknowledging *student disaffection* and the need to understand and explore the problems and issues to which this gives rise;

221

- placing a strong emphasis on the students' own sense of school *membership* and of the school as a community of learners;
- seeing *learning as a continuum* which necessitates close professional links with colleagues in feeder primary schools and close curriculum links with other key stages;
- focusing upon *individual progression* through systematic review procedures and curriculum target-setting and by offering opportunities for students to talk and write about their own learning; and
- seeking to establish with parents a *partnership* based on respect for the child as a developing learner and for the school as a place in which people go on learning.

Relating Values to Practice   What is interesting here is not so much the themes and starting points in themselves but the way in which they combine and – more importantly – what that combination tells us about the general approach adopted by these schools in trying to relate values to practice.

First, it is clearly an approach premised on the view that schools need to move forward on several fronts at once; that, for example, an exclusive concern with either student attendance or assessment procedures effects a different kind of change from that produced by a combined emphasis on both. The point is not simply that the one reinforces the other, but that together they mean something different. To atomize practice is, from this perspective, not just to devalue it but to render it educationally valueless.

Secondly, the approach would seem to be based on the assumption that movement forward on any front involves a strong element of reciprocity, and that organizational systems, if they are to be educationally effective, must be interactional and interpersonal. So, for example, target-setting needs to be systematic and consistent across the curriculum, but unless it also involves teachers and students talking and thinking together about the experience of learning it is reduced to a mere technical exercise. Again, from this perspective, any such reduction is one that, regardless of supposed gains in technical efficiency, necessarily squeezes the life – and with it the educational values – out of the practice.

Thirdly – and this is the crux – it is an approach that within the current political climate is necessarily oppositional. It is important to be clear on this point. I am not suggesting that all – or even some – of the teachers are politically motivated, nor that the schools are working to an explicitly alternative agenda. The point is that, given the policy framework that exists, the kind of approach being developed across these sites constitutes a kind of refusal. It is a tentative refusal – apologetic even – but a refusal nevertheless, because it challenges the assumption that teaching can somehow be separated out into a series of technical operations. In so doing, it affirms those values that help define and shape teaching as a profession.

CONCLUSION

'What needs above all to be changed', argue Trevor Blackwell and Jeremy Seabrook, 'is the current mix of what can be changed and what cannot be changed; and it is this perception that will liberate us from our present oppressive immobilism.'[20] We cannot – to return to that initial observation – change the fact that we live in the midst of an economic, technological and sociological earthquake. But we can change the way in which we respond to its varied upheavals. We can, for example, insist upon the importance of self-determination and agency, of collaboration and mutual support, even in the face of societal changes that perpetuate structural inequality and that are generating a new kind of underclass whose 'members cannot even get their feet on the first rung of the ladder'.[21] Moreover, we can do this in the name of a profession that is, by definition, committed to learning and to a learning society. For without that self-determination and agency, without that collaboration and mutual support, no real learning can take place. This is the change in perception that alone can open the pathway to action. 'There is another world,' suggest Blackwell and Seabrook, 'but it is this one.'[22]

NOTES AND REFERENCES

1. Hobsbawm, E., 'The crisis of today's ideologies'. *New Left Review*, **192**, pp. 55–64 (p. 57), 1992.

2. This project was funded by BP Chemicals as part of its Aiming for College Education programme. The fieldwork was conducted between 1992 and 1993. Further discussion of the findings can be found in Nixon *et al.* (op. cit., note 19). The focus of this enquiry developed out of an earlier case study of 'Milner School' (reported in Gilborn, D., Nixon, J. and Rudduck, J. *Dimensions of Discipline: Rethinking Practice in Secondary Schools*. London: HMSO, 1993).

3. *Guardian*, 2 July 1991.

4. Hall, S., 'Brave new world'. *Marxism Today*, **32** (10), pp. 24–9 (p. 24), 1988.

5. Williams, R., 'Problems of the coming period'. *New Left Review*, **140**, pp. 7–22 (p. 16), 1983.

6. Bauman, Z., *Intimations of Postmodernity*. London: Routledge, p. xxiii, 1992.

7. A very different position is adopted by Ernest Gellner (*Postmodernism, Reason and Religion*. London: Routledge, p. 75, 1992) who, in his diatribe against postmodernist theorizing, affirms his continuing commitment 'to the view that there is external objective, culture-transcending knowledge'.

8. Grace, G., 'Teachers and the state'. In Lawn, M. and Grace, G. (eds), *Teachers: The Culture and the Politics of Work*. London: Falmer Press, pp. 193–223 (p. 220), 1987.

9. The 1988 Education Reform Act applies to England and Wales. Comparable legislation includes, for Scotland, the School Boards (Scotland) Act 1988 and the Self-Governing Schools Etc. (Scotland) Act 1989; and, for Northern Ireland, the Education Reform (NI) Order 1989 and the Education and Libraries (NI) Order 1993.

10. Kelly, A. V., *The Curriculum: Theory and Practice* 3rd ed. London: Paul Chapman, p. 130, 1988.

11. Elliott, J., *Action Research for Educational Change*. Buckingham: Open University Press, p. 146, 1991.

12. Ranson, S., 'Markets or democracy for education'. *British Journal of Education*, **41** (4), pp. 333–52 (p. 334), 1993.

13. Ball, S., 'Education markets, choice and social class: the market as class strategy in the UK and USA'. *British Journal of Sociology of Education*, **14** (1), pp. 3–19, 1993.

14. Rorty, R., *Contingency, Irony and Solidarity*. Cambridge: Cambridge University Press, p. 77, 1989.

15. Department for Education, *Choice and Diversity: A New Framework for Schools* (White Paper). London: HMSO, 1992.

16. Sockett, H., 'Research, practice and professional aspiration within teaching'. *Journal of Curriculum Studies*. **21** (2), pp. 97–112 (p. 97), 1989.

17. Carr, W., 'Introduction: understanding quality in teaching'. In Carr, W. (ed.), *Quality in Teaching: Arguments for a Reflective Profession*. London: Falmer Press, pp. 1–18 (p. 11), 1989.

18. Fekete, J., 'Introductory notes for a postmodern value agenda'. In Fekete, J. (ed.), *Life After Postmodernism: Essays on Value and Culture*. London: Macmillan, p. i, 1988.

19. Nixon, J., Martin, J., McKeown, P. and Ranson, S., *Encouraging Learning*. Buckingham: Open University Press, 1995.

20. Blackwell, T. and Seabrook, J., *The Revolt Against Change: Towards A Conserving Radicalism*. London: Vintage, p. 4, 1993.

21. Dahrendorf, R., 'The changing quality of citizenship'. In van Steenbergen, B. (ed.), *The Condition of Citizenship*. London: Sage, pp. 10–19 (p. 15), 1994.

22. Blackwell and Seabrook, op. cit., note 20.

Name Index

Subject Index

228